BF
149
B3
1975

Bauer, Raymond Au-
gustine

Some views on So-
viet psychology

DATE DUE

SOME VIEWS ON SOVIET PSYCHOLOGY

Some Views on

SOVIET

PSYCHOLOGY

Edited by RAYMOND A. BAUER

GREENWOOD PRESS, PUBLISHERS
WESTPORT, CONNECTICUT

Library of Congress Cataloging in Publication Data

Bauer, Raymond Augustine, 1916–   ed.
  Some views on Soviet psychology.

  Reprint of the ed. published by American Psychological
Association, Washington.
  Includes bibliographies.
  1. Psychology—Russia—Addresses, essays, lectures.
I. Title. II. Title: Soviet psychology.
[BF149.B3 1975]   150'.0947   75-26671
ISBN 0-8371-8363-4

Originally published in 1962 by The American Psychological
Association, Inc., Washington, D.C.

Reprinted with the permission of American Psychological
Association

Reprinted in 1975 by Greenwood Press,
a division of Williamhouse-Regency Inc.

Library of Congress Catalog Card Number 75-26671

ISBN 0-8371-8363-4

Printed in the United States of America

CONTENTS

Preface

This volume is based on visits made to the Soviet Union by a number of American psychologists in the summer of 1960. The Human Ecology Fund furnished funds for most of these trips.

American psychologists have always maintained a lively interest in the work of their Soviet opposite numbers even during years when communications between the two countries were not as good as they now are. Since World War II, work in Soviet psychology has been surveyed at various times by Ivan London, Gregory Razran, and myself. More recently, Alexander Mintz has contributed reviews of Soviet psychological work at periodic intervals to the *Annual Review of Psychology*. When visiting between our countries became easier after 1956, a number of individual psychologists took the opportunity to travel back and forth. For example, Yvonne Brackbill, represented in this volume, has already reported on an earlier trip.

It was felt that, particularly with many American psychologists planning to attend the International Congress in Bonn during August of 1960, the time was propitious for a more extended group of visits with the explicit backing of the American Psychological Association. The intended merits of this procedure were dual. By having a considerable group of well-known American psychologists visit Soviet psychologists as individuals under the auspices of our professional association, it was hoped to improve communications further between psychologists of the two countries. In addition, and perhaps more directly to the point, a number of competent psychologists varying in their fields of interest would be in a position to report back to their American colleagues on the full range of work being done by our Soviet colleagues.

There is a special advantage to on-site visits by professionals competent in specific areas, and I am perhaps in a position to speak especially frankly of these advantages, having felt most strongly the disadvantage of their absence. When I wrote *The New Man in Soviet Psychology* about a decade ago, it was under the dual handicap of being restricted almost entirely to published sources and having to deal with areas of psychology which were outside my primary area of competence. Evaluation and understanding of what is being done is difficult under these circumstances. Even the translation of terms may suffer. Readers of translations of Soviet work must on many occasions wonder what a "Pavlovian approach" and other similar phrases mean in the specific contexts in which they appear. The contributors to this volume had the opportunity to ask for further elucidation, to see what was actually being done, and most of the time they were talking to psychologists in their own areas of competence in which they were optimally aware of the best English equivalences of the phenomena referred to.

The reader of this volume will discover that not all of these psychologists found much work parallel to their own. Gardner and Lois Murphy found much of interest to them in general, but not many psychologists doing the sort of social psychology to which they have devoted their own efforts. Fleishman found a good deal of educational psychology, but not nearly so much industrial psychology. Others, such as Brackbill, and Miller, Pfaffmann, and Schlosberg found much work going on in the areas in which they were most interested. Reitman found work on cognitive processes, but not always being done by psychologists.

Just who should be doing what line of work is of course a familiar argument for professionals of all lands. It is therefore no surprise that the boundaries of "psychology" and "psychologist" do not coincide perfectly in the U.S.A. and the U.S.S.R. In general, in recent decades the boundaries have been more narrowly drawn in the U.S.S.R. than in the U.S.A., but this in turn is changing. For example, Fleishman reports an awakening of interest in industrial psychology that antedates, to the best of my knowledge, the clear evidence for this trend in published literature. Even with a lag of two years between 1960 and the appearance of this volume, the reader can feel assured that in some respects at least he is getting a glimpse of imminent developments in Soviet Psychology.

Once the core papers of this book were prepared, it was felt that an introductory paper which would afford an appropriate setting would add to the value of the volume. Accordingly, Alexander Mintz, whose contributions to the *Annual Review of Psychology* have already been referred to, was asked to contribute a piece which would both offer historical perspective and a broad overview of recent developments in Soviet psychology to which the later, more specialized papers could be referred. Many of the writers were concerned over the possibility that their own coverage was selective, and over what they did *not* see and hear. The absence of an observation might mean either the absence of a given line of work, or merely the visitors ill chance in not having run across the relevant evidence. Mintz' paper helps to reduce this problem.

There are, of course, many persons who are due credit for their contribution to this volume. The authors of the various papers are identified by name.

John G. Darley, Executive Officer of APA, conceived of this venture, engineered it, and was ever willing and alert to see that it was pushed through to completion. His efforts were supported by Preston S. Abbott, Program Director of the Human Ecology Fund, and Samuel B. Lyerly, Research Director of the Fund. Alexander Mintz, in addition to writing the introductory chapter, reviewed the entire manuscript for points that might require clarification. The Human Ecology Fund is due a debt of gratitude for financing, not only the trips themselves, but a conference out of which the volume grew, and the preparation of the volume itself. Special credit should go also to Walter P. Pasternak and Hugh A. Bloom of the Editorial Department. Mr. Pasternak in particular worked extensively with the authors and the APA office in getting these papers together in book form.

The Soviet psychologists whose work is described and who furnished the information contained herein are mentioned by name throughout the manuscript. The authors wish to thank them as a group and especially those whose name occurs in several of the chapters for having been patiently hospitable to what must have seemed like a stream of American visitors. A number of the contributors sent drafts of their manuscripts to Soviet colleagues for comment and correction. The following authors wish to indicate the Soviet psychologists to whom they sent drafts of their manuscript and register their thanks to those who returned comments: Reitman—L. L. Gurova, F. N. Shemyakin, M. M. Bongard, P. Ya. Galperin, A. V. Napalkov; Brackbill—A. R. Luria, N. M. Shchelovanov, M. M. Koltsova, A. F. Tur; Miller, Pfaffmann, and Schlosberg—E. N. Sokolov.

The intent of these visits was to open up communication between American and Soviet psychology. This entire volume has been conceived in the same spirit.

RAYMOND A. BAUER

Cambridge, May 14, 1962.

CHAPTER I

Introduction to Contemporary Soviet Psychology

ALEXANDER MINTZ

HISTORICAL ANTECEDENTS

Contemporary Soviet psychology is a product of a long development and has varied historical antecedents. These antecedents include the work of Russian educators and educational theorists (beginning with the early part of the 18th Century), literary critics of the 19th Century, psychiatrists, physiologists, writers of books on psychology proper. A monograph by B. G. Ananiev (1947) presents a fair amount of information on the history of Russian psychology of the 18th and 19th Centuries, particularly information on early materialistic tendencies in Russian thought.

Tatishchev, a Russian educational writer of the early 18th Century, expressed the opinion that education should aim at achieving understanding, rather than memorization, on the part of students (Ananiev, 1947). Such an emphasis is also very characteristic of modern Russian educational psychology, as will be pointed out later in this chapter.

Lomonosov, a versatile Russian scientist and poet of the 18th Century, discussed human passions in his writings on rhetorics (B. G. Ananiev, 1947). Apparently he acknowledged the constructive aspects of the passions. He viewed the desirable intellectual qualities of man as products of interaction between intellect and passions. The tendency to accept the constructive aspects of emotional life is a characteristic feature of contemporary Soviet psychology (Mintz, 1958).

The first Russian book with a near-equivalent of "psychology" in its title, *Nauka o Dushe (Science of the Soul)*, appeared in 1796. Its author was a clergyman, but Ananiev states that the context of the book was similar to that of writings of British empiricists.

The first Russian book (by Liubovsky) with a title suggestive of empirical or experimental psychology (according to Ananiev, the book dealt with empirical psychology) appeared in 1815.

In 1834, a book by Galich appeared, expressing the idea that consciousness of the self is derived from the way one is perceived by others; one tends to view oneself as others view one (Ananiev, 1947).

In 1859, the famous Russian literary critic, N. A. Dobrolyubov, expressed in one of his essays the idea that an attempt to explain a man's personality requires knowledge of his development in childhood. He also stated that tyrannical behavior, as generally known, results from insecurity, and tends to produce tyrannical behavior in other people (Dobrolyubov, 1956).

Beginning with the 1860s, I. M. Sechenov (1871) a distinguished Russian physiologist, worked in the border area between physiology and psychology. He seems to have done much work on the inhibitory function of certain nerve impulses. He thought that behavior was of the type of reflexes, i.e. included responses to stimulation, mediated by a central coordinating apparatus. He used the term "reflex arc," but does not seem to have assumed that reflex arcs are relatively simple or anatomically fixed; he stated in one of his writings that it is not known how reflexes are produced. Consciousness, Sechenov believed, was a result of fuller elaboration of the functioning of the central components of reflex arcs. He viewed emotional states as capable of producing marked changes (both facilitating and inhibiting) of reflex functioning. He is reported to have been a vice-president of the First International Congress of Psychologists.

The first psychological laboratories in Russia were established by the psychiatrists V. M. Bekhterev (1886) and S. S. Korsakov (1888). A number of psychological laboratories were established at universities before the end of the 19th Century (Ananiev, 1947).[1]

The Psychological Institute of the University of Moscow opened in 1911. Its first director was G. I. Chelpanov, who had a high opinion of Wundt and Titchener. Chelpanov wrote a number of books on philosophy and on psychology. One of these (Chelpanov, 1915) was *Introduction to Experimental Psychology*, based on his course on this subject at the Institute. The book includes a long statistical section containing technical information not utilized by contemporary Soviet psychologists. The preface names several members of the Institute who helped to prepare the book, among them A. A. Smirnov, P. A. Rudik, N. I. Zhinkin, P. A. Shevarev. The supposition seems reason-

---

[1] Additional information on Russian psychology around 1900 is presented in Chapter V.

able that these men, all prominent in Soviet psychology, are (or were once) familiar with statistical methods, and refrain from using them for other reasons than lack of familiarity.[2]

STATUS OF PSYCHOLOGY AFTER THE REVOLUTION

The period following the revolution of 1917, in which the Communist Party seized power in Russia, was characterized by extensive theoretical discussions about the status of psychology among sciences and about the consequences of Marxist philosophy for psychological theory. A considerable range of viewpoints was represented in the discussions. Even Chelpanov, who favored the viewpoints of Wundt and Titchener, argued that his psychology was compatible with Marxism. Kornilov claimed that his psychology was the true expression of Marxist dialectical materialism. Bekhterev objected to psychology as "idealistic" and believed that it should be replaced by "reflexology." Pavlov was not opposed to psychology, at least not late in his scientific career (Pavlov, 1949); he thought that psychology had a legitimate function as the study of the subjective world, and that self-observation was a useful source of physiological theories. But he also believed that all true explanations of activities of living organisms were physiological ones, and some of his followers viewed psychology as superfluous. All in all, psychology during much of the 1920s was in a rather precarious position, with its continued existence uncertain. Bauer (1952) cites a short-lived decree of the Ukrainian Commissariat of Education, according to which psychology was to be replaced by reflexology as the basis of scientific pedagogy. According to B. M. Teplov (1947), reflexological opposition to psychology largely ended when Bekhterev died in 1927. A split occurred in the group of reflexologists, and some of them (Teplov names Ananiev and Miasishchev) became prominent as psychologists.

In 1928, three periodicals dealing with psychology and allied fields were established. Bauer (1952) gives the English equivalents of their titles as "Psychology," "Pedology" and "Psychotechnics"; however, these journals ceased publication a few years later, and there were no psychological periodicals in the Soviet Union from 1935 until 1955.

Soviet psychology of the 1920s and early 1930s exhibited theoretical influences and included topics later disapproved. A number of Russian psychologists are reported to have been influenced to a marked extent by American behaviorism (Bauer, 1952). There are

---

[2] See Chapters IV and VI.

many indications that gestalt theory and psychoanalysis had considerable influence in psychology and psychiatry of the Soviet Union in the late 1920s, and for a time in the 1930s. Thus Pavlov repeatedly referred disapprovingly to these influences, according to the published proceedings of his research seminars (Pavlov, 1949).

POLITICAL INFLUENCES ON SOVIET PSYCHOLOGY

Mental testing was prominent in psychology and allied fields (pedology, i.e. science of childhood, and psychotechnics) during the 1920s and early 1930s. But it came under attack increasingly on several grounds. Bauer cites evidence to show that a number of common results of mental testing were offensive to the ruling Communist Party. The objection was also raised that mental test scores are falsely treated as perfectly valid and permanently fixed. A further objection held that mental test scores could be produced by very different patterns of success and failure, representing qualitatively different performances. Quantitative test scores were therefore criticized as not having definite qualitative meaning. (Wertheimer raised much the same objection in his classes.) Judging by a sample of "pedological" literature (Blonsky, 1925), these objections—commonly raised by Soviet psychologists in critiques of Western psychology—are actually fair criticisms of Russian pedology of the 1920s and 1930s.

The context of Soviet psychology underwent several changes in the 1930s as a result of political influences. In 1929-30 Lenin's *Philosophical Notebooks* appeared in print. According to Teplov (1947), Lenin's theory of psychic life as the reflection of reality created considerable interest and was much discussed by psychologists. General acceptance of the Lenin reflection theory resulted in greatly increased interest in problems of sensation and perception.

In 1936, a decree issued by the Central Committee of the Communist Party condemned mental testing[3] and some other activities of the pedologists of the Soviet Union. Mental testing largely disappeared. According to Bauer, "the decree against pedology threw the Soviet psychologists into confusion and panic" and "departments of psychology were closed, and teachers of psychology wondered what to teach" (p. 129). But new tasks were found for psychology, particularly in education. In part, the decree against pedology was based on an optimistic view of educability of children. Thus a child's failure to make normal progress in school was attributed to improper instruction, inadequate preparation, and so on. The task of psycholo-

---

[3] Bronfenbrenner (Chapter III) cites a recent article by Kairov, which claims that the decree has been misunderstood and had not been intended to prohibit all testing and research utilizing tests.

4

gists was to conduct research on educational processes and procedures. Such research has been the most prominent feature of Soviet psychology since the late 1930s. (See, for example, discussions of the work of Galperin, Samarin, and others in Chapter II.)

Further changes in Soviet psychology followed World War II. In 1946 a decree was passed by the Central Committee of the Communist Party objecting to the supposedly exaggerated reliance of Soviet scientists on foreign sources, and the failure to credit Russian scientists sufficiently. A tendency developed among psychologists to cite exclusively Soviet sources, or only the "classics of Marxism-Leninism," and it became difficult to trace the influence of foreign sources in Soviet psychology. Bauer (1952, p. 155) cites a particularly clear example of suppression of a foreign source.

The Scientific Session of the Two Academies (Academy of Sciences and Academy of Medical Sciences), devoted to "utilization of the physiological doctrine of Pavlov," further illustrated political influences on Soviet science. The session seems to have been arranged by two of Pavlov's associates, K. M. Bykov and A. G. Ivanov-Smolensky, together with an unnamed high official, apparently Stalin.[4] The Session consisted of introductory and closing addresses (some of which were delivered by Bykov and Ivanov-Smolensky), and a large number of speeches accusing prominent Soviet scientists of departures from Pavlovian ideas, idealism, administrative inefficiency, failure to allow subordinates enough freedom, etc., defensive speeches and self-critical speeches. Several of the latter were by psychologists. Before the Session, Russian psychologists had said little about Pavlov's work, presumably because they regarded it mainly as physiology, and because they were not sufficiently familiar with it (Teplov, in *Nauchnaya Sessia*, 1950, pp. 153-159). After the Session, attention to Pavlovian ideas by Soviet psychologists gradually increased. The subsequent effects of Pavlovianism on psychological theory and research will be discussed later in this chapter.

There is a conspicuous omission among the principal historical sources consulted in writing these "historical remarks on Soviet psychology." Neither Teplov (1947) nor Bauer (1952) mentions the name of the distinguished Soviet educator and writer on education, A. S. Makarenko. His great influence on Soviet educational procedures and theories, and on Soviet theories of personality, are discussed in the second part of this introductory chapter, and also in

---

[4] In the published account of the Session *(Nauchnaya Sessia,* 1950) Orbeli, a distinguished Soviet physiologist, much criticized at the Session, hinted to that effect.

chapter III by U. Bronfenbrenner. The present writer has not traced the history of Makarenko's influence on Soviet psychology and education.

Recent Advances in Soviet Psychology[5]

In recent years two reports presenting the status of psychology in the Soviet Union have appeared in the volumes of the *Annual Review of Psychology* (Mintz, 1958, 1959). The work for the second of these reports was completed in the summer of 1958, the work for the first about a year earlier. During that year some apparently significant changes in the status of psychological thought in the Soviet Union were noted and were mentioned in the second paper. Therefore, the first task is to try to ascertain whether any new trends have appeared in Soviet psychology during the last two years.

As far as the available material is concerned the improved condition of psychology persists, and the picture of psychology presented in the preceeding papers continues to be substantially valid, or was valid in the early months of 1960. Whether it still is true, after the political events of that year, is not apparent. The present picture of Russian psychology appears to be substantially the same as that of two years ago, though there have been some advances within the same framework.

The information about psychological research in the U.S.S.R. has tended to increase in amount of detail; what was available a few years ago in the form of summary articles is now likely to be available as several research reports. In many instances there are now books on topics covered a few years ago in articles or proceedings of scientific meetings. Citations of authorities (even of Lenin) seem to have become more relevant than in the past, and the range of people who are likely to be quoted favorably seems to have increased; thus L. S. Vygotsky and Bekhterev are quoted more freely and favorably than they used to be. As for content, the general picture seems to be much the same as it was a few years ago.

Some of this framework, and the advances which have been made, is presented (partly on the basis of old material, partly by utilizing new material) in the sections which follow.

Books on General Psychology

A considerable amount of attention in the two reports was devoted to Russian books on general psychology. For this presentation, two

---

[5] The section of this chapter which begins here is an expanded and corrected version of an invited address presented at the 1960 Convention of the American Psychological Association, in Chicago.

books of very unequal value have been examined. One is the third edition of an elementary textbook by P. I. Ivanov (Ivanov, 1959). The first edition (Ivanov, 1955) had been unfavorably reviewed in the Russian psychological journal, *Voprosy Psikhologii;* the unfavorable criticism has not prevented the publication of additional editions. Two differences between the third and the first editions are striking. The name of Stalin has been eliminated from the author's list of greatest men of genius in the history of humanity, and the other three men on the author's list, Marx, Engels, and Lenin, are no longer asserted to be the greatest, but are listed only as examples of men of genius with a high degree of versatility. The other change has to do with the glowing portrait of what the author originally called the typical new Soviet man. The glow of the description has been toned down, and the description is now said to apply, not to the typical, but to the front-rank *(peredovoy)* Soviet man. These changes appear to represent increasing contact with reality in the author's writings.

The other book is the first volume of what appears to be a very informative handbook of psychology entitled, *Psychological Science in the U.S.S.R.* (Moscow Institut Psikhologii, 1959). Publication of a second volume is planned. The first volume deals mainly with cognitive functions—perception, memory, thinking, speech, etc.—and is a collection of papers by different Soviet psychologists. Included are a number of the best known psychologists in the Soviet Union, e.g. B. G. Ananiev, A. N. Leontiev, A. R. Luria, S. L. Rubinstein, P. G. Kostiuk, and others. Some of the papers are essentially research reviews with hundreds of references. Some are theoretical papers based on original experiments.

HISTORY-MINDEDNESS

As mentioned earlier, there is a tendency towards history-mindedness in Russian psychology. This tendency is still present. Recent issues of the Russian psychological journal, *Voprosy Psikhologii,* include three historical papers: Zakuev, 1959; Makovelsky, 1959; Ramul, 1960. One deals with the psychological contributions of medieval philosophers of the East who wrote in the Arabic language; their contributions are characterized as more advanced and more original than is generally believed by Western historians unable to read Arabic writings in the original. Another historical paper deals with courses in psychology taught at the University of Tartu (German name: Dorpat) in Estonia, from the late eighteenth century until 1918. The third paper deals with Spinoza's contribution to psychology.

Related to the history-mindedness of Soviet science is the tendency

7

to honor distinguished men of the past in various ways. Institutions of higher learning are likely to be named after political leaders (generally communists); liberal Russian writers of the nineteenth century; and scientists, usually but not always Russian (one scientific institute, for example, is named after Helmholtz). There are also scientific meetings commemorating anniversaries of births or deaths of distinguished scientists of the not-too-distant past, at which their contributions and topics, more or less related, are discussed. The proceedings of one particular meeting is devoted to the scientific contributions of the nineteenth century physiologist Sechenov; and a book of scientific papers is devoted to the contributions of the physiologist Vvedensky and their application in neurology and psychiatry.[6]

A paper by Ananiev summarized the research of his associates at the University of Leningrad (Mintz, 1959). The research dealt with the recognition of shapes of objects by means of the hand or hands. A report of the work is now available in much greater detail as a book, *The Touch Sense in Cognition and Work* (Ananiev, 1959).[7] The book provides descriptions of hand behavior in the examination of objects, subjects' drawings of shapes of objects, subjects' verbal reports, and results of experiments in which subjects examined objects indirectly, e.g. by means of sticks, etc. The authors reported, e.g. that active exploration of an object by a moving hand results in much better knowledge of the shape of an object than passive contact with the stationary object. When a right-handed person explores an asymmetrical object, the left hand tends to hold the object while the right hand explores it; if the object is symmetrical, the subject tends to explore it by synchronous movements of the two hands. If the object is asymmetrical, and the subject is required to explore it by synchronous movements of the two hands, interference phenomena like those in retinal rivalry are apt to be the result. In right-handed subjects, threshold measurements indicate that the left hand is superior to the right hand as a sense organ.

Inasmuch as the research deals largely with the questions (1) what

---

[6] Incidentally, there is evidence of people being honored who, during their lifetime, were anti-communists and had emigrated from Russia. For example, there have been references to a musical festival honoring the memory of Rachmaninov, a chess tournament commemorating Alekhin, etc.

[7] In Chapter VI there is an account of a visit to the recently established Leningrad Institute of Labor Psychology, in which research of the type in Ananiev's book is continued by Ananiev's associates. Additional research on sensory transmission of information (Shemyakin, Istomina) is presented in Chapter II.

actions of a subject lead to veridical perception? and (2) what are the demands of work situations on perception?, such research might be readily justified from the point of view of American functionalism. But since Lenin also believed that perception was likely to be veridical, Ananiev characterizes the research of his school as springing from the Marxist-Leninist dialectic-materialistic theory of psychic life as a reflection of reality.

EXPERIMENTAL WORK ON SPEECH

N. I. Zhinkin has written a book on speech (Zhinkin, 1959), which contains much information about such varied topics as the determination of the meaning of particular words by the context within which they occur, the symptomatology of stuttering, and so forth. The book also contains an account of many experiments performed by the author. The experiments fall into two main categories. For example, there are experiments on what may be called psychophysics of speech sounds. (A representative finding is that the accented syllable in a word is not necessarily the loudest; some vowels require less loudness than others, to be perceived as accented.) There are also numerous experiments on the mechanism of speech production. In many of these experiments X-ray photographs of the speech apparatus were used. Walter Reitman, who visited Zhinkin, provides an interesting and informative account of Zhinkin's work in Chapter II of this volume.

PAVLOV'S THEORIES

It is generally known that Soviet psychologists, psychiatrists, physiologists, and others concerned with the study of human behavior think highly of Pavlov's theories. The high opinion persists,[8] although the frequency of citations of Pavlov's ideas seems to have decreased, probably because of the apparent disappearance of numerous irrelevant citations of Pavlov. However, the admiration of Pavlov's ideas can easily be misconstrued. It does *not* indicate the prevalence of a viewpoint which holds that behavior is produced by automatically functioning inherited and acquired stimulus-response bonds. Such an interpretation of Pavlov's ideas may fit some of his early writings and some contemporary Russian medical writings. It does not fit Pavlov's later ideas, which have been presented in many modern psychological and physiological writings. Many of these ideas were originally expressed by Pavlov orally at his research seminars; the pro-

---

[8] The veneration of Pavlov by Soviet scientists is discussed in Chapter VIII. Relevant information about Pavlovian influence is also to be found in Chapter VII.

9

ceedings of these seminars were eventually published under the title *Pavlovian Wednesdays* (Pavlov, 1949).

To Pavlov, a reflex was not a local automatism. A reflex is an organism's activity, which occurs in response to stimulation. The activity need not be simple. Thus Pavlov referred to exploratory behavior as the "investigatory reflex," to an animal's struggle against confinement as the "freedom reflex," to an animal's disturbed behavior if left alone as evidence of a strongly developed "social reflex," and so on.

One of Pavlov's complex reflexes was called the "orientational reflex."[9] This idea acquired (and apparently is continuing to acquire) a more precise meaning as a result of experimental work by E. N. Sokolov and his associates.[10] A previous summary (Mintz, 1958) discussed Sokolov's arguments in favor of his view that vascular changes, as recorded by a finger plethysmograph, are indicators of readjustments which go on in the organism and which prepare it for response to stimulation. Some other papers dealing with other components of the orientational reflex (GSR, EEG), and with possible clinical applications have also been summarized (Mintz, 1958, 1959). Since then, at least three books dealing with the orientational reflex and related topics have appeared. One of them, Sokolov's *Perception and the Conditioned Reflex* (Sokolov, 1958) was an impressive account of a large amount of painstaking research aiming to disentangle the complex relations among perception, adaptation phenomena, conditioned adaptation, the orientational and conditioned orientational reflexes, and defensive and conditioned defensive reflexes. What amounts to operational definitions of adaptational reflexes, orientational reflexes, and defensive reflexes are given in terms of different patterns of change in the case of the different physiological measures which were used.

To Pavlov, a conditioned reflex was not based on an acquired S-R sequence; a conditioned reflex was thought to be based on a "temporary bond" between the cortical portions of sensory "analyzers." The cortical representations of the conditioned and unconditioned stimuli are synthesized, and the conditioned stimulus becomes, as a result of this synthesis, a signal of the unconditioned one. There are complicated induction relations between conditioned reflexes. The sum total of an organism's conditioned reflexes (other than those in-

---

[9] Another translation is "orienting reflex." "Orientational" is a slightly more precise translation because it is, like the Russian term, an adjective derived from a noun, while "orienting" is a participle.

[10] See also the Chapters written by Miller, Pfaffmann, and Schlosberg, and by Murphy and Murphy in this volume.

volving speech) form a "signal system." Man has, in addition, a "second signal system" involving speech,[11] and the two signal systems interact; normally the second signal system is the leading one. There seems to be no necessary implication of participation of effectors in conditioned reflexes. In one passage, Pavlov referred to perception as belonging to the category of conditioned reflexes; in another passage he stated that Helmholtz's unconscious inferences were conditioned reflexes. There are even papers which make a distinction between reception theory and Pavlovian reflex theory of perception. The latter implied only that perception was to be viewed as an active process, rather than as passive reception.

However, papers by Leontiev (1959) give reflex theory of perception a more definite interpretation. He suggests that the functioning of the efferent branch of reflex arcs may be an essential component of perception, and cites experimental findings in favor of such a view. In one of the experiments tone-deaf people were trained to reproduce musical tones by singing them; they were then informed about the success of their attempts. Leontiev reports that the training in intonation was successful, and that at the same time the tone deafness of the subjects disappeared in other situations.[12] Leontiev suggests that pitch discrimination may be a complex skill based on the ability to reproduce tones by vocal intonation and that most people acquire this ability without special effort. A few, the tone deaf, fail to acquire it in the natural course of events; they can acquire it through special training.

Another experiment attempted to obtain a conditioned reflex to an invisible beam of light shining on the palm of the subject's hand. Infra-red rays were filtered out. The experiment succeeded, but only if the subjects were told that the unconditioned stimulus would be preceded by a warning. As a conditioned reflex developed, the subjects reported that they felt something, although they could not describe it further.[13]

In the last years of his life, Pavlov devoted considerable attention to what he called "sistemnost" (a neologism translatable as systemness or systemity) of conditioned reflexes, which, he felt, tended to form dynamic systems. The products of synthesis can be re-synthe-

---

[11] The characterization of the second signal system as involving speech follows Pavlov's formulation; but Pavlov's use of the term was not always consistent with this formulation. A possibly better formulation is to be found in Chapter VI.

[12] See Chapter VII.

[13] Interviews with Leontiev are reported in Chapters II, VII and VIII.

sized into larger units. In case of regular sequences of conditioned reflexes to different conditioned stimuli, the places in the sequence may become the effective conditioned stimuli, so that changing the order of conditioned stimuli may have no effect on the accustomed sequence of the conditioned reflexes.[14] Relations can also function as conditioned stimuli.

SWITCHING OVER PHENOMENA

The relation between conditioned reflexes and complex stimuli has received considerable attention in recent years. The work of E. A. Asratian, for example, on "switching over" phenomena (the meaning of "switch" is similar to that in railroad switch) is particularly interesting. A conditioned stimulus may produce one conditioned reflex in one set of circumstances, when it is a part of one stimulus complex. The same conditioned stimulus may lead to another conditioned reflex in other circumstances; in such case the changed circumstances act as a "switch," and "switch over" from one conditioned reflex to the other. The sound of a buzzer may be regularly followed by food in one experimental room, by an electric shock in another. In such a case the experimental room is likely to become the switch which determines whether the sound of the buzzer leads to salivation (and other components of the food reflex) or to defensive reflexes. The experimenter or the time of the day may also function as "switch" stimuli. Asratian reported this material at the International Congress of Psychology in Montreal in 1954, and in articles. He has stated that the switching phenomena afford an explanation of the great flexibility of acquired behavior in higher animals and contribute to their ability to adjust to changing circumstances.

More recently, he wrote a book (Asratian, 1959) based on his lectures in England. The book presents what may be called modern Pavlovian ideas on the physiology of the central nervous system. In this account, for example, Pavlov's ideas have at times surprising resemblance to those of Goldstein. Pavlov's conception of the reflex is characterized as involving complex dynamic interaction within the central nervous system, rather than the functioning of specific anatomically defined pathways. The cerebral cortex participates in the production both of conditioned and unconditioned reflexes. Asratian views the mechanisms which produce reflexes as multi-level reflex arcs. He comments on the great complexity and variety of the neural mechanisms which enable organisms to compensate for defec-

---

[14] This is known as a stereotype. Recent research on stereotypes in children, as conducted in Koltsova's laboratory, is reported in Chapter V of this volume.

tive functioning. The last chapter of Asratian's book deals with his experiments on switching phenomena.[15]

EDUCATIONAL APPLICATIONS OF PAVLOVIAN THEORIES

Pavlov's theories on analysis and synthesis, on resynthesis of products of synthesis, on conditioned stimuli as signals, on the two signal systems, and on the normal dominance of the second signal system in man can be readily utilized and have been utilized in Russian educational psychology and in psychology of perception, thinking, and speech. The Pavlovian educational psychologists do not favor the utilization of repetitive drill in school instruction. There are, however, references to the Pavlovian principles of analysis and synthesis, to the interaction between the first signal system of the senses and the second signal system of speech, and to learned performances as complex hierarchical structures with many components.[16]

LEARNING POTENTIALITIES OF CHILDREN

In his well known textbook of psychology, Hilgard distinguishes between learning as habit formation, which includes conditioning, and learning as acquisition of understanding. Katona, who used to be one of Wertheimer's associates, makes the same distinction in the title and content of his book, *Organizing and Memorizing.* The Russian educational psychologists appear to be very much in favor of organizing, and quote from Pavlov's late writings to that effect. The expressed attitudes of educational psychologists towards the potentialities of children are invariably optimistic. There is the general conviction that practically all children can achieve good understanding of school subjects if only the teacher uses sound educational techniques, and instructional procedures appropriate for different children.[17]

Two other items of information on Russian educational writings are of interest. One is the unquestioning acceptance of the intrinsic value of education. Russian educational psychologists never question that children should understand algebra or grammar or be able to spell "properly." They assume these are desirable objectives. The

---

[15] A much more comprehensive account of Asratian's work on switching is given in Chapter VII.

[16] Chapters II, V and VIII contain more detailed information about educational research in the U.S.S.R. In addition, Chapter VI discusses the achievement of understanding as one of the objectives of the training of industrial workers. Soviet workers are trained to solve problems and think in a flexible manner.

[17] The related views of one psychologist, Krutetsky, are explored in some detail in Chapter II.

other point concerns the belief, prevalent in the United States, that Russian schools are organized solely for the benefit of the all-powerful state and ignore the rights of individual children. Whether this represents the attitude of the Soviet government is not clear, but it certainly does not represent the expressed attitudes of Soviet educational psychologists.

PHASE PHENOMENA

There are other Pavlovian theories which should be mentioned here. One is the theory of "hypnotic phases" or "phase phenomena" (*fazovye yavlenia*).[18] Normally, an increase in the intensity of a conditioned stimulus increases the intensity of the conditioned reflex. But under certain conditions this so-called "rule of intensity" ceases to operate. In the equating phase, intensification of the stimulus fails to exert an influence on the magnitude of the reflex. In the paradoxical phase, intensification of the stimulus weakens the reflex. In the ultra-paradoxical phase, stimuli which ordinarily produce excitation acquire an inhibitory function, and normally inhibitory stimuli become excitatory. These "phase phenomena" were viewed by Pavlov as effects of inhibition of cortical cells. This inhibition may serve the function of protecting the cortical cells from damage by overstrong trans-marginal stimulation. The stimulation can become transmarginal as a result of a strong drive. The inhibitory state can be produced by various influences which have a weakening effect on the nervous system, so that ordinary stimuli begin to function as trans-marginal ones. Phase phenomena were also treated by Pavlov as appearing in sleep-like states and in hypnosis, which were thought to be characterized by widespread cortical inhibition. The theory of phase phenomena has obvious applications in psychopathology. Pavlov himself suggested a number of such applications when, at 75 years of age, he became interested in psychopathology. Ultra-paradoxical phase phenomena may be used, whenever a patient exhibits ambivalent attitudes. The paradoxical phase is suggested, for example, by confusions between fantasy and reality; the patient's reactions may be in response to the normally weaker factor, *fantasy*, rather than the normally stronger *reality*. Pavlov interpreted catatonic stupor as a state of widespread protective inhibition. Tests of the functioning of conditioned reflexes to establish whether pathological phase phenomena are present frequently are reported in Russian psychiatric literature.

---

[18] The theory of the "phase phenomena" is Pavlovian; the term, however, appears to have originated after his death.

Types of Nervous Functioning

Another Pavlovian contribution is his doctrine of types of nervous functioning. According to an article by the Russian psychologist Teplov,[19] Pavlov's typology underwent a long and complicated development. In the last form of the typology (1935) while Pavlov was alive, there were three dimensions within the first signal system. These Pavlov called strength, balance between excitatory and inhibitory processes, and mobility, i.e. the ease or difficulty of changing over conditioned reflexes to particular stimuli. In addition, there were the two additional dimensions of balance between the first and second signal systems, and between cortical and subcortical centers. (The latter seems to be mentioned only in discussions of psychopathology.) Pavlov had characterized his own personality as psychasthenic with pronounced dominance of the second signal system. The Pavlovian typological ideas are widely utilized (not always in the same form) in Russian literature dealing with personality and psychopathology. Apparently, experimental work on Pavlovian typology is continuing in Soviet psychology. The publication of a second volume of typological studies by the school of Teplov has been announced.[20]

Analysis Through Synthesis

There are still other examples of research inspired in part by Pavlovian ideas. Rubinstein has written a small book on psychology of thinking (Rubinstein, 1958) which overlaps to a considerable extent his chapter in *Psychological Science in the U.S.S.R.* The book deals with experiments in which the author asked subjects to solve mathematical puzzles and to think aloud while solving them.[21] In Rubinstein's formulation of the nature of problem solving, based on his experimental notes, he uses the expression "analysis through synthesis." He maintains that problem solving is generally accomplished in the course of exploratory attempts at solution. These trial solutions place the requirements of the problem in relation to different aspects of the situation (synthesis). The accumulation of a number of such

---

[19] B. M. Teplov, Tipologicheskie osobennosti vysshey nervnoy deiatelnosti. (Typological characteristics of higher nervous activity.) A.P.N. R.S.F.S.R., Moscow, U.S.S.R., 1956.

[20] Information concerning current research by Teplov's associates is given in Chapter VII of this volume.

[21] Rubinstein criticizes the formulations of the nature of problem solving by Selz, who was a member of the Wurtzburg school, and Koffka. His discussion indicates that he was very familiar with the ideas both of the Wurtzburg school and the gestaltists and expected his readers to be familiar with them.

syntheses leads to the discovery and isolation of the relevant aspects of the situation. This is what Rubinstein means by "analysis through synthesis."

INFERRED INTERACTIONS IN THE BRAIN

E. I. Boyko (Moscow Institut Psikhologii, 1957) edited and wrote parts of a book called *Higher Neuro-dynamics of Man*. The book deals in some instances with material in earlier versions, but there are also new variations of experiments reported earlier. Thus in one study (by Schwartz) the effects of practice on the threshold of recognition of visual shapes were investigated. A similar study reviewed earlier reported large practice effects, but only with some methods of practice. On the basis of subjects' introspective reports, of generalization to other shapes and of recognition times, the author views the effects as perceptual, rather than based on the use of secondary criteria. Several studies deal with a number of effects of hypothesized or inferred interactions in the brain. One such interaction effect presumably accounts for joint utilization of items of information originally acquired separately. Boyko, unlike many other Russian psychologists, views this process of "intellectual placing together" as based on a physiological process different from that of formation of temporary bonds or conditioning. The book includes an account of experiments (by N. Kostomarova) requiring subjects to find common parts of previously memorized visual patterns which were presented incompletely or completely. Rather surprisingly, "intellectual placing together" worked more effectively with patterns which were presented incompletely and had to be compared "from memory," than with patterns presented completely. In another experiment (by N. I. Chuprikova), the author attempted to time "intellectual placing together." Interactions between consecutive reaction time experiments are studied in other papers; the spatial distance between consecutive stimuli, the time intervals between them, and the presence or absence and location of visual signals to which the subject is asked not to respond, are some of the independent variables. The effects on the reaction times are interpreted in terms of the Pavlovian ideas of initially irradiated, and later concentrated, cortical response to stimulation. There is a paper on electromyograms obtained from muscles controlling wrist movements, taken during reaction time experiments. Results show that electrical oscillations in the muscles precede hand movements, and the muscles which control the hand not to be moved also show electrical activity.[22]

---

[22] Accounts of visits to Boyko's laboratory may be found in Chapters II and VII.

N. I. Krasnogorsky, one of Pavlov's earliest associates still living, published a book (1958) summarizing his work on conditioned reflexes in children. He states that his first paper dealing with this topic appeared in 1907. The book is largely an exposition of Pavlov's ideas, illustrated by the results of experiments (mostly on salivary conditioning) with children. There are interesting variations of experiments on semantic conditioning; thus the author reports that, if a conditioned salivary response to the number ten is established, the child is also apt to salivate in response to the request, "add five to five." The author reports on experiments studying functions other than salivation, e.g. speech, pressing a key, etc. There are accounts of experiments establishing two conditioned salivary reflexes to two different signals by using two kinds of food.[23] Subsequently, after the subjects were satiated for one of the foods, the corresponding conditioned reflex tended to disappear. There also are accounts of disturbances both of unconditioned and conditioned reflexes in a variety of cases of disease. One chapter deals with neurasthenia in childhood, with advice to parents, stressing kindness, regular routines, and protection of the neurotic child against over-stimulation and against fatigue.

Incidentally, some of Pavlov's ideas seem to be ignored in practice. Thus Pavlov tended to ridicule Ivanov-Smolensky's technique of motor conditioning with verbal reinforcement on the grounds that it neglects the differences between man and dog; nevertheless, this technique is very widely used.

MAKARENKO AND PLANNED UTILIZATION OF COLLECTIVES

Another influential factor in Russian psychology not to be overlooked is the tradition which originated in the work of the Soviet educator and writer on educational subjects, A. S. Makarenko. Makarenko, who died in 1939, was a school teacher and a communist sympathizer. His writings are frequently cited, always favorably, in present-day Russian research accounts and other writings on personality development, moral education, and related subjects.[24] Makarenko's first major piece of writing was his *Pedagogical Poem* (translated as, *The Road to Life*, 2nd edition, 1955). This work has the sub-title, "A Novel," but some time after its publication, Makarenko stated in an article that the story of the book is true.

---

[23] For a recent report on related work, see A. R. Luria, "Verbal Regulation of Behavior," *The Central Nervous System and Behavior*, New York: J. Macy, Jr. Foundation, 1960.

[24] Chapters III and V present examples of research on these topics.

17

(This has been questioned in Russia.) The work is limited by the fact that the conversations were not recorded verbatim but are reconstructions from memory. The reason for believing in the essential truthfulness of the book is that, although the author was a communist sympathizer, he made no attempt to hide the post-revolutionary confusion, administrative inefficiency and trickery of his colleagues in dealings with the administrative agencies.

The story concerns an institution for juvenile delinquents, established in an old orphanage abandoned by staff and inmates during the civil strife following the revolution. Makarenko's first task was to recover furniture and equipment stolen by neighborhood peasants. When the first group of juvenile delinquents (about 12 youths) arrived, they behaved like teen-age "hoods"—stealing from neighboring farmers, from each other, and from some members of the institution's staff. They ridiculed the staff for taking care of them, refused to help with household chores and even staged a number of holdups. Makarenko's educational ideas apparently developed initially out of improvisations in emergencies arising in the course of his institutional work. He worked for many years in institutions and seems, also, to have been an educational consultant to families. Several books, monographs, and articles written by him, have been collected in seven volumes. Some of his educational ideas (as cited by Krutetsky & Lukin, 1959) were as follows:

The best way for an educator to influence children is through one (or more) of the collectives of which they are members, e.g., the family collective, the school class collective, the school collective, the young pioneers collective, etc. Much of the business of the collective is transacted at meetings at which discussion takes place. The educator should place demands before the collective. The educator may attempt to influence the collective through a select few, informal leaders, or the so-called "active." It is very important that members of the "active" *not* receive special privileges. It is advisable that the collective be initially organized around a task of unquestionable social usefulness. With time, the demands of the educator presented to the collective tend to become the collective's own demands.[25]

How common and widespread are the applications of Makarenko's ideas in Soviet educational practice? Some of the stories seem almost too remarkable. For example, Korotkov—in a paper presented at a teachers' conference—gives this account (Institut Psikhologii, Moscow, 1959, pp. 89-104) of pupil initiative in an overcrowded school with inadequate plumbing. By their own labor, and on the recommendation of their collective, the pupils constructed a water line between school buildings—at a saving that assured construction of an addi-

---

[25] Chapter III includes an account of a detailed plan for step-wise building of classroom collectives.

tional classroom. Later, the pupils participated in building other classrooms, eventually expanding the school from nine to thirteen rooms. The school's needs were first presented by the teachers for discussion at a meeting of the relevant pupil collective. Action by the pupils followed.

THEORY OF PSYCHOGENIC DISORDERS AND PSYCHOTHERAPY

From our point of view, the status of the theory of psychogenic disorders and psychotherapy in the Soviet Union presents some curious features. The existence of psychogenic disorders and the appropriateness of psychotherapy were acknowledged in Russian psychiatric textbooks but the origin of the former and the techniques of the latter were, for the most part, not revealed.[26] More recent sources, e.g. some issues of the *Journal of Neuropathology and Psychiatry;* two textbooks of neurology (V. V. Mikheev, 1958; Liapidevsky, 1959); a small book by K. A. Skvortsov (1958) on psychotherapy for patients afflicted with organic diseases; a Congress or Conference on Psychotherapy (U.S.S.R. Ministertvo Zdravookhranenia, 1958); a recently published book on psychotherapy, by K. Platonov; a first volume of a new textbook on psychiatry (O. V. Kerbikov, 1958); a book on hypochondria (Pashchenkov, 1958); and a book on schizophrenia (Ye. N. Kameneva, 1957) present the following impressions: (1) The *Journal of Neuropathology and Psychiatry* is practically all neuropathology and contains hardly any psychiatry. (2) As far as the newer textbooks are concerned, they are still largely uninformative on the subject of psychogenic disorders; exceptions to this rule are disorders provoked by the physicians or iatrogenic disorders. (3) The book on psychotherapy, for organically ill patients, discusses only one formal psychotherapeutic procedure, i.e. hypnosis. Striking successes of hypnosis, as far as relief from suffering is concerned, are recounted. The author also points out that all patient-physician contacts are apt to have psychotherapeutic or psychotraumatic consequences and presents many illustrative examples. (4) The proceedings of the Congress of Psychotherapy (published as *Voprosy Psikhoterapii*), which consists of about fifty papers, deals mostly with hypnosis. However, there are three papers which deal with other matters. One, by V. N. Miasishchev, states that there are two kinds of psychotherapeutic procedures, suggestion and persuasion. Two procedures, re-education and distraction, are later added. He disapproves of psychoanalysis, but his therapeutic procedures seem often to resemble those of unorthodox psychoanalysts. Thus one pas-

---

[26] Chapter IV mentions the availability of Freud's writings in libraries in the U.S.S.R.

sage states (my translation) "the psychiatrist by his skilled approach to the patient helps him to disentangle the history of his life—the complicated and tangled non-understandable or incorrectly understood circumstances of the past and present." He states that this leads to the trust, respect, and love of the patient for the physician, which are likely to be decisive therapeutic influences. Emotion, a very important factor in neurosis, is often overlooked: "Dry speech by the physician-pedant won't cure any man." Miasishchev states that "pathogenetic analysis" is, as a rule, necessary. He make the distinction between essentially normal people who have developed neuroses as a result of severely traumatic situations, and people whose character structure is neurotic. The former may be cured by hypnosis; the latter require other procedures. Disorders with complex psychogenic bases require "deep psychotherapy." The author also indicates and illustrates, by examples, that symptoms may be deceptive and that their true meaning may be different from what they seem to be.

Platonov's paper largely deals with hypnosis and his own "combined psychotherapy" (anamnestic conversations, clarifying and persuasive conversations, hypnotic removal of affect, hypnotic sleep as rest). There are, however, some new points. For example, the author refers to the hidden desire of some people to remain sick. He refers to the danger of direct removal of symptoms by hypnosis in a small minority of people, e.g. those with a "weak nervous system, preponderance of the first signal system and hysterical character." He complains also about the lack of instruction in psychotherapy in medical schools.

M. Lebedinsky views psychotherapy in Pavlovian terms, as restoration of normal neurodynamics which have been disrupted by collision of excitation and inhibition. He views the patient's confidence in the therapist as particularly important. The physician's honesty in dealing with the patient and his concern for the patient, as well as his thoroughness in investigating the symptoms contribute greatly to the patient's confidence in the therapist. The therapist may play a supportive role. The real trauma may be masked by another. The author objects to narcoanalysis, and also to what he calls "catharsis" (he does not explain what he means by catharsis), as being potentially dangerous and tending to disturb the patient-therapist relation. He cites some cases of symptoms substitution, which indicates that such cases are not unknown to Russian psychiatrists.

The Compatibility of Materialism With the Theory of Psychogenic Disorders and Practice of Psychotherapy

Apparently, awareness of psychogenic disorders and practice of psychotherapy exist in Russia, although not on a large scale.[27] Undoubtedly there are many people in the United States who believe that this state of affairs is an unavoidable consequence of Pavlovian materialism and reflex doctrine. Although the relative neglect of psychogenic disorders and psychotherapy in Russia is due, to a considerable extent, to a persistence of certain ideas of Pavlov, these ideas are not necessary consequences of his materialism or reflex doctrine.[28] In his discussions of psychopathological problems Pavlov tended to utilize certain components of his system, rather than other components. Thus he might have placed more emphasis on psychotherapeutic interviews than he actually did, as providing opportunities for the extinction of undesirable conditioned emotional reflexes, and for interaction between the two signal systems. Instead, Pavlov favored therapeutic procedures aiming to restore the patients' disturbed nervous functioning by means of excitatory and inhibitory drugs, or by rest. Similarly, he tended to interpret psychopathological states in terms of "inert foci of excitation," "sick cortical points," "ultra-paradoxical phase," "protective inhibition," "over-strained excitatory (or inhibitory) process," etc. As a rule, he did not recommend thorough investigations of the development of the patients' systems of conditioned reflexes during their life histories, or of the relations between this development and the content of the symptoms. He might have, considering that he repeatedly expressed the idea that conditioned reflexes, once established, do not completely go out of existence, but are only inhibited or covered up by layers of later acquisitions. Sometimes the inhibited conditioned reflexes reappear. The concept of regression was included in Pavlov's theoretical system. Pavlov spoke of the lasting effects of the early living conditions on the later behavior of his laboratory dogs. He referred with approval to the fact that, in his laboratories, the same dogs were used again and again as subjects in different experiments, thus making what amounts to longitudinal studies possible.

Pavlov also spoke of the possibility of inferring experience from behavior and underlying brain processes from experience. One particularly interesting example of Pavlov's utilization of a person's experience in constructing a physiological theory had to do with the origin of his famous experiments on experimental neurosis. He set

---

[27] Neither the Davids, the Murphys, nor Brackbill report encountering any psychotherapeutic procedures resembling those discussed by Miasishchev or Platonov. The Davids (Chapter IV), however, report the existence of a post-doctoral course in psychotherapy at a hospital they visited.

[28] A contrasting viewpoint may be found in Chapter IV.

out to produce what he called a collision between excitation and inhibition because he inferred such a "collision" in the case of Elizabeth von R., one of Freud's early cases (Pavlov, 1949).

Pavlov's theories of behavior as "higher nervous activity" have components which can serve as a basis for detailed systematic theories of psychogenic disorders and psychotherapeutic interviews. Apparently, Miasishchev and like-minded people are currently engaged in an elaboration of these components of Pavlovian theory without giving up materialism. Pavlov's theories are capable of being expanded as far as the interpretation of symptoms is concerned, just as they were expanded to justify the emphasis on understanding in education.

Do Ideological Differences Make Cooperation Between American and Soviet Psychologists Impossible?

Previously in this chapter it was pointed out that Russian educational psychologists emphasize understanding of school subjects by pupils (as contrasted with memorization), and justify this objective as springing from true Pavlovian doctrine. The educational ideas of the Soviet psychologists, like the psychopathological viewpoints which were discussed in the paragraphs immediately preceding this one, illustrate the great flexibility of major theoretical systems (Pavlov's doctrine of higher nervous activity, materialism) and their capacity to incorporate the most diverse facts. Such an apparent lack of a direct or unambiguous or necessary relationship between the broad theoretical system favored by a psychologist and his attitudes on concrete psychological issues appears to be a very common state of things.

The opinion has been expressed (both in the U.S.A. and the U.S.S.R.) that collaboration between psychologists of the two countries is not likely to develop because of ideological differences. Generally, Russian psychologists accept the ideology of Marxism-Leninism (combined with Pavlovian ideas), which is not popular in the U.S.A. Nevertheless, it is difficult to see any consequences of Marxism-Leninism for the typical research projects of Soviet psychologists, e.g. one dealing with the use of live flowers in classroom instruction in botany, or one concerned with the effectiveness of certain methods of remedial instruction in arithmetic, geometry, and grammar, or one investigating the course of extinction of the orientational reflex in normal and feebleminded children, or one of the uses of discussions of literary heroes in moral education of children and adolescents.

Ideological considerations appear to exhibit more influence on the treatment of psychological topics which are rejected in the Soviet Union, e.g. social psychology and mental testing. In some instances, there is probably a tendency to avoid topics wherein facts are apt to be discovered contradicting certain Marxist theories. Thus the American "proletariat" has remarkably little Marxist class-consciousness and intelligence tests indicate the existence of differences between the distributions of the test scores of people belonging to different social classes. Soviet psychologists seem unaware that findings such as these have no unanimously-accepted interpretation in American psychology, and can be incorporated into different ideological contexts. The lack of class-consciousness of the American working class need not be interpreted as an argument for the preservation of the present social order; it is probable that some American psychologists are dissatisfied with the present social order and view the comparative lack of social-class consciousness as an obstacle to social progress. Similarly, intelligence tests have not been invented for the purpose of freezing the social order, as a number of Soviet psychologists apparently believe; these tests serve a number of useful purposes in educational and vocational situations. Their use often serves to reduce the numbers of students of whom either too much or too little is likely to be demanded, considering their degree of readiness for school work of various degrees of difficulty. Some of the other main uses of mental tests have to do with prediction of future vocational success of individuals. The users of tests in American psychology undoubtedly vary widely in their opinions on political and social issues. Tests are used both by defenders of the present social set-up, and by champions of the social "underdog." The use of tests does not presuppose a belief either in their unfailing accuracy or the hereditary determination of the test scores. Though there are differences of opinion about their degree of validity and about the share of heredity in the variance of test scores, estimates of validity as close to 1.00, or the opinion that test scores are wholly hereditary, are held by few if any psychologists. By and large, mental tests seem to be treated in American psychology as empirical instruments which are useful in predicting future performance, in spite of their only moderate degree of validity and their uncertain theoretical basis.

For the most part, ideological differences as obstacles to communication between American and Soviet psychologists are not impressive. On the other hand, ignorance in each of the countries about psychological work in the other cannot be discounted. It has been reported that some Soviet psychologists claim that American psychological literature is well known to the Soviet psychologists. It is difficult to believe these claims;[29] they are contradicted by the paucity of references to American publications in Russian psychological literature (often only old American sources are cited), by misinformation about the state of American ideas on psychology, by apparent lack of information and the non-utilization of methodological procedures which are commonly used in the U.S.A., such as many statistical techniques. Even more impressive is the ignorance concerning Soviet psychology (and related fields) on the part of many people in the U.S.A. For example, very few people in this country have heard of Makarenko's techniques of utilization of collectives in reeducation of juvenile delinquents, or about the method of teaching children the concepts of mathematics or grammar by utilization of what amounts to operational definitions of these concepts. Nor are many people aware that Pavlovian theory of the conditioned reflex is not (at least for the most part) a theory of simple sensory-motor habits, but one of formation of temporary bonds within the afferent system.

Psychology in both countries could profit from better acquaintance with scientific work in the other. There are a number of ways in which this may be accomplished. Translation of books, articles surveying the literature, lecture tours, books of articles specially written for the collection, and visits by psychologists or groups of psychologists are all useful steps towards better acquaintance with each others' work, and are actually being practiced. Some additional steps which might be put into effect include the exchange of research findings and critical reviews by psychologists of both countries for publication in professional journals. The teaching of suitable courses by visiting professors in the two countries might also prove advantageous, e.g. a course on statistical methods, or on test construction and standardization by Americans in Russia, or on "higher nervous activity" by a Russian in America. Last but not least, cooperative research by psychologists of the two countries, particularly in areas where marked disagreement prevails, might prove mutually beneficial. Thus in the U.S.A., low I.Q.'s are apt to be treated as justifying an unfavorable educational prognosis for children (particularly so if there is no evidence indicating that the apparent intellectual retardation is a result of emotional problems), in which case psychotherapy tends to be recommended. In the U.S.S.R., psychologists express more favorable attitudes towards the potential efficacy of instructional procedures with educationally retarded children, pro-

---

[29] Chapter II contains information confirming the impression of inadequate information about American psychology in the U.S.S.R., and even less information in the U.S. concerning Soviet psychology.

vided that the children do not have damaged brains, and that the missing components of the complex educational skills are located by appropriate experimentation. There is the possibility that a Russion psychologist working in an American institution for the feeble-minded, using Russian non-test experimental techniques, may be able to find the educationally neglected children who can be rehabilitated by the instructional methods which have been developed by Russian educational psychologists.[30] On the other hand, an American psychologist using psychometric tests may be able to identify the children in a Russian remedial school who are not likely to benefit from remedial instruction; or he may use projective tests and interviews in order to identify the children who need counseling or play therapy. There are undoubtedly many additional research problems, the solution of which may be advanced by cooperation between American and Russian psychologists. One such research problem, for example, could stem from the many Russian reports of successful applications of Makarenko's techniques of work with collectives of children and young people. An attempt at utilization of these techniques in the problem schools of our own large cities, or in community work with delinquent youths, in collaboration with a Russian consultant who is an expert on these techniques, may prove fruitful.

[30] Dr. B. F. Riess mentioned a conversation with a Russian psychologist in which the latter suggested the desirability of such an investigation, to be conducted by a Russian psychologist in the U.S.A.

REFERENCES

Ananiev, B. G. *Ocherk istorii russkoy psikhologii 18 i 19 vekov. (A sketch of the history of Russian psychology of the 18th and 19th Centuries.)* Moskva, Gospolitizdat, 1947.

Ananiev, B. G. and others. *Osiazanie v protsessakh poznania i truda. (The touch sense in the processes of cognition and work.)* Moskva, Izd-vo APN R.S.F.S.R., 1959.

Asratian, E. A. *Lektsii po nekotorym voprosam neiro-fiziologii. (Lectures on some questions of neuro-physiology.)* Moskva, Iz-vo AN S.S.S.R., 1959.

Bauer, R. A. *The new man in Soviet psychology.* Cambridge, Mass., Harvard Univ. Press, 1952.

Blonsky, P. P. *Pedologia.* Moskva, Rabotnik prosveshchenia, 1925.

Chelpanov, G. I. *Vvedenie v experimentalnuyu psikhologiu. (Introduction to experimental psychology.)* Moskva, Kushnerev, 1915.

Dobrolyubov, N. A. *Selected philosophical essays.* Moscow: Foreign Languages. Publishing House, 1956.

Ivanov, P. I. *Psikhologia. Moskva, Uchpedgiz, 1955.*

Ivanov, P. I. *Psikhologia.* izd. 3. Moskva, Uchpedgiz, 1959.

Kameneva, E. N. *Shizofrenia, klinika i mekhanizmy shizofrenicheskogo breda. (Schizophrenia. Clinical picture and mechanisms of schizophrenic delusional state.)* Moskva, 1957.

Kerbikov, O. V. *Uchebnik psikhiatrii. (Textbook of psychiatry.)* V. 1, Moskva, MEDGIZ, 1958.

Krasnogorsky, N. I. *(Vysshaya nervnaya deyatelnost u rebenka. (Higher nervous activity in the child.)* Leningrad, MEDGIZ, 1958.

Krutetsky, V. A. and Lukin, N. S. *Psikhologia podrostka. (Psychology of the adolescent.)* Moskva, Uchpedgiz, 1959.

Leontiev, A. N. O mekhanizme chuvstvennogo otrazhenia. (About the mechanism of sensory reflection.) *Voprosy Psikhologii,* 5th year, 1959, No. 2, 19.

Liapidevsky, S. S. *Osnovy nevropatologii. (Foundations of neuropathology.)* Moskva Uchpedgiz, 1959.

Makarenko, A. S. *Pedagogicheskaya Poema. (The road to life; an educational epic.)* 2nd edit. Moscow: Foreign Languages Publishing House, 1955.

Makovelsky, . . Benedikt Spinoza i ego mesto v istorii psikhologii. (Benedictus Spinoza and his place in the history of psychology.) *Voprosy psikhologii,* 6th year, 1959, No. 2, 71-78.

Mikheev, V. V. *Nervnye bolezni. (Nervous diseases.)* Moskva, MEDGIZ, 1958.

Mintz, A. Recent developments in psychology in the U.S.S.R. *Annual review of psychology,* 1958, 9, 453-504.

Mintz, A. Further developments in psychology in the U.S.S.R. *Annual review of psychology,* 1959, 10, 455-487.

Moscow Institut Psikhologii. *Voprosy izuchenia vysshei neirodinamiki v sviazi s problemami psikhologii. (Questions of research on higher neurodynamics in connection with problems of psychology.)* E. I. Boyko, edit. Moskva, Izd-vo APN R.S.F.S.R., 1957.

Moscow Institut Psikhologii. *Psikhologicheskaya nauka v S.S.S.R. (Psychological science in the U.S.S.R.)* V. 1, 1959a.

Moscow Institut Psikhologii (ed. Dragunova, T. V. and Kabanova-Meller, E. N.) *O nekotorykh metodakh obuchenia i vospitania. (Of some methods of instruction and upbringing.)* Moskva, Izd-vo APN RSFSR, 1959b.

Nauchnaya sessia posviashchennaya problemam fiziologicheskogo uchenia Akademika I. P. Pavlova. Stenogrammy dokladov. Moskva, Izd-vo Akad. Nauk S.S.S.R., 1950. (Scientific session dedicated to the problems of the physiological doctrine of Academician I. P. Pavlov.)

Pavlov, I. P. *Pavlovskie Sredy. (Pavlovian Wednesdays.)* Moskva, Izd-vo AN S.S.S.R., 1949. V. 1, 2, 3.

Ramul, K. A. Psikhologia v Tartuskom Universitete. (Psychology in Tartu University) *Voprosy psikhologii,* 1960, 6, No. 2, 128-134.

Rubinstein, S. L. *O myshlenii i putiakh ego issledovania. (On thinking and ways of its investigation.)* Moskva, Izd-vo AN S.S.S.R., 1958.

Sechenov, I. M. *Reflexy golovnogo mozga. (Reflexes of the brain.)* 2nd edit. St. Petersburg, Trubnikov, 1871.

Skvortsov, K. A. *Ocherki po psikhoterapii somaticheskogo bolnogo. (Sketches on psychotherapy of the somatically ill.)* Moskva, Vsesoyuz. obshch. nevropatol. i psikhiat., 1958.

Sokolov, E. N. *Vospriatie i uslovnyi reflex. (Perception and conditioned reflex.)* Moskva, Izd-vo Moskovskogo Universiteta, 1958.

Teplov, B. M. *Sovietskaya psikhologicheskaya nauka za 30 let. (Soviet psychological science over 30 years.)* Moskva, Pravda, 1947. .

U.S.S.R. Ministerstvo Zdravookhranenia. Institut Psikhiatrii, *Voprosy psikhoterapii.* (M. S. Lebedinsky, ed.) Moskva, MEDGIZ, 1958.

Zakuev, A. K. Araboyazychnaya psikhologia na Blizhnem i Srednem Vostoke v srednie veka. (Arabic-language psychology in the Near- and Middle East in the Middle Ages.) *Voprosy psikhologii,* 5th year, 1959, No. 4, 30-38.

Zhinkin, N. L. *Mekhanizmy rechi. (Mechanisms of speech.)* Moskva, Izd-vo APN R.S.F.S.R., 1959.

CHAPTER II

Some Soviet Investigations of Thinking, Problem Solving, and Related Areas[1]

WALTER R. REITMAN[2]

This chapter is based on a visit to the U.S.S.R. from May 12 to June 5, 1960. The trip was made to establish contact with scientists investigating thinking, problem solving, and related areas, with special emphasis on research using computer modeling or other simulation techniques. Moscow and Leningrad were the only cities visited, and the discussion is limited accordingly to work under way at these centers.

The materials are organized under three rough and very general headings: (1) experimental investigations, (2) pedagogically oriented studies, and (3) cybernetic[3] studies, and research on sensory mechan-

1. A draft version circulated earlier was entitled "Notes on Conversations with Soviet Investigators of Thinking and Problem Solving."

2. The writer is indebted to the Human Ecology Fund which provided, through the American Psychological Association, most of the funds for the visit to the U.S.S.R. upon which this paper is based. Also gratefully acknowledged are a Faculty Research Fellowship and supplemental funds from the Social Science Research Council, as well as a month's release from regular academic obligations by the Graduate School of Industrial Administration, Carnegie Institute of Technology. Credit for whatever is conveyed here of the methods and intent of Soviet work in this field is due primarily to the many Soviet scientists who patiently explained what they were about, and also in many cases went out of their way to assist in making interview arrangements with colleagues. In this connection, the writer is especially grateful to three psychologists, A. N. Leontiev, A. R. Luria, and A. A. Smirnov; to A. P. Ershov, of the Computing Center of the U.S.S.R. Academy of Sciences in Moscow; and to L. A. Chistovich, of the Pavlov Institute of Physiology in Leningrad. Finally, very helpful reviews of the manuscript in Alexander Mintz and Josef Brozek, and the resourceful support of John G. Darley at all stages of the project also are deeply appreciated.

3. The term is used with very broad meaning in the U.S.S.R., covering work in such areas as artificial intelligence, self organizing systems, automatic programming, and automata studies, to mention only a few. A. V. Napalkov has very kindly acquainted me with a comprehensive and up to date survey of Soviet developments in this area. It is: A. I. Berg (Ed.) (Cybernetics—to the service of communism). Moscow: (State Energy Press), 1961,—the first of a projected three-volume series. See also E. A. Feigenbaum, Soviet cybernetics and computer sciences, 1960. Commun. ACM, 1961, 4, 566-579.

isms. Some of this work is perhaps not directly relevant to thinking and problem solving, as these terms are understood in the United States. In doubtful cases, however, particularly where material appeared likely to be of general interest, it seemed worthwhile to include it, even at the risk of blurring already vague boundaries. Wherever possible, we have focussed throughout on concepts, formal and informal assumptions, and methodological characteristics.

Almost all of the materials presented here derive from interviews. And while the writer speaks Russian, these discussions often involved terms, concepts and methods well outside his competence. To minimize inaccuracies, the chapter has been checked against published materials in several cases, and copies of an earlier version were sent in August, 1961, to all individuals and groups in the U.S.S.R. whose work is described here in any detail. The corrections received in correspondence from the U.S.S.R. through the end of 1961 have been incorporated in this final draft. No doubt a number of errors of fact and interpretation remain, but it seems reasonable to suppose that there are none so serious as to interfere with the overall useful‚ ness of the chapter as an informal report on Soviet work in this general area.

EXPERIMENTAL INVESTIGATIONS

This first section discusses work by F. N. Shemyakin and Z. M. Istomina, N. I. Zhinkin, A. N. Sokolov, A. N. Zakharov, and L. L. Gurova, all of the Laboratory of Thinking and Speech at the Institute of Psychology in Moscow, as well as some experiments from the Laboratory of Higher Nervous Activity at the same Institute.

Since almost all of the members of the Laboratory of Thinking and Speech are represented in what follows, a few words on the overall organization of the Laboratory may be helpful at this point. To begin with, it is one of the six laboratories of general psychology at the Institute. "Laboratory," incidentally, is best understood as a synonym for "group," at least in this case. Each of the members is an independent investigator, although all are united by common bonds of interest in the same general area.

Studies are initiated by research proposals from the individual members. These are reviewed, and accepted or rejected by senior officers of the Institute, and perhaps in some cases by officers of the parent organization—the Academy of Pedagogical Sciences, as well. At the end of the year, each investigator writes a report to the Director of the Institute, for information and for evaluation of his work.

In many ways these procedures would resemble quite closely those obtaining in the United States were our department heads, deans, and foundation officers all integrated into a single hierarchy. But there are at least two important potential differences to be remarked. First, the pluralistic organizational structure in the U. S. may result in a somewhat weaker and less consistent set of formal and informal pressures on and guides for research content and method. Second, there would seem to be somewhat more administrative control exercised over individuals as compared with American practice. For example, in the U.S.S.R. the head of an institution must approve all work submitted for publication by its members; and unpublished materials otherwise apparently may not be sent abroad.

F. N. Shemyakin is one of the senior investigators of the Laboratory of Thinking and Speech, as well as the administrative Head of the Laboratory. His first remarks provided a general overview of the current status of psychology in this area as he sees it. Very briefly, Shemyakin considers that the old associationistic psychology, based on the kinds of concepts available to John Stuart Mill, has run up against a revolution in modern physical science. The basic elements of this revolution are: (a) the development of non-Euclidean geometry; (b) the paradoxes of set theory; (c) the theory of relativity; (d) the statistical mechanics of quantum physics; and (e) information theory and cybernetics. This modern scientific revolution is claimed to have markedly affected psychology: classical associationism no longer is tenable, and has given way to a statistical, non-deterministic point of view. Shemyakin traced the development of this newer viewpoint back to Clarapède and William Stern, as well as to the Gestalt psychologists (especially Wertheimer). He did not, however, explicitly relate his own research efforts to this new position, nor was it clearly evident in the presentations of the other investigators in the Laboratory.

RESEARCH ON PERCEPTION

The empirical investigations conducted by Shemyakin and his associate, Z. M. Istomina, are best classified from a Western viewpoint as research on perception, with the main focus on the transmission of sensory information. Only the barest summary will be presented here.[4] The first of these studies deals with the development of internal representations of spatial coordinates. Subjects are seated in chairs, and told the direction of different objects, e.g. the

---

4. Full descriptions of these investigations are contained in a new volume *Thinking and Speech* (11) just received through the kindness of Professor Shemyakin. The volume also reports in a great deal more detail some of the investigations by N. I. Zhinkin and A. N. Sokolov discussed here.

railroad station, the airport, etc., and then rotated at various angles. After enough time to allow for damping out of movement in the labyrinthine canals, they are asked to indicate the locations of these objects. Among the findings for rotations of 180 degrees, for example, are that objects directly in front of and behind the subjects are located accurately. The perceived locations of objects on either side shift, however. Comparable investigations with blind subjects also have been carried out. Shemyakin was interested to learn of the somewhat related investigations by Werner and Wapner, although it proved difficult to make any direct comparisons between his investigations and theirs.

Other work is being conducted (primarily by Istomina) on the availability and use of color information by children as a function of age. Principal concerns are the development of color discrimination, the use of color names, and the way in which names and color discriminanda become associated. Using various matching methods, the investigators find, for example, that hue discriminations can be made at around three years of age. Combined hue and brightness discriminations are made correctly only somewhat later. Discrimination of color sensations, on the one hand, and acquisition of color names, on the other, proceed quite separately. Completely correct discrimination and naming of colors may not occur until as late as seven years of age. These investigations, it should be noted, are only one phase of a broad program of research into the apperception and symbolization of color sensations at all ages and in several languages now being carried out by Shemyakin, Istomina, and their associates.

MECHANISMS OF SPEECH

Of the several members of the Laboratory of Thinking and Speech, N. I. Zhinkin is probably the man most interested in the actual mechanisms of speech,[5] and in the relation of these mechanisms to the thinking process. Zhinkin believes that the organs and mechanisms of speech have been subject to intensive investigation, but from a number of independent and mutually isolated points of view. Linguists, psychologists, physiologists, and others have accumulated massive bodies of facts, without, however, attempting to integrate these specialized collections of information across the boundaries of their respective disciplines. It is just such a broad generalized scheme that Zhinkin is trying to develop.

To illustrate the benefits to be achieved through such an approach,

---

5. A. R. Luria (3, p. 29) indicates that Zhinkin's *The Mechanisms of Speech* very soon will be reviewed in the journal *Contemporary Psychology*. See also fn. 4.

Zhinkin described his work on the mechanisms involved in pronouncing the letters of the alphabet. For a long time, he pointed out, we have known the apparently trivial fact that vowels and consonants are not pronounced at the same volume level in normal speech, i.e. they do not all require a constant amount of energy. The fact seemed trivial because no one could say what it might mean. The original research had been done by linguists, who were concerned only with speech organs located in and around the mouth—principally the lips and the tongue. But these organs are responsible only for speech "segments"; equally important are those organs involved in the phonology or prosody of speech—the pharynx, the diaphragm, and the bronchial passages of the lungs. Zhinkin investigated the two sets of organs at the same time, using roentgenogram and kymoroentgenogram techniques, and discovered an unanticipated set of complementarities. The diaphragm descends, for example, when the vowel "ah" is spoken, but ascends in pronouncing the sound "ee." This compensates, Zhinkin stated, for the relatively smaller amount of energy required for "ee" than for "ah." In brief, the previously unexplained difference in volume now appears to be one of several complexly related manifestations of a general regulatory mechanism in the brain, which governs both sets of organs as a single system.

The pharynx, diaphragm, and bronchial apparatus are entirely outside the sphere of voluntary control, however, and this raises another very interesting problem involving the relation between these organs and the regulatory centers of the central nervous system. Somehow or other, a very complex pattern of involuntary movements in these organs has to be learned if a child is to acquire the ability to pronounce the sounds of his language. Zhinkin suggests that a feedback system of the following sort may be involved. The organism has access to the correct sounds, first supplied from without and then gradually internalized. Differences thus may be generated between the auditory feedback from the imperfect utterances of the organism, and the model sounds or their traces. The organism, in effect, strives to reduce these differences, selecting and retaining those involuntary movements which do so even though it cannot elicit them directly.

The critical factor here is the feedback. If this is eliminated, one would expect that correct involuntary movement patterns never would be acquired. But in those who are deaf from birth, there is no such feedback mechanism operative. How then do the deaf learn to speak?

Zhinkin first of all pointed out that the speech of those born deaf actually sounds quite different from that of normal adults. Only those who become deaf after their third or fourth year, having learned reasonably well to articulate the basic sounds of their language, approximate normal speech. Because those who are born deaf cannot match model sounds with their own auditory feedback, they never do acquire the proper patterns for the involuntary apparatus. To support his argument, Zhinkin exhibited roentgenograms which he said demonstrated that there is no pharyngeal movement whatsoever during the speech of those born deaf.

Zhinkin's work on speech control mechanisms has led him to conceive a very interesting theory of stuttering. He sees stuttering as the outcome of a conflict between two mechanisms, one subserving breathing and the other speech. The breathing control is a two-stage reciprocal mechanism. In the first stage, the diaphragm descends and the lungs expand; in the second, the lungs contract. When one talks, however, a new sound-making system imposes itself on the lower level breathing system. Zhinkin proposes that stuttering develops when an individual has experienced a situation in which he wanted to talk but could not, due to some fear stimulus. Under the influence of fear, the autonomic nervous system preempts control of breathing from the speech coordinating center. A vicious cycle develops. The individual comes to fear loss of his ability to speak, and this perpetuates the conflict between the two control systems. The cycle feeds on itself, and Zhinkin noted that the later treatment of stuttering begins, therefore, the more difficult it is to correct.

As a final illustration of the range of Zhinkin's interests, we may note his work in comparative psychology, on the vocalizations and cries of chimpanzees. (The work is being carried on at the well known chimpanzee colony at Sukhumi, in Georgia.) Chimpanzee vocalization, he finds, consists of a fixed set of 18 sounds, fixed in the sense that, in contrast with human speech, if there is a cry that sounds like "ak," there will not be one that sounds like "ka." Chimpanzees show no evidence of possessing the vocal co-ordination, transition, and control mechanisms that enable humans to build up large vocabularies by permuting elementary phonemic units. Interestingly enough, he also has pointed out important differences in primary vocal apparatus between humans and chimpanzees. For example, the roof of the pharynx, or epiglottis, is significantly higher in the chimpanzee, so that there are two distinct resonating chambers, whereas humans have one combined chamber, running from the mouth down through the pharynx. Finally, the pharynx has no role in the vocalizations of the chimpanzee, which thus are comparable in at least this one respect with the speech of humans born deaf.

Zhinkin's psychological terminology consisted primarily of Pavlovian concepts, which he seemed to find easy and convenient to his basic analytic tools. Asked about this, he pointed out that Pavlov in his opinion was the first to provide a "modern" conceptual system, in the sense that, like cybernetics, it viewed the human organism as functioning much like an adaptive machine. Notions like "feedback," therefore, which are essential to his thinking, fit in very well, and require no major reworking of the theoretical superstructure he uses.

The complexity and interdisciplinary character of Zhinkin's experimental work requires a variety of special apparatus, little of which is available at the Institute of Psychology. Roentgenograms and kymoroentgenograms, for example, both must be made with equipment located at other scientific centers. As Zhinkin commented, however, procurement of such devices by the Institute would hardly be justified, since he could not ensure a sufficient work load either for the apparatus or, still more important, for the skilled people who would be required as operators.

A. N. Sokolov's extremely interesting research on silent speech during reading is described by Miller, Pfaffmann, and Schlosberg elsewhere in this volume.[6] The few added points reported here were made in the course of fairly casual, speculative conversation; they may, however, be useful in indicating something more of the conceptual framework Sokolov brings to bear on his data.

Sokolov considers that the movements of the speech musculature picked up in his recordings during silent reading, in fact, reflect the inner saying of the words. This inner speech is in turn held to be substantially correlated, perhaps even identical, with thinking. Sokolov seems quite capable of determining from his recordings how relaxed a subject is as he reads. He does not, however, as yet appear able to provide convincing empirical support for a close relation between thinking and inner speech.

Among other very interesting speculations on the role of the musculature, Sokolov suggested that it might be viewed as a resonator, selecting and temporarily preserving information to be used by the brain, the main information processor in the system. He used this idea in discussing one curious result he had obtained, the fact that lip recordings showed more activity prior to rather than during utterances. If lip muscle activity depends primarily on inner speech, or thinking, and speech itself occurs only *after* what is to be said has been thought out, then it is quite reasonable that the recordings

---

6. See Chapter VII.

show a relative drop in activity during actual speech. Sokolov has tried to pin down this hypothetical role of feedback from the musculature, for example, by asking subjects to repeat constantly a single syllable while reading to themselves. Apparently, however, he has not had any conclusive results.

Thinking and Problem Solving

A. N. Zakharov and L. L. Gurova, two of the younger members of the Laboratory of Thinking and Speech, might be characterized as those on the staff most concerned with thinking and problem solving as the typical western psychologist would understand the terms. In fact, Zakharov's principal published work derives from a study by J. W. Whitfield (13), which compared the amount of information subjects require to solve a set of classification problems with the theoretical minimum needed.

Zakharov was a student of philology before becoming interested in psychology. At present, he is one of the few psychologists[7] in the Soviet Union with a strong interest in the application of mathematical and computer models in the study of psychological processes. He has acquired most of his mathematical training independently, and the contacts he has with mathematicians appear to be maintained largely through his own initiative. He undertook to follow up Whitfield's research in part as a kind of training exercise, to develop familiarity with the theory and methodology involved. Once he got into the problem, he found himself wondering whether Whitfield's results were not to be explained more in terms of mnemonic processes than by the characteristics of human thinking, and so what originally had been intended as a replication study developed into an original investigation instead.

The study itself is available in an English translation (14), and therefore only the main findings are mentioned here. In brief, Zakharov was able to support Whitfield's results. In addition, he concludes that psychological difficulty is a function of the form of information feedback, and is smallest for the conditions of his experiment when information is presented all at once. Finally, Zakharov relates the efficiency of information utilization to the previously acquired heuristics which his subjects bring to the experimental situation.

Gurova primarily is concerned with the role of conscious awareness *(osoznavanie)* in the problem solving process. Her experiments

---

7. As the term is defined organizationally in the U.S.S.R. Scientists from other disciplines make considerable use of these tools, as the subsequent discussion of research on cybernetics and sensory mechanisms demonstrates.

are intended to clarify basic general relationships; she is not concerned with events at the microprocess level. She described briefly two unpublished studies to illustrate her objectives, methods, and results. (They have since been published. See 5, 6.) Both make use of moderately difficult problems in geometry such as might require five minutes of a very good student, and a good deal more for less capable individuals. Her subjects generally had not recently been studying geometry, and so did not have basic theorems and proofs readily at hand.

In describing the results of her first study, Gurova divides her subjects into three groups, those who are "good," those who are "average," and those who fail entirely to solve her problems. She finds that "good" subjects immediately see how to approach the problems and begin at once to carry out necessary constructions. "Average" subjects must spend some time in preliminary analysis before they discover how to proceed. Those who fail to solve the problems never seem to raise the question of appropriate approaches, and they show surprise when questioned about their approach afterwards. She concludes that "good" problem solvers can think through the approach question without conscious awareness of what they are doing. She further concludes that conscious thinking is necessary for all successful subjects after the approach question has been decided, when the specific operations necessary for solving the problems are at issue.

Gurova's results will be of direct relevance and interest in connection with the increasing number of American studies of problem solving which make use of "thinking aloud" techniques for gathering data, since these studies have not in general been concerned with the potential effects of conscious awareness upon the thinking process.

Gurova's investigation employed a somewhat different set of methods. For example, she did not ask subjects to think aloud as they worked, but instead asked for a report of what they had been doing after they either had finished or else had failed to find a solution. Investigations utilizing thinking aloud techniques (e.g. 4, 9, 10) have not at least as yet suggested a relation between degree of conscious awareness and the success or failure of a particular attempt to solve a problem. The absence of such awareness that Gurova reports in subjects who fail, for example, thus may reflect this difference in methods. So far, in fact, there seems to be little or no difference in actual experimental findings, since in a recent personal communication, Gurova mentions preliminary data indicating that "reasoning aloud appears to be one of the methods which stimulates conscious thought." The difference is rather one of interpretation of the results. Gurova views the two experimental techniques as generating different kinds of thought processes in the subjects, whereas those in the U.S.A. now trying to simulate the thought processes inferred from thinking aloud protocols probably would prefer to assume that the thinking processes do not differ basically in the two cases. On this assumption, Gurova's results then might be taken to indicate that problem solvers do not store in memory detailed information about attempts they make to solve problems when these attempts turn out to be unsuccessful. Further research on this question should be of considerable interest and importance, since it concerns both basic concepts of the thinking process and also fundamental problems of data interpretation.

Gurova's second study is an investigation of the effects of visual aids on the solving of similar multi-stage geometry problems requiring construction in order to arrive at a solution. The visual aids are three-dimensional plexiglass structures, some representing correct intermediate steps in the solution, others representing incorrect steps. These representations are shown to the subject, and he is asked to distinguish correct steps from incorrect ones.

Her conclusions are quite interesting. In the first place, she finds that these visual aids have little effect on her subjects as a group. They appear to help only about one individual in ten. In the second place, what effectiveness they have depends upon the subjective structure of the problem as the individual reports it. More specifically, the visual aids assist only those who recognize that a given representation is one of several possible constructions, i.e. those who realize that a given line, for example, might go here *or* there, *or* in some third position. What in effect amounts to the awareness of a disjunctive set seems to be associated with a conscious search for additional information to decide among the several possibilities. Those who already have arrived at a poor construction seem unaware that it is poor, and that there are better possibilities. They are not looking for, and do not make use of, the information provided by the visual aids.

HIGHER NERVOUS ACTIVITY

In describing the overall organization of the Institute of Psychology, the Director, Professor A. A. Smirnov, noted that research relevant to thinking and problem solving also was under way in several other laboratories within the Institute, and he pointed out in particular the work of the laboratory headed by E. I. Boyko, which has as its problem the study of the general laws of higher nervous activity. (I can do no more than note here the arrival of a new volume received through the kindness of N. I. Chuprikova, T. N. Ushakova, and M. M. Vlasova while this chapter was in galley proof.

It is: E. I. Boyko (Ed.) (*Borderline problems of psychology and physiology.*) Moscow: APN R.S.F.S.R., 1961. The book contains comprehensive and authoritative reports of the experiments discussed below, and of a number of other investigations by Boyko and his associates as well.) A group consisting of N. I. Chuprikova, T. N. Ushakova, and M. M. Vlasova undertook to describe some of these investigations. They began with a general description of their underlying interests. The focus of their research is what Pavlov termed the *second signal system*.[8] This is specific to humans, Ushakova explained, enabling them to react adaptively not only to immediate information, but also to information concerning the past and the future. They are trying, for one thing, to learn how the brain centers associated with the second signal system facilitate or inhibit neural activity in other brain centers in response to instructions from the experimenter: this work provides a specific example of the group's overall interest in the physiological bases of higher psychological processes, e.g. thinking.

This description of their interests suggests research primarily neurophysiological in technique. But while there is some work with EEG recordings elsewhere in the laboratory, the studies described by Chuprikova, Ushakova, and Vlasova actually employ only behavorial tasks and measurements. The principal method discussed involves latencies on a switch throwing apparatus in response to visual cues under varying instructions. Much of the conversation centered, therefore, on the relation between these experimental techniques and the neurophysiologically framed theoretical concepts in terms of which the results were interpreted.

Consider these four typical experimental tasks.

1. Subjects are instructed to respond, for example, by closing a specified switch, when a spot of light appears on the left side of a

---

8. While there is no generally accepted distinction in western literature corresponding to it, the Pavlovian classification of all human information processing mechanisms into two groups, the first and second signal systems, is basic to Soviet psychological conceptualizations, perhaps especially so in the area of thinking. In Leningrad, for example, a physiologist wishing to communicate the nature of our common interests introduced the writer to colleagues as a psychologist doing research on the second signal system.

Smirnov defined the first signal system as common to men and animals, comprehending the mechanisms underlying the development of (non-verbal) conditioned reflexes, and the second signal system as that based in linguistic and symbolic processes. According to W. H. Bridger (3, pp. 425-426), Pavlov meant by these concepts ". . . that, in common with other animals, man has unconditioned or inborn reflexes and instincts, as well as primary conditioned responses, formed from a first signaling system, such as sensations, perceptions, and direct impressions of their environment. In addition, he believed that man has a second system of signals of reality which includes speech, ideas, or verbal thoughts, abstractions, and generalizations."

See also further comments on the Pavlovian concept of signal systems in Chapter I of this volume.

screen, and to make no response when the spot appears on the right side.

2. Subjects are instructed to respond similarly to one of a pair of tones, but not to the other.

In both cases, response latency is measured as a function of similarity relations between positive and negative stimuli.

3. Five switches are provided in a row. Each switch is paired with a light. A subset of four adjacent switches in the row is designated, and subjects are instructed to respond when one of the corresponding four lights goes on by closing the switch with which it is paired. No response is to be made when the fifth light goes on. Response latencies for the four positive switches are studied as a function of proximity to the fifth switch.

4. Four lights and four switches are provided. The subjects are instructed to determine which switch is paired with each of the lights. There are two training trials, and two test trials. In the first training trial, two of the four lights—for example, lights B and C—are indicated, and the subjects learn which pair of switches goes with this pair of lights. On the second trial, a new pair of lights, consisting of one from the previous set, say B, and a new light, perhaps D, is designated. The subjects learn that these lights are associated with a second pair of switches, one from the previous set, and one new one. On test trials, subjects must indicate which switch is associated with the light common to both pairs, and which is associated with the remaining light—in this case, light A.

In interpreting response data from experiments such as these, three assumptions seem to be applied:

1. Response latency is a function of the readiness status of the neural locus immediately determining the particular response just prior to the presentation of the stimulus to which the response occurs. This status ranges from a high degree of *excitation* to a high degree of *inhibition*. Short latency is a sign of high prior excitation, long latency, of high prior inhibition.

2. Verbal instructions achieve their effect through the neural centers of the second signal system, by causing neural loci activated by a particular instruction to send facilitating or inhibiting impulses which influence the excitation status of the motor centers receiving the impulses.

3. There is a one-to-one correspondence between degree of similarity among stimuli (or among responses) on the one hand, and degree of functional interconnection among the corresponding neural loci on the other, such that the more similar two stimuli (or responses) are to one another, the greater the inhibitory or excitatory

interaction between the corresponding neural centers.

These assumptions lead to the following sorts of interpretations and explanations when applied to the results observed in experiments of the sort described above.

These investigators find in the first two experimental situations that the more similar the positive and negative stimuli, the greater the latency in response to the positive stimulus. This is attributed to the joint effect of the verbal instructions and the changing functional relation between the neural loci associated with the two stimuli. As a result of the instructions, the neural area associated with the negative stimulus is in an inhibited state. The more similar the two stimuli, the more interconnected the two corresponding neural loci, and thus the greater the inhibitory influence exerted by the negative locus upon the positive one. It is this increased inhibitory influence upon the positive locus which accounts for the longer response latency.

A correspondingly direct neurological interpretation is given for the third experiment, where they find that response latencies vary inversely with proximity to the no-response light-switch pair. This physical proximity parallels the functional interconnectedness of the corresponding neural loci. The closer the other neural loci are to those associated with the no-response pair, the greater the overflow to them of inhibitory potential.

In the test trials of the fourth experimental situation, subjects correctly associate the common light with the common switch, and the remaining light with the remaining switch. This is interpreted as evidence for (and, as in the preceding cases, is explained by) the assumption that, relative to the other loci, the twice activated loci corresponding to the common switch and the common light are in a more highly excitatory state; and similarly, relative to the other neural loci, those associated with the remaining switch-light pair are in a less highly excitatory state.

Ushakova readily agreed that the results obtained in this fourth experimental situation might be derived quite well from many models, e.g. by means of elementary terms and operations in symbolic logic, but she and her associates clearly preferred to make use of the physiologically-oriented Pavlovian concepts referred to above.

Since, as far as could be determined, these investigators have not sought to discover directly neurophysiological correlates of the loci and potential changes they postulate, a few hypothetical examples were presented to elicit further information on their usage of terms such as *inhibition*. Vlasova began by stating that the meaning of the term was quite clear, and that it referred to a state of increased resistance to firing within the nerve cell. The following two problems then were posed:

1. Consider a subject faced with a highly complex problem, one requiring that he go through many stages in order to solve it. The end result is a decision either to throw or not to throw a single switch.

2. Consider a person engaged in a very involved argument. At one point he suddenly comes upon a phrase which seems to clinch his case. But just before he speaks, he observes that the phrase might be misunderstood, and does not utter it.

The general consensus was that considerable information processing had gone on in both of these hypothetical cases. But while Vlasova agreed that there might well be different kinds and degrees of inhibition, she considered that "inhibition at one level of the nervous system—of a somewhat different kind, but still inhibition—" provided the key to the explanation of a null response in these cases, just as it did in their experiments.

PEDAGOGICALLY ORIENTED RESEARCH

Most Soviet psychology is organized under the Academy of Pedagogical Sciences of the Russian Soviet Federated Socialist Republic, and consequently reflects a much greater emphasis on working on important problems of educational practice than is the case in the United States. The primary intent of a great part of Soviet research on thinking and problem solving is probably best understood in this light. But while aims and methods thus vary somewhat from typical American practices in this area, often these investigations contain much that is relevant and important to an understanding of complex mental processes. The explicit concern for educational practice very likely also will make the work described in this section of interest to investigators of instructional methods as well as to those concerned with current trends in Soviet education. Work by P. Ya. Galperin, V. A. Krutetski, and Yu. A. Samarin serves as the main focus of the discussion, and some related investigations by their associates and others also are very briefly described.

Galperin is in the Department of Psychology, Moscow University. The center of a lively theoretical controversy in recent issues of the Soviet psychological journal, *Voprosy Psikhologii,* Galperin has an orientation to problem solving behavior which might be compared in some respects to H. F. Harlow's. Like Harlow, he is interested in how children and adults "learn to learn" to solve problems, and he also believes that problem solving behavior develops through several stages. He is investigating these processes in order to work out improved teaching methods.

Quite unlike Harlow, however, Galperin believes that learning to solve problems can occur without trial and error experience. In fact, he treats the occurrence of trial and error as a sign that the teacher has not adequately analyzed the stages involved in learning the behavior, and so is unable to lead the student through the steps of the learning process without his making mistakes.

Galperin and his associates distinguish among three varieties of learning process. Trial and error learning is the first of these. The second is insightful learning, in the sense of the Gestalt psychologists, which involves perception of underlying relations on the basis of previous trial and error experience. Galperin holds that there is a third variety of learning process, which he believes superior to the other two. Basic here is the development of appropriate heuristics for analysis and performance in the problem area. Once these have been acquired, the essential conditions of new problems may be discovered directly, without trial and error. Taught to learn in this third mode, subjects make no errors, require shorter training periods, and exhibit a broader and more general ability to transfer what has been learned to new problems. This results from the awareness achieved of the key elements common to the problem area, and from the acquired analytic heuristics, which enable the subject to make adjustments appropriate to the conditions of new situations so as to avoid errors in transferring what has been learned.

To clarify the essential features of his training method, Galperin discussed three concrete examples of the work of his group. These three instances—teaching writing to young children, teaching grammar, and teaching basic mathematical concepts—illustrate their methods of analyzing problems, providing basic problem orientations, and inculcating appropriate problem solving procedures.

As an example of their method for teaching young children how to write the letters of the alphabet, Galperin demonstrated the way in which a child might be trained to make the letter "o." The teacher first draws the letter on graph paper, and then marks it off into roughly linear segments with a set of superimposed pencil marks. He next puts down a corresponding set of points elsewhere on the graph paper, and asks the child to connect the points. Now the teacher gradually removes himself from the problem. Where earlier he put down the corresponding points himself, he now merely indicates where the points are in the original figure. At last, even this support is omitted, and the child now has an integrated set of behavior patterns for writing the letter "o." To do this for each letter would be tedious, of course, but it is not necessary. The child may next be taught how to analyze any letter into such segments, and once he has learned this, he is able to proceed entirely on his own.

43

In training students in grammatical analysis, Galperin and his associates begin with single words. The teacher may say *"karandash"* (pencil), and then ask what the student heard. If the student answers that the teacher was talking about pencils, he is given another word, the plural of "pencil," and asked to state the difference in meaning between the two words. By this kind of comparison across grammatical variants, the student comes to see that specific meanings are associated with basic phonemic units, and he gradually becomes accustomed to thinking of these units as the functional carriers of meaning. The same kind of training continues at the next higher level, as students are presented with sets of related words and so acquire an understanding of the basic functions of roots, prefixes, suffixes, and so on. At the same time, the student acquires the analytic heuristics he needs in order to proceed still further on his own. Only after he has acquired a knowledge of grammatical functions, incidentally, is he taught their names.

Galperin claims that with forty-five minute individual lessons several days a week, students acquire in three weeks a good understanding of basic grammar. At the same time, they develop a problem-solving orientation towards language—an important surplus benefit from the experience, since it gives them a lively interest in language as an integrated subject area with problems which may be attacked in much the same fashion one attacks problems in other sciences.

Traditional practice in the teaching of mathematics, with regard both to the basic concepts utilized and to the ways in which they are taught, have been criticized by Galperin and his associates. The concept of quantity, for example, usually is introduced by contrasted presentations of many and few objects. Children are expected to induce their idea of the number *one* from concrete examples, e.g. *one* bottle, *one* pencil, *one* lemon, etc. Galperin believes that under these conditions children acquire not real mathematical concepts, but ideas about the physical objects to which mathematical concepts may be applied.

Galperin thinks of a number as a measure on a set of objects. To communicate this, he proceeds by defining an arbitrary unit of measurement which is then to be applied in some measurement activity. The arbitrary unit might be a measure of length, for example, defined by the length of three matchboxes laid end to end. Children might then be asked to determine the length of a table in these units. In this way, the concept of the number *one* is established as a *relation* between some arbitrary standard measure and a comparable unit in the object being measured. Given the concept of *one, zero* is taught as taking one unit from one unit, leaving nothing, and the rest of the natural numbers are induced as a sequence of measures derived by successive unit increases. Using this technique, Galperin and his associates find that students learn not only addition and subtraction, but also multiplication and division, all at the same time. This results from the fact that the arbitrary units employed actually consist of several physically separable sub-units. Multiplication and division thus can be taught as operations involving redefinition of the basic unit.[9]

Successful utilization of his methods for teaching how to learn presupposes two requirements, Galperin noted. First, the basic functional units which comprise the problem materials must be determined and set forth clearly. Second, the teacher must discover and then impart to the student methods of analysis which allow the student to discern and work with these units. Both of these requirements imply a reasonably well structured subject matter, and in fact Galperin and his associates have had to modify the materials of both grammar and mathematics as taught in conventional elementary classes. Thus he does not teach morphology, emphasizing instead the functional significance of grammatical variation. Similarly, as was indicated, the usual notions introduced in elementary mathematics have been replaced with concepts derived from modern set theory.

Discussing the significance of his results, Galperin stated that his research had convinced him that Piaget's observations on the peculiarities of quantitative judgment in children were artifacts of the mathematical training to which they had been exposed. Piaget describes children who were shown a set of saucers, each of which held a cup. Asked how many cups and saucers there were, the children reported an equal number of both. When the cups were removed from the saucers and lined up separately, however, the children reported more saucers than cups. For Galperin, this is evidence that these children had not been taught mathematical thinking as a separate way of approaching the physical world. Most elementary mathematical training builds instead on the primitive ability to perceive quantitative distinctions among objects and collections of objects. Galperin considers that Piaget's results would not have taken the form he reports had his subjects been introduced to numbers as arbitrary measures, rather than as a refinement of primitive percep-

---

9. Something very similar to this view of the psychological relation between addition and subtraction on the one hand and multiplication and division on the other also is to be found in Wertheimer (12, p. 44, fn. 11).

tions of relative magnitude, and he indicated that subjects of comparable age taught by his methods did not respond as Piaget's subjects had.

Since the prospect of efficient, transferable, and error-free learning of complex heuristics seemed likely to arouse a considerable amount of interest among American psychologists, Galperin was asked to indicate what he considered to be the content areas to which his methods of analysis and training might usefully be applied. He would not predict how far they might be carried in training people to work at problems requiring considerable creativity. Otherwise, he anticipated that these methods would be quite generally helpful.

One of Galperin's colleagues, Z. A. Reshetova, has in fact applied many of these same techniques in working out procedures for training machine tool operators. Reshetova first observed that master operators themselves often are not very good teachers, since they tend not to see the task from the viewpoint of the novice. Discussions of operating principles also are of little help to the typical novice. At best, he learns how to describe the operations, although still unable to apply his knowledge in practice. At worst, he learns nothing, and ends up with a marked dislike for "theory." She emphasized the importance of "getting the learning in the hands."

Reshetova also distinguishes several levels of training. At the first level, workers are acquainted with the details of the task and what it is they are to do. Next, they are taken through the correct procedure, step by step, and shown how to check the results as they proceed. Once a task has been mastered at this level, a more advanced form of instruction is begun. Now a detailed, step by step list of requirements for the task is provided. Some of these lists may run to three pages in length. The workers are asked to read the list, not to learn it, but to familiarize themselves with the overall task. Once this context has been established, mastery of the details of a new task proceeds easily. Workers may keep the list as long as they wish, although as they repeatedly work through the sequence of requirements they make less and less frequent use of it. Workers who have acquired adequate skill at this second level now are ready for training on the third. Just as children who have learned to copy one letter next are taught how to break any new letter down into simple segments, so the workers now are given guided experience in taking complex tasks and breaking them down into simple functional components. Once they have acquired the appropriate analytic heuristics, they may be left entirely on their own. This kind of problem solving training also leads to a good appreciation of the usefulness of theoretical descriptions, and a much better attitude towards theory, much as Galperin had noted that a problem solving approach to the learning of grammatical rules leads to an interest in the analysis of language. Finally, Reshetova finds that workers attain the third level more easily when they are trained on several similar machines or tasks, perhaps because this procedure serves to distinguish the essential invariants from the unimportant details.

The work on higher mental processes of Zh. I. Shif and her associates, in the Laboratory for the Psychological Study of the Mentally Retarded at the Institute of Defectology in Moscow, is described elsewhere in this volume; we will only note here the several very interesting conceptual and methodological similarities between some of this research, particularly that of N. I. Nepomnyashchaya, and the work of Galperin and his associates. Nepomnyashchaya is studying methods for training mentally retarded children. In describing her results, she also emphasized the importance of first dividing even the simplest counting tasks into almost trivial component parts, and then of guiding the children step by step through the proper sequence. With these children, too, actually doing the task is essential; there is little or no learning with even the most careful attempts to explain the task in words.

Regarding for the moment Galperin's insistence on errorless learning as a normative proposition about an ideal case, one is struck in viewing what these Soviet psychologists actually do by the unexpected but marked apparent resemblances to the positions of some American investigators, notably B. F. Skinner and the advocates of programmed teaching. Galperin, it should be remarked, is unfamiliar with both. Nonetheless, on either side of the Atlantic there is the same tendency to ask "what is necessary so that at every point the subject does the appropriate thing" in preference to "what kind of formulation best predicts the behavior observed in this situation." There also is much the same emphasis on breaking down the problem into very small stages, and then guiding the learner sequentially through the maze. If there is a major difference of principle, it would seem to be that Galperin and his associates treat this stage of the learning process as only the first of several, and try to go beyond it, to the development of problem solvers who are able to analyze new situations successfully and transfer previously learned behavior adaptively. Put another way, Galperin wants to train individuals who not only do well what they have been taught, but who also can induce appropriate solutions for unfamiliar problems. There is probably a good deal to be learned (by those attempting to develop intelligent behavior in computers, as well as by those studying human learning and intelligence) from carefully conducted studies along the lines laid out by Galperin and his colleagues.

MATHEMATICAL ABILITY

V. A. Krutetski, at the Institute of Psychology in Moscow, is among the several Soviet psychologists interested in aspects of thinking and problem solving from a somewhat more molar point of view. Krutetski is concerned primarily with the development of mathematical ability *(sposobnost')*. An ability, for Krutetski, is a personality attribute which enables an individual to do well in a variety of related task areas. He noted that the German concept of *Fähigkeit* is rather similar to his meaning. Ability so defined is a broader concept than that used by Thorndike, whom Krutetski characterized as interested primarily in the development of skills—relatively limited, local abilities. As Krutetski sees it, mathematical ability is not something superimposed on the normal processes of perception, thinking, and imagination. It is rather a characteristic turn of mind *(sklad uma)* which these processes take in certain individuals. In common with Galperin and many other Soviet psychologists studying comparable problems, Krutetski defined his primary task in applied terms: to find methods which would make it possible to improve and develop mathematical ability.

Krutetski considers it quite likely that those who later show great mathematical ability may at birth differ in brain physiology and function from those who do not. And in general, he holds that babies will differ in the kind and extent of their physiological preconditions of ability, or gifts *(zadatok)*. But while Soviet psychology does not necesarily view all people as having equal abilities, it does consider that abilities *per se* are not directly a function of genetic endowment. For regardless of initial structural and functional differences among individuals, ability develops only through activity. If an individual never engages in activities which allow the development of an ability, then it will not develop. So convinced is he of the existence of underlying physiological differences between those who manifest striking mathematical gifts and those who do not, that he intends to make use of Boyko's methods and apparatus to investigate them directly.

His analytic framework did not appear to be very different from that which might be used by American psychologists working in the same area and having comparable methods and goals, with the following exception. In speaking of one highly gifted subject, described in more detail below, he spoke of the remarkable *strength* of her nervous system. The distinction between strong and weak nervous systems is basic to the Pavlovian typology, and has to do with resistance to fatigue under continued stimulation. It is interesting to note,

48

however, that Krutetski's use of the concept varied somewhat from Pavlov's. Krutetski pointed out that his subject showed no unusual resistance to fatigue when reading, although she enjoyed reading a great deal. In contrast, however, she could work for as much as two hours on a difficult mathematical problem without tiring. Thus Krutetski considers, as apparently Pavlov did not, that there is no such thing as a unique "strength of nervous system" factor, but rather separate strength factors for functionally different parts of the overall system.

Krutetski's principal research method is the qualitative longitudinal study of individual cases. In explaining his concept of mathematical turn of mind as a characteristic of the overall psychological functioning of mathematically gifted individuals, for example, he illustrated his points with material from the case mentioned above. When his subject learned poetry, she looked for mathematical laws governing the distribution of syllables. When she studied music, rather than listening for melodic interest, she looked for mathematical relations among the notes. Krutetski believes that this characteristic form of mental activity appears very early. In this same subject, for example, he reported an event which apparently had taken place before she was four years old. Her older brother's teacher had unwittingly reversed the numbers in a homework problem, so that he was required to subtract fifteen from ten. Because mathematics often is taught in terms of physical objects in the U.S.S.R., students encounter great difficulty in performing such manipulations. How can there be less than no apples? But Krutetski's subject, when she saw the problem, is reported to have answered without assistance that the answer was "five apples less than none."

Krutetski, apparently in common with the great majority of Soviet psychologists, did not look favorably upon the use of tests of ability for selection purposes. The test situation is strange, and the results may not be representative. To support his position, he noted that the subject described above had blocked when he tried to tape record her behavior. A casual observer assessing her performance under these conditions would no doubt have concluded that her mathematical abilities were no better than average. The best selection criterion, he asserted, is evaluation by skilled teachers who have observed the behavior in question over a long period of time. Krutetski's objection to tests and measures is not categorical, however. He himself is developing a series of tasks which will be of assistance in studying mathematical imagination—the ability to visualize spatial and other kinds of complex relationships.

The number of highly gifted subjects he works with is quite small, primarily because he has been able to discover only three or four children at this level in all of Moscow. He recognizes that there will be many problems in relating findings for this group to questions about mathematical ability in average children. He anticipates, however, that this kind of investigation will provide important new information on the problems he has defined for himself, namely: what is mathematical ability, and how do we develop it?

Recent Developments in Soviet Pedagogical Policy

Krutetski also had some observations on recent developments in Soviet pedagogical policy on the training of mathematically gifted students which may be worth brief mention here. At one point, they had planned to open special mathematical schools, analogous to their special schools for students of the ballet. Children with great mathematical ability would be singled out at an early age, and enabled to develop it to the fullest. This plan did not go through, Krutetski stated, because the Soviets feared to develop an elite. Krutetski pointed out that there is a great danger of harm to the ability you wish to develop if a child comes to believe that it makes him something special or unique. (He noted that he himself regularly reminds the gifted children he deals with that, yes, they have a special gift for mathematics, but then Johnny has a special gift for music, Peter is able to run very fast, and so on.)

While the Soviet Union has not gone ahead with plans for full-time special schools in mathematics, there are attempts to provide special training on a part-time basis. This training is accomplished in special schools, by highly qualified people—candidates for higher degrees, Krutetski stated, and sometimes even academicians. At present, even such part time training is available only to children fourteen to fifteen years of age. They may attend for an hour and a half to two hours at a time. Those who do well may be selected for still further training. While highly gifted children certainly would benefit from special attention to mathematics at a far earlier age, Krutetski pointed out that these part-time training schools are an important step forward in discovering and developing the mathematically gifted.

Current techniques for recognizing the mathematically gifted also are of interest. Krutetski mentioned two. First, use is made of the many already existing informal mathematical groups or "circles," in which youngsters meet to discuss and solve difficult problems. Such circles may be associated with schools, clubs, and even branches of universities. Second, there are regular mathematical "olympiads." Those who excel in these contests are, of course, made note of, as possibilities for further attention.

50

Much of the work on thinking and problem solving by pedagogical psychologists in Leningrad seems to involve similarly qualitative but detailed longitudinal studies of individuals and small groups. Yu. A. Samarin, of the Leningrad Institute of Pedagogy, indicated that he and his associates were concerned with the development of organized systems of information as students learn. They follow Pavlov in viewing these information systems as emerging via temporary connections,* developing from the very simple to the very complex.

Samarin believes that the child begins with very isolated associations; there is no overall structure, and the same element may be represented in a number of isolated associations, with no connections among them. Often these isolated structures are purely verbal. Samarin illustrated this with the case of a child who knew the heights in meters of a group of mountains. But if he forgot a figure, he might guess that the height was anywhere from a hundred meters to a million meters. Rather than having a well integrated information structure, the child had acquired only an isolated, mutually unrelated set of associations (to be thought of, perhaps, as analogous to associations between paired nonsense syllables).

Given these isolated associations, Samarin says the teacher's function is to encourage the development of hierarchical association systems. A child reads something from a school book, for example. Asked to relate what he has read, he tends initially to repeat sentences, in the order in which they were read. It is up to the teacher, by questions and discussion, to work this into a more integrated system. Such a system will reflect the multiple relations among elements more adequately, distinguishing between principal and secondary or incidental items of information, and unifying the material in terms of the cardinal principles and main ideas involved.

In senior classes, Samarin pointed out, the problem is similar, although at a higher level of organization. Now material must be integrated across broader areas. What happens in this chapter must be related to what happened in the last one. Finally, at an even higher level, what are useful ways of encouraging students to think through relationships across content areas, e.g. between psychology and biology? At each level, there are the same two empirical questions to be explored: how are knowledge systems to be built up from simpler elements, and under what conditions does this knowledge become useful, in the sense that it is capable of effective application in concrete situations.

---

* Used in the Soviet Union as a synonym for CR.

A very brief description of the work of Samarin's colleagues and associates will clarify further the orientations and specific interests of this group.

A. A. Liublinskaia, of the Gertzen Pedagogical Institute, is studying thinking in children to differentiate those aspects which vary with content, age, or instructional method from those features which seem to be invariant. While she has done a good deal of work on various systematic test materials, her basic methodology is observation of classroom teaching; in this context, she has investigated many practical problems, e.g. the effects upon learning of homework vs. no homework.

S. E. Drapkina is working on the acquisition of scientific knowledge by students in the twelve-to fifteen-year-old age group. Her methods involve detailed examination of the acquisition of specific concepts—for example, the notion of *air pressure*—especially where the new concept to be learned depends upon functional relations among components which are themselves complex scientific concepts. Both of the basic concerns to which Samarin referred are evident here. Drapkina wishes to comprehend the manner in which these conceptual structures are developed, and also to be able to provide teachers with a description of the misunderstandings likely to develop at various stages, so as to increase effective use of the resulting information structures.

Among other investigations under way in this same conceptual context are several by O. I. Galkina and by I. I. Finkelstein. Galkina is exploring the development of spatial representations in children, while Finkelstein is working on the ways in which children learn, and learn to apply, mathematical knowledge.

In all of this work, as in related studies by other investigators, such as those of D. N. Bogoyavlensky, discussed by Fleishman elsewhere in this volume,[10] there is the same pervasive concern for fine structure and microprocess previously noted in the work of Galperin and his associates. There certainly are formidable difficulties in store for American psychologists who wish to make use of the findings and reports of these investigators, both because of the qualitative nature of the work and, of course, the problems involved in securing translations into English. On the other hand, there quite likely is a wealth of important ideas and observations to be had from these findings, and further efforts to surmount the communication barrier are certainly to be encouraged.

---

10. See Chapter VI.

There seems to be little reason to challenge the often repeated claim that "cybernetics" has become almost a household word in the U.S.S.R. The consequences of this popular attention are difficult to assess, of course, but a glance at recent issues of the *Soviet Review,* which has been translating about one article per month on such topics as "cybernetics and medical diagnosis" and "cybernetics applied to legal problems," will provide a rough indication of the widely varied forms it takes. This same interest is reflected in a broad range of current research projects in the U.S.S.R., and in the formation of multi-discipline discussion groups in several places, to consider the interdisciplinary implications of the cybernetic point of view.

The research discussed below does not, in fact, seem to share any very precisely defined common assumptions, but it will serve as a small sample of some of the more psychologically pertinent work now under way in this general area. The distinguishing feature of this kind of work may be thought of as a preference for approaching psychological phenomena in terms of concepts and processes not limited in their reference to human systems alone. It is interesting to note that while Shemyakin, Zhinkin, Sokolov, and Zakharov[11] all made some use of cybernetic elements in their thinking, much of the most explicitly cybernetic research with psychological implications is the work of scientists from other disciplines.

Among the most outspoken advocates of a cybernetic frame of reference for the analysis of living systems are the members of the Experimental Laboratory[12] of the Institute of Psychiatry, U.S.S.R. Academy of Medical Sciences. A. P. Ershov, then at the Computing Center in Moscow, also wishing to know more of the work of this group, very kindly made arrangements for both of us to visit the Laboratory.

The members of this Laboratory are engaged in a great variety of investigations, including physiological research and studies of psychotic disturbances. In addition to the Director of the Laboratory, S. N. Braines, who together with two associates, A. V. Napalkov and V. B. Svechinski, is the author of a book on *Problems*

---

11. There no doubt are other psychologists who make use of cybernetic concepts in their work, notably E. N. Sokolov (see the description of his work by Miller, Pfaffmann, and Schlosberg in this volume). Those listed above were the only ones available for interview during the visit on which this chapter is based, however.

12. Located in suburban Moscow at No. 2 Zagorodnoe Shosse.

of Neurocybernetics,[13] the staff includes specialists in mathematics, electrical engineering, and in other related disciplines. Thus although rather smaller in size, it might be compared with such multidiscipline research establishments in the United States as the Mental Health Research Institute in Ann Arbor. Only a series of experiments on problem solving in chimpanzees will be described here.

The chimpanzee experiments were demonstrated by I. Mirzane and S. L. Novoselova, a former student of Leontiev's. The primary aim seems to be to explore learning and problem solving in the animals as a process involving development of more and more complex chains of conditioned reflexes. The conceptualization is not far from the notion of secondary reinforcement training, in that new links in the chain are engrafted onto the old with former conditioned stimuli as reinforcement for the new learning.

To illustrate, Novoselova put one animal through the following sequence. First, part of an orange was wrapped in newspaper and stuffed into a tube perhaps fifteen inches long. The chimp was given the tube and a thin stick, and he proceeded to push the little bundle out of the tube with the stick, and then to eat the orange. The animal next was given a second tube containing another piece of orange similarly wrapped, but now with a rather larger piece of wood—too large to fit into the tube. Using its teeth, the chimp broke a strip of wood off from the larger piece, and seemed to check it visually, to see whether it would fit into the tube. Finding that it would not, the chimp "recursed," continuing to break off additional fragments until he had a piece adequate for the job at hand. Then, as before, the orange was pushed out, unwrapped, and eaten.

A bit of orange also served as the reward in a second demonstration of a complex learned sequence. But now the orange rested atop a flat piece of wood, at some distance from the animal's cage. A long string was passed through a hook screwed into the wood. The two ends of the string were led back so that the chimp could just reach them with one arm, but not both at the same time. The chimp proceeded to push the two pieces of string together, and then when he had them close enough, he grasped them in his one hand and slowly and carefully pulled the wood towards the cage. When the orange was within reach, he grabbed it and ate it. Novoselova pointed out that the animal had to have simpler conditioned reflexes available before it could evolve more complicated sequences of adaptive be-

---

13. Now available in an English translation, dated 18 October, 1960, from the Office of Technical Services, U. S. Dept. of Commerce, Washington 25, D.C., as OTS:60-41, 639; JPRS 5880.

havior. A naive animal, given the two ends of the string at some distance from one another, was unable to learn to solve the problem. On the other hand, when the present animal first had to secure the orange with the two strings close together, it learned how to do it. Next, given the two strings at some distance from one another, it responded initially by pulling one end of the string until it almost passed through and separated from the hook. Gradually, from trial to trial, the chimp pulled the single ends less and less until finally, pulling one end just a bit and noticing, apparently, the retrograde movement of the other end, the animal stopped and began instead to push the two ends together.

The language in which these results were conceptualized was largely Pavlovian, with the addition of several cybernetics concepts such as feedback. It is difficult to judge, however, on the basis of these demonstrations, the extent to which the cybernetics orientation of this research group basically affects either the kinds of experiments run or the conclusions which may be drawn from them.

A detailed cybernetically oriented model of the problem solving and learning processes involved in the development of such complex behavior is presented in *Problems of Neurocybernetics*. The main intent of the book is theoretical and methodological, however, and although the formulation itself is extremely interesting, it is hard at this point to assess the adequacy with which it would enable detailed prediction of behavior as it develops in experimental studies of the sort just described.

PERCEPTUAL AND COGNITIVE TRANSFORMATIONS

M. M. Bongard[14] is a biophysicist, and works under the auspices of the Institute of Biophysics of the U.S.S.R. Academy of Sciences.[15]

While he considers that we now know almost nothing of the physiological functions involved, Bongard's central long range concern is with thinking, and more specifically, the way in which thinking processes are realized in the brain. At the present time, he and his associates are engaged in a broadly based and highly imaginative

---

14. A portion of this discussion is reproduced, with permission, from (10). The presentation here also makes use of additional detail from Bongard's own recently published report (1).

15. The Institute itself is at No. 33 Leninskii Prospekt, but Bongard and several associates are located in a separate section, on the fourth floor of a building at No. 10 Frunze Street. (However, a wrapper received late in 1961 containing a reprint of Bongard's study gives his address as "Institute of Biophysics, AN U.S.S.R., No. 7 Profsoyuznaya Street, Building 1, Moscow.") The assistance of A. N. Leontiev and A. R. Luria, who pointed out the relevance of Bongard's work and made arrangements for an interview with him, is gratefully acknowledged.

program of research into the neurophysiological mechanisms underlying perceptual and cognitive transformations. He proceeds in two directions, carrying out direct experimental studies of retinal function, and at the same time investigating some of the perceptual and cognitive information processing mechanisms involved, by means of computer simulation.

Explaining his interest in the retina, Bongard pointed out that for object and concept identification to take place, the nervous system must preserve certain invariances over sets of transformations which alter both the position and the elements of retinal objects. The retina should be a good place to study the mechanisms underlying these transformations, both because it is known to be the locus of complex neural interactions,[16] and also since it actually develops as an outgrowth of brain tissue. Achievement of better representations of retinal functioning thus should lead to useful models of neural interaction within the brain itself.

Bongard's use of computer programming differs somewhat from that employed in comparable investigations of cognitive processing in the United States. In contrast, for example, to Newell, Shaw, Simon (9) and others,[17] Bongard is not trying to simulate human information processing directly. Instead, he has programmed a system designed to achieve results comparable to those attained by humans in learning to recognize as such concrete instances of complex concepts.

His program handles problems of the sort given in a matrix such as this.

A	B	C
4	2	8
9	3	27
5	5	5
2	4	?

We might ask a human faced with this matrix to induce a simple arithmetic rule in A and B which gives the indicated value for C in the first three lines and yields a prediction of C in the fourth line. One immediate hypothesis might be $C = A \times B$. This holds for the first two lines, but fails for the third. All three lines, however, are consistent with $C = A^2 \div B$, and this hypothesis yields 1 as the prediction for C in the fourth line. Bongard believes that humans induce hypotheses such as these working from characteristics or features of the lines of numbers which serve as clues. If A and B are small, for

---

16. For a vivid and suggestive discussion, see (7).

17. See (10) for a description of current investigations in this general area.

example, and C is large, this suggests some sort of multiplicative relation. Again, if A is 4, B is 3, and C is —5, then subtraction must be involved.

Bongard's computer program accepts as input a given or initial set of completed arithmetic matrices of this sort, each of which embodies a different rule or expression. (The program is *not* given the rules themselves.) After processing these matrices, it is able to specify for any new test matrix which one of the rules represented by the initial matrices it is consistent with. The program consists of two parts, one concerned with "learning" the set of given matrices and the other with "recognizing" test matrices. In the learning phase, the program has access to and makes use of a stock of simple expressions in A, B, and C, e.g. A + 2B. Application of such an expression to a line of a matrix yields a number, which, in turn, may be classified as whole or fractional, greater or less than zero, etc. These resulting binary variables next are combined to yield logical functions which play the role of attributes, with a given matrix having a value of either zero or one for each such attribute. Thus at the end of the learning phase, each matrix in the given set has associated with it a particular string of ones and zeros. The program uses two criteria in selecting the functions characterizing any particular given set of matrices. Attributes yielding roughly equal numbers of zeros and ones as values over the set of matrices are preferred, and attributes yielding overlapping, nonindependent patterns of zeros and ones are avoided. Thus the information transmitted by the final set of attributes is at a maximum. The "recognition" portion of the program identifies a test matrix by comparing the string of values generated for it by the series of attributes with the strings associated with each of the initial matrices.

Bongard has run a number of experiments with his program. These are described in detail in his published report (1). We may note that the program achieves perfect recognition with sets of six, eight, or nine initial matrices, each embodying a different rule. In terms of a numerical ratio, an index of guessing which he defines, Bongard reports almost perfect recognition with as many as 24 different rules represented in the set of given matrices. Still more impressive, the amount of guessing remains at the same very low level—roughly three per cent, even when the set of attributes developed to characterize one set of matrices is taken over wholesale and used to characterize another set obeying 24 totally different rules. Thus attributes defined with the learning phase of this program display a very large degree of universality over the domain of such problems.

57

In still another of these experiments, an attempt was made to determine whether a program which had derived a good set of attributes for identifying arithmetic matrices would also be able to distinguish among logically different matrices. These are based on rules such as "A always less thán B," or "A always divisible into B," and so on. The results indicate that when the program has learned to differentiate among arithmetically different matrices, it is unable to distinguish logically distinct matrices, and vice versa. Like humans, it behaves as if the ones it has been trained on are quite different among themselves, and the ones it has not been trained on are all pretty much alike.

The questions motivating Bongard's research are explicitly psychological. He notes, for example, that subjects shown pictures of various animals have no difficulty in identifying a test picture of one of these animals in quite a different position. In his view, we have not as yet an adequate theory of the processes which make this achievement possible. Bongard does not consider that a problem solving formulation along the lines of the Newell, Shaw and Simon models (9) can be extended directly to these kinds of processes. He noted that the time required to respond in this situation is on the order of one tenth of a second, far too little for the numerous comparisons and tests a problem solving interpretation would require. Bongard believes, as was indicated above, that the results are achieved instead by complex transformations which preserve critical invariances, and he is attempting in these investigations to clarify the mechanisms which underlie these transformations. To the extent that he is able to do so, he may well succeed in providing a neurologically reasonable foundation for the concepts of *symbol,* and *symbol* manipulating processes which lie at the heart of information processing interpretations of psychological activity (8, 9).

Finally, it is important to point out the relevance of the really exciting studies under way at the Pavlov Institute of Physiology[18] to the trends discussed in this section. Some of these investigations, in particular those of L. A. Chistovich, are discussed elsewhere in this volume by Miller, Pfaffmann, and Schlosberg.[19] Chistovich's experimental work, for example, is almost entirely in the area of audition, but she is actively interested in a broad range of problems having to

---

18. The Pavlov Institute of Physiology is located at 6 Naberezhnaya Makarova, in Leningrad. Chistovich worked in a separate section of the Institute, at 3a Petrovskaya Street. According to Dr. E. Feigenbaum she has now been called to a new post in Moscow. Once again, thanks are due A. N. Leontiev and A. R. Luria for the initial contacts. L. A. Chistovich also went out of her way to suggest and arrange additional interviews.

19. See Chapter VII.

do with the conceptualization of sensory mechanisms and their relation to central processes; her personal library includes an impressive variety of advanced materials in several languages on electronics, mathematics, and cybernetics, as well as diverse physiological subjects. Similarly, V. D. Glezer, who is concerned mainly with retinal processes, also demonstrated a sophisticated awareness of recent developments in cybernetics, and he has published several papers involving mathematical treatment of retinal mechanisms as components of complex adaptive systems. Both of these investigators are in contact with Bongard, incidentally; and all three illustrate the highly competent level of interest in the cybernetic analysis of complex psychological processes which seems to be developing in the U.S.S.R.

CONCLUSION AND POSTSCRIPT

While a few similarities and contrasts with American work have been noted where it seemed they might point up particular characteristics of Soviet work, the foregoing largely has been a report on a set of interviews. In this conclusion, however, a few very personal impressions and reactions to relations between Soviet and American work in the general area covered in this report may be of interest to the reader.

First, it is one thing to know that Soviet psychology is grounded in Pavlovian concepts, and quite another to listen to people who think that way, trying to figure out what in the world it is they *really* mean. They really mean, of course, just what they are saying. But even after the sense of unreality subsides, and one accepts the fact that research in the U.S.S.R. has developed its own quite independent framework, it still takes a good deal to follow through the logic of an argument set forth in a language which is no less foreign conceptually than it is linquistically. Matters are not helped much, incidentally, by the fact that, in the absence of operational definitions for most concepts in this area, usage of terms like "inhibitions" seems to vary as much in the U.S.S.R. as usage of terms like "motive" does in the U.S.A.

The next shock comes at the lack of familiarity, not infrequently accompanied by a lack of interest, shown by many Soviet investigators in the work of counterparts in the West. Then one quickly recalls that however great this ignorance and lack of interest, as the typical western bibliography in this area will show, we almost certainly know and have cared less about their work than they do about ours. Furthermore, individual Soviet investigators vary widely in this respect: researchers at the Pavlov Institute of Physiology, to cite just one example, exhibit a firm grasp of non-Soviet work, and in several cases could be said without qualification to be operating in a fully international context, in the best sense of the phrase. Finally one must admit that, given the state of the art in the area covered in this chapter, it is by no means self evident that either group would gain enough to warrant the investment it would require to become truly conversant with the work of the other. But in areas such as this, however, which lack common empirical referents, neither side is likely even to be able to make a good estimate of the value of the other's work until much broader competence is acquired in the conceptual language in terms of which that work is set forth.

Several features of Soviet pedagogically oriented research seemed striking. In general, the interest in thinking *processes*, investigated via qualitative longitudinal studies, differs of course from the American emphasis on precisely determined input-output correlations under well specified experimental conditions, but in a somewhat complementary way. Soviet psychologists, much more willing to speculate on the basis of such qualitative evidence, have as a result constructed some extremely interesting theories of thinking, and of the growth and development of higher mental functions. They may be at many points quite unsupported by experimental evidence; but lacking such evidence ourselves, we quite frequently also seem to lack even the systematic speculations necessary to decide what evidence we ought to collect.

The consistent distinction made in the U.S.S.R. between "applicable" learning and verbal learning (i.e. the learning of relations among *names*, for example) seems worthy of closer attention, set as it is in terms of a detailed position on the way in which long term learning results in various kinds of information structures. Given such a position, Soviet psychologists are able to suggest answers to important practical questions (including one now perplexing our schools of education—what relation *what* to teach should have to *how* to teach) from systematic propositions about how thinking develops with learning. The propositions may be as yet unverified by our standards, but certainly they do not seem untestable; in fact, careful study of such propositions very likely could suggest direct experimental tests of the sort at which we excel.

Finally, the relatively recent change in attitude toward cybernetics is very interesting. Soviet scientists now are engaged in many of the same arguments on the comparative advantages of men vs. machines which are to be found in the West. And Soviet research reflects this new orientation, although it is still too early to comment at length on the results. Only one instance could be found, for example, of the use of a computer program model in a psychologically relevant investigation. No one should be too surprised, however, if future visits reveal impressive achievements sprung from these beginnings. Worth noting, also, is the fact that research utilizing computer models may be described in a common language which is largely free of conventional Soviet or western psychological concepts. Bongard's study (1), for example, is presented without the use of a single Pavlovian concept. This common conceptual framework, together with the freedom from non-operational and subjective notions achieved by expressing a theory in program form, allow us to hope that further investigations in this vein may well provide a convenient and fertile ground for more extensive interactions among the scientists and the scientific endeavors of the two countries.

REFERENCES

1. Bongard, M. M. (Modeling the process of recognition on a digital computer.) *Biofizika*, Vol. IV, No. 2, 1961.
2. Braines, S. N., Napalkov, A. V., and Svechinski, V. B. *(Scientific notes: problems of neurocybernetics.)* Moscow: U.S.S.R. Acad. Med. Sci., 1959.
3. Brazier, Mary A. B. (Ed.) *The central nervous system and behavior: transactions of the third conference.* New York: Josiah Macy, Jr. Foundation, 1960.
4. Feldman, J. An analysis of predictive behavior in a two choice situation. Unpublished Doctoral Dissertation, Carnegie Institute of Technology, 1959.
5. Gurova, L. L. (The role of conscious awareness of thinking operations during the solution of spatial transformation problems.) Doklady A P N R.S.F.S.R., No. 4, 1960.
6. Gurova, L. L. (The influence of visual aids on the process of solving spatial problems.) Doklady A P N R.S.F.S.R., No. 5, 1960.
7. Lettvin, J. Y. Maturana, H. R. McCulloch, W. S., and Pitts, W. H. What the frog's eye tells the frog's brain. *Proc. IRE*, 1959, 1940-1951.
8. Newell, A. On programming a highly parallel machine to be an intelligent technician, *Proc. WJCC*, 1960, 267-282.
9. Newell, A., Shaw J. C. and Simon, H. A. Elements of a theory of human problem solving, *Psychol. Rev.*, 1958, *65*, 151-166.
10. Reitman, W. R., Programming intelligent problem solvers, *IRE Trans. PGHFE*, 1961, *2*, 27-33.
11. Shemyakin, F. N. (Ed.) [Thinking and speech.] *Izvestiya A P N R.S.F.S.R., 113*, Moscow: R.S.F.S.R Acad. Ped. Sci. Press, 1960.
12. Wertheimer, M. *Productive thinking* (enlarged edition). New York: Harper, 1959.
13. Whitfield, J. W. An experiment in problem solving. *Quart. J. Exp. Psychol.*, 1951, *3*, 184-197.
14. Zakharov, A. N. A comparison of the theoretically possible and actual procedures used in problem solving. T-126. Santa Monica, Cal.; RAND Corp., 1960 (translated by A. Kozak from *VOPR. PSIKHOL.*, 1959, 110-118.)

CHAPTER III

Soviet Studies of Personality Development and Socialization*

URIE BRONFENBRENNER

SIMILARITIES AND CONTRASTS

Viewed against the perspective of its American counterpart, Soviet work on problems of personality development and socialization presents a study in contrasts. In each country, such investigations are associated with different branches of psychology (social psychology in the U.S., educational psychology in the U.S.S.R.), with emphasis on different methods of analysis (quantitative-analytical vs. qualitative-holistic); different social settings (the family vs. the school); different foci of attention (the individual vs. the collective); different time perspectives (retrospective vs. future-oriented); different dynamics (affectively-loaded unconscious forces vs. externally-mediated rational decisions); and different spheres of practical application (psychotherapy vs. character education). Yet, underlying these sharp differences in context, method, and interpretation is a strikingly similar conception of the basic process through which personality is formed.

This paradoxical state of affairs was brought home to me at each of the five research centers I visited (Leningrad, Moscow, Odessa, Tbilisi, and Kiev), in my reading of Soviet psychological literature, and in informal conversations with Soviet teachers, parents, youth workers, and school children. In attempting to communicate what I learned, I shall abide by the lessons of current communication theory and begin with the minimally-dissonant—the similarity that I discerned in the Soviet and American approaches. Also, rather than present my own interpretation of what I saw and heard, I should prefer to let Soviet psychologists speak for themselves. One of the longest and most informative conversations I had on the subject was with Professors V. N. Miasishchev and A. G. Kovalev, in

---

* With comment by Professor Otto Klineberg, who also traveled for the APA under a grant from the Human Ecology Fund.

Leningrad. The former is Director of the Bekhterev Institute and erstwhile Head of the Department of Psychology at the University; the latter is Professor of Psychology at the University. I have since discovered that much of what they told me is expressed even more succinctly in their jointly-authored two volume work entitled *The Psychological Characteristics of Man* (1957). Here are some translated excerpts from Volume I, sub-titled *Character.*

The formation of character begins in early childhood. As a function of conditions of life in the family, of relationships developing between the parents and between parents and child, and of the nature of this upbringing, the child develops one or another habitual orientation toward people, objects, and obligations; in short, his behavior and character are formed.

It is well known that the dominant relationships within the family are determined by the way of life of the society and class to which the particular family belongs . . . . These relationships become the decisive factor in the character development of the growing generation. Over and above the basic characteristics that Soviet families share in common are certain special features specific to each particular family; that is, different relationships and opinions, different ways of life, different personality characteristics in the parents, which in turn exert different influences and impose different demands—all of which cannot help but affect the individual habits of others. Children take on the relationships of the parents, they imitate these relationships and use them as criteria for their own conduct. Not infrequently one can observe that the child treats his father in the same way that the mother treats him and, conversely, the child excuses his own behavior on the basis of his mother's or father's behavior.

If the child first of all appropriates the behavior of the parents, copies their relationships, then the social will be reflected in the personal; that is, the child will reflect the family's mode of life and relationships (pp. 188-189).

With only minor modifications, the preceding passage would hardly be out of place in an American text on personality development or social psychology. And, it is representative of the predominant thesis that I heard and read repeatedly in the course of my explorations of Soviet work in this area: *man is the product of his social relationships.*

Soviet Psychology as Viewed in the Soviet Union

How is it, under these circumstances, that social psychology is not recognized as a discipline in the U.S.S.R.? I directed this question to my Soviet colleagues everywhere that I went. Their replies are paraphrased as follows:

Ah, you Americans, you are so confused as a society; you don't know what to do, and you don't know whom to do it with, and so you try to get science to give you an answer. For this reason, you spend much time and energy on research on motivation and interpersonal relations. We in the Soviet Union are not confused by such problems. We know what we want to do and with whom to do it. We arrive at answers to these questions deductively from scientific principles and hence do not have to study them empirically. Our main concern is not what, why, or with whom but *how*. We need to improve our skills for doing what we want to do, and it is on this general problem that we focus our researches.

*   *   *

We are interested in the problems you describe, but the work is done primarily by educators and party people, rather than by scientists. Every activity is evaluated for its effectiveness, and reports are sent to higher authority for evaluation and action. In such reports, social factors receive great emphasis. If an educational or industrial enterprise is poorly organized, if there is poor communication among key persons or organizational units, this fact is noted and remedial measures taken. There are principles of social organization that are studied by specialists concerned with such matters, but we do not view these as problems especially appropriate for the psychologist.

*   *   *

To understand this matter you have to know something of the history of psychology in our country. You must recognize that the Great October Revolution was not just a revolution of men but a revolution of ideas. In psychology it meant the rejection of idealism and the adoption of materialism as the proper solid foundation of science. It is clear that the problems of motivation and of social relationships, of which you speak, are extremely difficult and also are particularly susceptible to the errors of idealism. When one has to rebuild a science from its very foundation, it is unwise to tackle first the problems that are most difficult and most likely to lead one astray. Thus in rebuilding Soviet materialist psychology, we started with the more simple classical problems. Even then, eager as we were to make some progress also on the more complex issues, we began, in the late twenties and early thirties, to work on questions of personality and individual differences. But we were not ready and in trying to avoid Scylla, fell upon Charybdis. In our efforts to escape the dangers of idealism we fell into the error of extreme mechanism. Thus in the era of pedology and psycho-technology we relied too heavily on tests and simple formulas. Fortunately through the aid of dialectic materialism,[1] we recognized our mistakes and rejected the misleading approaches, which are still followed in your country. In recent years, however, our science has matured so that we feel truly ready to tackle the difficult problems of which you speak. Some work in this area is already appearing, and you will be seeing more in the years to come.

One might think that these three informants were living in different worlds and that all three statements could not possibly be true. Yet my observations lead me to believe that all three are valid descriptions of reality, but a reality that is in process of change.

Thus it is true that, unlike their American colleagues, Soviet psychologists are little interested in studying individual differences in motives and interpersonal relationships, and are primarily concerned with the development of group skills. What my first informant failed to make clear, however, was that in many instances the skills were those for developing common motives for the group and the optimal translation of these motives into effective group performance.

An Illustrative Experiment. To illustrate the last point, as well as the methods typically employed in Soviet research in this sphere, I shall describe an experiment recently completed by N. F. Prokina, at the Laboratory on the Psychology of Upbringing, Institute of Psychology, Moscow. Her study is one of a series of investigation at the Laboratory, based on and supporting the general thesis that "personality

---

[1] This took the concrete form of a decree of the Central Committee of the Communist Party. (Cf. p. 81 of this chapter.)

characteristics develop as a result of the incorporation by the child of certain aspects of his social activity." Prokina's study was described as involving four stages: (1) defining a specific desirable mode of behavior for children; (2) arousing the motive to behave in the appropriate manner; (3) providing for systematic practice in the desired behavior; (4) determining whether the behavior persists after special measures for evoking it are discontinued.

The particular "desirable behavior" selected as the focus of investigation was that of orderly forming of ranks prior to leaving the classroom. This behavior was chosen both for methodological and substantive reasons. On the former grounds it had the advantages of being readily observable, lasting a short time, and recurring several times each day. But the primary basis of choice was "practical importance." According to the investigator, before the experimental procedures were instituted, children spent as much as eight to ten minutes lining up after every class, so that in the course of a single day they could lose as much as an hour-and-a-half on this single routine.

The subjects in the experiment were the entire class (30 children) in the first grade at a Moscow boarding school. The class had been chosen because it had the reputation of being one of the most difficult and disorganized. In the first "experiment" the children were simply told about the specific behaviors that necessarily entered into orderly lining-up (e.g. rise when the bell rings, stand quietly, etc.). Upon then being asked to perform these actions, the pupils did so quickly and well. The investigator viewed this phase of the experiment as essential in demonstrating that the pupils had the ability to engage in the desired behavior, even though they might not make use of this ability on particular occasions.

The aim of the second experiment was to translate the "latent capacity into an active and enduring form." For this purpose the children were divided into six groups of five persons each. A chart was made showing six stairways with series of steps equalling the number of "line-ups" required each day. Successful performance was recognized immediately afterwards by allowing the team's representative to move a little red flag up the steps. The "competitive motive" aroused by this procedure proved highly effective, but not enduring. At the first lining-up, time was reduced to one minute but by the end of the day it had lengthened to the customary interval of seven minutes.

Accordingly, in a series of further experiments, the investigator sought to increase the duration of improved performance by evoking additional motives. The most effective of these proved to be the "motive of play" aroused by designating competing teams as pilots, soldiers, or sailors, and asking each group to line up quickly and well, "the way real sailors do." Although performance improved with this additional incentive, there was still marked retrogression over the course of the day. Further observation revealed that, despite being able and motivated to form straight lines quickly, as the day wore on pupils became easily prone to distractions (casual conversation, looking out the window, fiddling with objects, etc.). To meet this problem the investigator employed a three-minute sand-timer that was started as soon as the bell sounded. As a result children continued to line up promptly throughout the day.

As a final step in perfecting performance, times were taken at successive phases of the lining-up process and teams given points for the most rapid completion of each phase (standing, walking, sitting, etc.). In consequence, the entire procedure was completed in an average duration of one-to-one-and-a-half minutes. This level of performance was maintained to the end of the academic year, three months after the "game" had been discontinued.

In the investigator's view, the series of experiments establishes three major conditions as facilitating enduring changes in behavior: (1) there must be arousal of a strong motive (competitive play) insuring positive orientation toward acquisition of the desired behavior; (2) the behavior to be learned should be broken up into component elements; and (3) the child should be instructed to relate the corresponding behavioral elements to the time intervals allotted to them.

SOVIET METHODOLOGY FOR THE
STUDY OF PERSONALITY DEVELOPMENT

The foregoing investigation is typical, both in method and substance, of Soviet work in this area. Indeed, so far as research design is concerned, the study is more structured than the average: the number of subjects is specified (although age and sex are not), and some results are expressed in numerical form. But, viewed in the framework of American psychology, this is not, strictly speaking, an experiment but an observational study of an experimental program. As such, it exemplifies Soviet preference and practice. Especially in the study of personality and social process, Russian psychology eschews the analytic, quantitative approach so characteristic of the American scene in favor of an almost anecdotal, holistic orientation. This view, expressed in virtually every center visited, has recently been stated systematically in a definitive paper by V. A. Krutetski

(1960). Writing on problems of method in the study of personality, Krutetski asserts:

Soviet psychology categorically rejects the possibility of building personality study on the basis of different types of tests and questionnaires. The mechanistic approach to man, the subjective interpretation of results, the attempt by primitive, standardized methods to "analyze" a most complex and ever-changing object, giving quantitative form to personality characteristics and manifestations—all this which is organically inherent to tests and questionnaires, has prompted Soviet psychologists once and for all to repudiate this antiquated method.

Soviet psychology has established a set of principles for the scientific study of personality: (1) personality should be investigated in an analytic-synthetic manner with proper regard for its wholeness; (2) personality can be studied only on the basis of objective material, i.e. in investigating character one must proceed from concrete behavior, man's actions and the motives they reveal; (3) personality can be studied only with due regard to the determining influences of external and internal conditions (conditions of life and upbringing, the state of the organism and its life-activity); (4) personality characteristics must be examined in their genetic development and change; (5) individual personalities can be studied only in the collective, through the collective, and against the background of the collective, in which character forms and develops . . .; (6) personality must be studied in the perspective of its development . . . that is, personality must be viewed not only as an object of investigation but also as an object of training; (7) investigation must have an activistic character, have the goal of controlling the process of personality formation. . . .

The specific methods for the study of personality accepted in Soviet psychology conform to the foregoing principles. These methods include observation, naturalistic experimentation, laboratory experimentation, as well as the biographical method, interviews, the analysis of products of activity, techniques which are ordinarily applied together thus supplementing, correcting, and controlling one another (pp. 67-68).

Although Soviet psychologists, by and large, agree in their con-

69

demnation of the statistical, variable-oriented approach of much American research, they differ among themselves in the degree to which they prefer one or another of the approved methods listed above. For example, the psychologists at the University of Leningrad are suspicious of the validity of experimental methods for the study of personality. Indeed, Professor Kovalev has stated flatly, "It is entirely clear that the laboratory experiment cannot serve as a means for studying the essential characteristics of the school age child." (Bozhovich, 1960, p. 225.) A contrary position is taken by Moscow University psychologists, who look to the laboratory as the most hopeful source of progress in child psychology. But even though their researches are conducted in the laboratory, their methods have more in common with those employed in Leningrad than in any leading research center in the United States.

AIM, SUBSTANCE, AND SOURCE OF
SOVIET PERSONALITY STUDIES

Turning from method to content, we may note (in examples already cited) the characteristic features of Soviet research on personality development. To begin with, the line between research and reform is difficult to draw. Indeed the distinction is often explicitly rejected, as in the quotation from Krutetski cited above. The principal focus of virtually every study I heard about or read was the application of a training procedure designed to remedy a defect or, even more commonly, to maximize the development of some desirable character trait such as motivation for study, initiative, self-awareness, responsibility, self-confidence, moral judgment, self-control, etc. And despite the diversity of these characteristics, each investigation tended to follow the same general pattern already illustrated in the Prokina study. The elements in the pattern are as follows: concrete manifestation of the desirable behavior is identified, the behavior is motivated and monitored by introducing collective competition and social control, the behavior is "rationalized" (i.e. analyzed into its component segments), and opportunity for extensive practice is provided under optimal conditions of social motivation and control.

This implicit theoretical model reveals how deeply Soviet psychology has been permeated by broader conceptions of communist theory, at least so far as studies of personality are concerned. For emphasis on objective reality, activism, rationalization of tasks, and collectivist motivation and control are all hallmarks of Marxist-Leninist thought and application. But, as I discovered early in the course of my visit, Soviet studies in personality and socialization have an even more immediate ideological source. Almost invariably when I told Soviet psychologists and educators of my special interests, they would nod and say: "Oh yes, and of course you have read Makarenko." And when I innocently confessed that I had not, my Soviet colleagues were visibly shocked. I soon learned that for a child psychologist not to know the works of Makarenko was as inconceivable in Russia as for an American pediatrician to be ignorant of Spock. Makarenko's influence, however, is even more widespread, for his ideas have affected theory and research as much as practice. There is hardly a Soviet study in the area of personality development that does not cite his works as a major source of inspiration or interpretation. At the same time, there is scarcely a manual for the training of communist teachers, parents, or youth workers that does not quote him as the principal authority on problems of character education. His works have been translated into many languages and are apparently widely read, not only in the Soviet Union, but also in the satellites (notably East Germany) and in communist China. Since English translations are not readily available in the United States, it may be useful to summarize the major ideas of this influential educator-psychologist and to present one or two excerpts from his writings.

MAKARENKO'S WORK AND IDEAS

I first learned about A. S. Makarenko and his theories and techniques from the director of teacher training at the Gertsen Institute in Leningrad, who generously devoted two hours to my education. We began with a biographical account.

In the early 1920's, Makarenko, then a young school teacher and devout communist, was handed the assignment of developing a rehabilitation program for some of the thousands of homeless children who were roaming the Soviet Union after the civil wars. The first group of such children assigned to Makarenko's school, a ramshackle building far out of town, turned out to be a group of boys about 18 years of age with extensive court records of housebreaking, armed robbery, and manslaughter. For the first few months, Makarenko's school served simply as the headquarters for the band of highwaymen who were his legal wards. But gradually, through the development of his group-orientated discipline techniques, and through what can only be called the compelling power of his own moral convictions, Makarenko was able to develop a sense of group responsibility and commitment to the work program and code of conduct that he had laid out for the collective. In the end, the Gorky Commune became known throughout the Soviet Union for its high morale, discipline, and for the productivity of its fields, farms, and shops. Indeed, Makarenko's methods proved so successful that he was selected to head a new commune set up by the Ministry of Internal Affairs (then the Cheka, later to become the GPU and NKVD). In the years which followed, Makarenko's theories and techniques became widely adopted throughout the U.S.S.R. and now constitute the central core of Soviet educational practice.

To turn to the ideas themselves, we may begin with an excerpt from what is possibly the most widely read of Makarenko's works, *A Book for Parents*. This 400-page volume is exactly what its title implies. Despite frequent reprintings, it is typically out of stock and I had a great difficulty obtaining my own copy (which is from a 1959 edition of 75,000 copies published especially for the Karelian Soviet Socialist Republic). The excerpt follows:

But our (Soviet) family is not an accidental combination of members of society. The family is a natural collective body and, like everything natural, healthy, and normal, it can only blossom forth in socialist society, freed of those very curses from which both mankind as a whole and the individual are freeing themselves.

The family becomes the natural primary cell of society, the place where the delight of human life is realized, where the triumphant forces of man are refreshed, where children —the chief joy of life—live and grow.

Our parents are not without authority either, but this authority is only the reflection of societal authority. The duty of a father in our country towards his children is a particular form of his duty towards society. It is as if our society says to parents:

You have joined together in good will and love, rejoice in your children and expect to go on rejoicing in them. That is your personal affair and concerns your own personal happiness. Within the course of this happy process you have given birth to new human beings. A time will come when these beings will cease to be solely the instruments of your happiness, and will step forth as independent members of society. For society, it is by no means a matter of indifference what kind of people they will become. In delegating to you a certain measure of societal authority the Soviet State demands from you the correct upbringing of its future citizens. Particularly it relies on you to provide certain conditions arising naturally out of your union; namely, your parental love.

If you wish to give birth to a citizen while dispensing with parental love, then be so kind as to warn society that you intend to do such a rotten thing. Human beings who are brought up without parental love are often deformed human beings (Makarenko, 1959, p. 29).

Characteristic of Makarenko's thought is the view that the parents' authority over the child is delegated to him by the state and that duty to one's children is merely a particular instance of one's broader duty toward society. A little later in his book for parents, the author makes this point even more emphatically. After telling the story of a boy who ran away from home after some differences with his mother, he concludes by affirming: "I am a great admirer of optimism and I like very much young lads who have so much faith in the Soviet State that they are carried away and will not trust even their own mothers" (pp. 37-38). In other words, when the needs and values of the family conflict with those of society, there is no question about who gets priority. And society receives its concrete manifestation and embodiment in the *collective,* which is an organized group engaged in some socially useful enterprise.

This brings us to Makarenko's basic thesis that optimal personality development can occur only through productive activity in a social collective. The first collective is the family, but this must be supplemented early in life by other collectives specially organized in schools, neighborhoods, and other community settings. The primary function of the collective is to develop socialist morality. This aim is accomplished through an explicit regimen of activity mediated by group criticism, self-criticism, and group-oriented punishments and rewards.

Makarenko's ideas are elaborated at length in his semi-biographical, semi-fictional accounts of life in the collective (1949, 1953). It is in these works that he describes the principles and procedures for building the collective and using it as an instrument of character education. More relevant to our purposes, however, is the manner in which these methods are applied in school settings, for it is in this form that they become the source and substance of much psychological research.

SOCIALIZATION IN THE SCHOOL COLLECTIVE

Although schools were closed at the time of my visit, I heard several descriptions of the Makarenko method from professors, school teachers, and school children. But no description was as graphic and informative as that I found in a manual (Novikova, 1959) for the training and guidance of "school directors, supervisors, teachers, and Young Pioneer leaders." It was put together by staff members of the Institute on the Theory and History of Pedagogy at the Academy of Pedagogical Sciences. I have since seen several others published under the same auspices and very similar in content.

The present volume carries the instructive title: *Socialist Competition in the Schools*. The same thesis is echoed in the titles of individual chapters: "Competition in the Classroom," "Competition between Classrooms," "Competition between Schools," and so on. It is not difficult to see how Russians arrive at the notion, with which they have made us so familiar, of competition between nations and between social systems. Moreover, in the chapter titles we see reflected the influence of dialectical materialism: *conflict at one level is resolved through synthesis at the next higher level, always in the service of the communist collective.*

It is instructive to examine the process of collective socialization as it is initiated in the very first grade. Conveniently enough, the manual starts us off on the first day of school with the teacher standing before the newly-assembled class. What should her first words be? Our text tells us:

> It is not difficult to see that a direct approach to the class with the command, "All sit straight!" often doesn't bring the desired effect since a demand in this form does not reach the sensibilities of the pupils and does not activate them.

How does one "reach the sensibilities of the pupils" and "activate them?" According to the manual, the teacher should say, "Let's see which row can sit the straightest." This approach, we are told, has certain important psychological advantages. In response,

> The children not only try to do everything as well as possible themselves, but also take an evaluative attitude toward those who are undermining the achievement of the row. If similar measures arousing the spirit of competition in the children are systematically applied by experienced teachers in the primary classes, then gradually the children themselves begin to monitor the behavior of their comrades and remind those of them who forget about the rules set by the teacher, who forget what needs to be done and what should not be done. The teacher soon has helpers.

The manual then goes on to describe how records are kept for each row from day to day for different types of tasks so that the young children can develop a concept of group excellence over time and over a variety of activities, including personal cleanliness, condition of notebooks, conduct in passing from one room to the other, quality of recitations in each subject matter, and so on. These activities emphasize the externals of behavior in dress, manner, and speech. There must be no spots on shirt or collar, shoes must be shined, pupils must never pass by a teacher without stopping to give greeting, there must be no talking without permission, and the like. Great charts are kept in all the schools showing the performance of each row unit in every type of activity together with their total overall standing. "Who is best?" the charts ask, but the entries are not individuals but social units—rows, and later the "cells" of the communist youth organization which reaches down to the primary grades.

At first it is the teacher who sets the standards. But soon, still in the first grade, a new wrinkle is introduced: responsible monitors are designated in each row for each activity. In the beginning their job is only to keep track of the merits and demerits assigned each row by the teacher. Different children act as monitors for different activities and, if one is to believe what the manual says, the monitors become very involved in the progress of their row. Then, too, group achievement is not without its rewards. From time to time the winning row gets to be photographed "in parade uniforms" (as in pre-Revolutionary Russia, Soviet children wear uniforms in school), and this photograph is published in that pervasive Soviet institution, the wall newspaper. The significance of the achievements is still further enhanced, however, by the introduction of competition *between* classes so that the winning class and the winning row are visited by delegates from other classrooms in order to learn how to attain the same standard of excellence.

Now let us look more closely at this teacher-mediated monitoring process. In the beginning, we are told, the teacher attempts to focus the attention of children on the achievements of the group; that is, in our familiar phrase, she accentuates the positive. But gradually, "It becomes necessary to take account of negative facts which interfere with the activity of the class." As an example, we have the instance of a child who, despite warnings, continues to enter the classroom a few minutes after the bell has rung. The teacher decides that the time has come to evoke the group process in correcting such behavior. Accordingly, the next time that Serezha is late, the teacher stops him at the door and turns to the class with this question:

75

"Children, is it helpful or not helpful to us to have Serezha come in late?" The answers are quick in coming. "It interferes," "one shouldn't be late," "he ought to come on time." "Well," says the teacher, "how can we help Serezha with this problem?" There are many suggestions: take up a collection to buy him a watch, exile him from the classroom, send him to the director's office, or even to exile him from the school. But apparently these remedies are either not appropriate or too extreme. The teacher, our text tells us, "helps the children find the right answer." She asks for a volunteer to stop by and pick Serezha up on the way to school. Many children offer to help in this mission.

But tragedy stalks. The next day it turns out that not only Serezha is late, but also the boy who had promised to pick him up. Since they are both from the same group, their unit receives two sets of demerits and falls to lowest place. Group members are keenly disappointed. "Serezha especially suffered much and felt himself responsible, but equal blame was felt by his companion who had forgotten to stop in for him."

In this way, both through concrete action and explanation, the teacher seeks to forge a spirit of group unity and responsibility. From time to time, she explains to the children the significance of what they are doing, the fact "that they have to learn to live together as one friendly family, since they will have to be learning together for all of the next ten years, and that for this reason one must learn how to help one's companions and to treat them decently." And in concrete instances, whenever any of the children go out of their way to help a classmate, the teacher makes a point of this fact and praises the pupil for his contribution to collective living. "Today Peter helped Kate and as a result his unit did not get behind the rest."

By the time the children are in the second grade, the complexity of their responsibilities increase. For example, instead of simply recording the evaluations made by the teacher, the monitors are taught how to make the evaluations themselves. Since this is rather difficult, especially in judging homework assignments, in the beginning two monitors are assigned to every task. In this way, our text tells us, they can help each other to do a good job of evaluation.

Here is a third grade classroom:

> Class 3-B is just an ordinary class; it's not especially well disciplined nor is it outstandingly industrious. It has its lazy members and its responsible ones, quiet ones and active ones, daring, shy, and immodest ones.
>
> The teacher has led this class now for three years, and

she has earned the affection, respect, and acceptance as an authority from her pupils. Her word is law for them.

The bell has rung, but the teacher has not yet arrived. She has delayed deliberately in order to check how the class will conduct itself.

In the class all is quiet. After the noisy class break, it isn't so easy to discipline yourself and to quell the restlessness within you! Two monitors at the desk silently observe the class. On their faces is reflected the importance and seriousness of the job they are performing. But there is no need for them to reprimand: the youngsters with pleasure and pride maintain scrupulous discipline; they are proud of the fact that their class conducts itself in a manner that merits the confidence of the teacher. And when the teacher enters and quietly says be seated, all understand that she deliberately refrains from praising them for the quiet and order, since in their class it could not be otherwise. . . .

During the lesson, the teacher gives an exceptional amount of attention to collective competition between "links." (The link is the smallest unit of the communist youth organization at this age level.) Throughout the entire lesson the youngsters are constantly hearing which link has best prepared its lesson, which link has done the best at numbers, which is the most disciplined, which has turned in the best work.

The best link not only gets verbal approval but receives the right to leave the classroom first during the break and to have its notebooks checked before the others. As a result the links receive the benefit of collective education, common responsibility, and mutual aid.

"What are you fooling around for? You're holding up the whole link," whispers Kolya to his neighbor during the preparation period for the lesson. And during the break he teaches her how better to organize her books and pads in her knapsack.

"Count more carefully," says Olya to her girl friend. "See, on account of you our link got behind today. You come with me and we'll count together at home."

In the third grade still another innovation is introduced. The monitors are taught not only to evaluate but also to state their criticisms publicly. Here is a typical picture:

It is the beginning of the lesson. In the first row the link leader reports, basing his comments on information submitted by the sanitarian and other responsible monitors: "Today Volodya did the wrong problem. Masha didn't write neatly, and forgot to underline the right words in her lesson, Aloysha had a dirty shirt collar."

The other link leaders make similar reports (the Pioneers are sitting by rows).

The youngsters are not offended by this procedure: they understand that the link leaders are not just tattle-telling but simply fulfilling their duty. It doesn't even occur to the monitors and sanitarians to conceal the shortcomings of their comrades. They feel that they are doing their job well precisely when they notice one or another defect.

Also in the third grade, the teacher introduces still another procedure. She now proposes that the children enter into competition with the monitors, and see if they can beat the monitor at his own game by criticizing themselves. "The results were spectacular: if the monitor was able to talk only about four or five members of the row, there would be supplementary reports about their own shortcomings from as many as eight or ten pupils."

To what extent is this picture overdrawn? Although I have no direct evidence, the accounts I heard from participants in the process lend credence to the descriptions in the manual. For example, I recall a conversation with three elementary school teachers, all men, whom I had met by chance in a restaurant. They were curious about discipline techniques used in American schools. After I had given several examples, I was interrupted: "But how do you use the collective?" When I replied that we really did not use the classroom group in any systematic way, my three companions were puzzled. "But how do you keep discipline?"

Now it was my turn to ask for examples. "All right," came the answer, "Let us suppose that ten-year-old Vanya is pulling Anya's curls. If he doesn't stop the first time I speak to him, all I need do is mention it again in the group's presence; then I can be reasonably sure that before the class meets again the boy will be talked to by the officers of his Pioneer link. They will remind him that his behavior reflects on the reputtaion of the link."

"And what if he persists?"

"Then he may have to appear before his link—or even the entire collective—who will explain his misbehavior to him and determine his punishment."

"What punishment?"

"Various measures. He may just be censured, or if his conduct is regarded as serious, he may be expelled from membership. Very often he himself will acknowledge his faults before the group."

Nor does the process of social criticism and control stop with the school. Our manual tells us, for example, that parents submit periodic reports to the school collective on the behavior of the child at home. One may wonder how parents can be depended on to turn in truthful accounts. Part of the answer was supplied to me in a conversation with a Soviet agricultural expert. In response to my questions, he explained that, no matter what a person's job, the collective at his place of work always took an active interest in his family life. Thus a representative would come to the worker's home to observe and talk with his wife and children. And if any undesirable features were noted, these would be reported back to the collective.

I asked for an example.

"Well, suppose the representative were to notice that my wife and I quarreled in front of the children (my companion shook his head). That would be bad. They would speak to me about it and remind me of my responsibilities for training my children to be good citizens."

I pointed out how different the situation was in America where a man's home was considered a private sanctuary so that, for example, psychologists like myself often had a great deal of difficulty in getting into homes to talk with parents or to observe children.

"Yes," my companion responded. "That's one of the strange things about your system in the West. The family is separated from the rest of society. That's not good. It's bad for the family and bad for society." He paused for a moment, lost in thought. "I suppose," he went on, "if my wife didn't want to let the representative in, she could ask him to leave. But then, at work, I should feel ashamed." (He hung his head to emphasize the point.) "Ivanov," they would say, "has an uncultured wife."

The preceding incident calls attention to the pervasiveness of group criticism and self-criticism as mechanisms of social control in Soviet society. These procedures are employed at every level of the Soviet social structure, from the elementary school through the upper echelons of party and government. Indeed, the conversation with the three school teachers had occurred in part because I had been unable to talk with anyone at the Psychological Institute that afternoon. No one there was available for conference since the entire staff, from the director down to the janitor, were involved in a two-

and-a-half hour group criticism session of "all aspects of the Institute's activities."

APPLIED SOCIAL PSYCHOLOGY IN THE U.S.S.R.

I have gone into some detail on these matters because of their profound import for Soviet studies of personality development and socialization. In observing and training school children under conditions of social competition and control, Soviet psychologists are studying and teaching skills that have enduring relevance to life in Soviet society.

Moreover, psychologists represent but a small segment of the many professional groups engaged in what is in effect applied social psychology on a massive scale. It is in this sense that the second of my three informants was substantially correct in stating that what we call social psychology is carried on in the Soviet Union primarily, not by psychologists, but by educators and party workers. For this reason, future Western students of social psychology in the U.S.S.R. should not confine their attention to work in psychological departments and institutes but should, also, give careful attention to applied social psychology as it is practiced in schools, youth organizations, farms, factories, and governmental bodies.

Although scientific psychology plays a proportionally small role in these areas, there are many indications that in the immediate future this role will expand both in scope and method. The principal impetus for such development comes from the recent educational reform and the universal emphasis it places on training in practical education, character building, and early experience in collective living. In connection with this reform, several new types of educational institutions are to be developed on a massive scale. The most important of these is the "internat," or boarding school, in which youngsters are to be entered as early as three months of age, with parents visiting only on weekends. The internat is described in the theses announcing the reforms as the kind of school which "creates the most favorable conditions for the education and communist upbringing of the rising generation." (*Ob Ukreplenii Svyazi*, 1958.) The government plans to increase the number of boarding schools in the U.S.S.R., during the current seven-year plan, from the 1958 level of 180,000 to 2,500,000 in 1965 (figures cited in *Pravda*, November 18, 1958), and according to I. A. Kairov, head of the Academy of Pedagogical Sciences, "No one can doubt that, as material conditions are created, the usual general educational school will be supplanted by the boarding school." (Kairov, 1960)

The implications of these developments for psychology are spelled out in an address by Kairov published in the official Soviet educational journal, *Sovetskaya Pedagogika,* in which he criticizes psychologists and others for failing to give adequate attention in research to problems of "Society and the School." Such recommendations are reflected at the operational level in the direction of developing research in three of the centers I visited (the Department of Psychology at Leningrad, and the Institutes of Psychology at Moscow and Kiev) and in programmatic statements published recently by leading Soviet psychologists (Bozhovich, 1960; Kovalev, 1959; Krutetski, 1960; Smirnov, 1959).

Especially noteworthy in this connection is the call, on the part of several of the foregoing authorities, for guarded reconsideration of one or another approach characteristic of psychology in the West and regarded over the past quarter century as reactionary. Kairov (1960, p. 12), for instance, criticizes Soviet psychologists for too narrow an interpretation of the 1936 Decree of the Central Committee on "pedological distortions," with resultant neglect of the important problem of individual differences.

> . . . Certain of our workers in the pedagogical sciences, having failed to examine this decree as they properly should have, adopted an incorrect attitude. Contrary to common sense, they began simply to deny the need and the orthodoxy of any research whatsoever into differences between children, to be used for pedagogical purposes. . . . They attacked as "pedological" all methods involving research into age and individual differences of school children which went beyond the bounds of simple observation and the common methods of checking their knowledge.
>
> Despite the fact that over 20 years have elapsed since that decree, this incorrect and one-sided attitude has yet to be subjected to criticism, and continues to interfere seriously with the development of true Marxist teachings on children. Meanwhile, there is no doubt that, without studying the personality of the youngster, it is impossible for a teacher to carry on his practical educational activity on a scientifically sound basis. The most important thing here is the careful compilation of materials giving the specific developmental history of the child's individuality, the history of the development of children's collectives, and the history

of the inter-relations formed within those collectives. But, having cut out research on the age and individual differences of children, pedagogy became essentially "childless."

In another sphere, Bozhovich re-opens the possibility of conducting research on unconscious processes.

Soviet psychologists have shown a fully understandable tendency to oppose with the supremacy of the conscious the "unconscious" of Freud and other representatives of "depth psychology," to demonstrate that man is by no means a mere marionette dancing at the whim of certain dark powers, but instead is the master of his own behavior, capable of governing his actions and deeds on the basis of consciously-posed tasks and consciously-taken decisions.

However, in the course of battle against its domination the "unconscious" came to be viewed as the demiurge of personality. It was thought that one had only to convince a child, to develop his conscious awareness, and his total personality would be developed. One cannot agree with such an over-estimation of the role of conscious processes. In our investigations, we constantly encounter phenomena that do not lie within the child's conscious awareness, but which nevertheless cannot be overlooked either by the psychologist or the pedagogue. For example, in the course of investigating motives for academic performance in school children, we have established on the basis of obtained data that the main motives of learning, those which express the social needs most significant for the child and which thereby constitute the principal instigators of academic performance are, as a rule, not recognized by the child himself.

In the investigation of the development of the affective aspects of personality, we likewise constantly come face to face with the fact that moral feelings and habits which arise in the course of social activity determine the behavior of the child often quite independently of his consciousness and even in direct contradiction to it. . . .

In the light of these considerations, it seems to us of the utmost importance in further studies of problems in the psychology of personality to give special attention to the investigation of psychological phenomena which arise in the course of the child's life and activity but of which he remains unaware. It is necessary to study the character-istics of such phenomena, their origins, and their role in the behavior of the child as well as in the formation of his personality (Bozhovich, 1960, p. 223).

But perhaps the most revolutionary change urged by a leading Soviet psychologist is Kovalev's proposal (1959) to redeem social psychology from its purgatorial status and reinstate it as a legitimate sphere of investigation for Soviet science. Acknowledging as entirely proper and justified the severe criticism of bourgeois social psychology which appear in the definitive article on that subject in the *Great Soviet Encyclopedia,* Kovalev nevertheless challenges the official view, as expounded most recently by the late dean of Soviet psychology, S. L. Rubinstein, that to express interest in social psychology is to "defend that which is so dear to the hearts of reactionaries, that which, in the last analysis, is an attempt to psychologize sociology; that is, to drag in idealism into the scientific study of social phenom-ena" (Kovalev, 1959, p. 70).

Such a position, Kovalev suggests, forces one to question the legitimacy of studying "philosophy, political economy, sociology, and psychology" since these subjects too might be "dear to the hearts of reactionaries." The real question, the author argues, is whether or not an objective social reality exists; if it does exist, then it is neces-sary to find methods appropriate for its study. He then cites Soviet philosophers in support of the thesis that "social psychology is a real phenomenon made manifest in the psychology of a given society, a given class; and in the psychological character of national groups; social psychology is the sum total of social feelings, attitudes, exper-iences, habits, illusions, etc." Citing the work of the "great Soviet educator, A. S. Makarenko," Kovalev asks,

Are not Soviet pedogogues and psychologists investigating questions of the psychology of upbringing in essence work-ing on one of the most important problems of social psy-chology? The question of the formation of the collective (and for that matter of public opinion) and of the develop-ment of personality in the collective, through the collective and for the collective constitutes precisely such a problem. It follows that in actuality social psychology is already being investigated in Soviet pedagogical science. . . .
The majestic program of developing socialist construction approved after all-union discussion at the 21st Congress of

83

the Communist Party of the Soviet Union poses great and responsible tasks, not only for the natural, but also for the social sciences.

The program laid down for the communist upbringing of the Soviet peoples, at the center of which stand the problems of developing a communist orientation toward work and collectivism as hallmarks of the personality of the new man, make imperative the investigation of social psychology, which must make its contribution to the solution of these most vital problems (pp. 79-81).

American social scientists will be watching with interest the future of this "new look" in Soviet psychology.

COMMENT
Otto Klineberg

Professor Bronfenbrenner's chapter brings out a number of important and interesting aspects of Soviet psychology, and I find myself in general agreement with his conclusions. There are, however, two issues on which I should like to comment. The first refers to the contrasts he has drawn between Soviet and American psychology; the second to the status of social psychology in the Soviet Union.

The "sharp differences in context, method, and interpretation" undoubtedly exist, and Bronfenbrenner has rightly drawn attention to them. It should be kept in mind, however, that these are differences in relative emphasis, and that they are by no means complete or absolute. Bronfenbrenner speaks of the American concern with the social setting of the family, and the Soviet concern with the school. True, but American psychologists interested in personality development and socialization have also stressed the influence of peer cultures. Conversely, in the Soviet Union the family is by no means neglected, as Bronfenbrenner's quotation from Makarenko, in fact, indicates. The same point can probably be made for all his "contrasts," namely, that they are relative rather than absolute. This holds even for concern with the unconscious. One Soviet psychologist spoke to me about the important contributions made by psychoanalysis, and remarked with some pride that many of the works of Freud were to be found in the library of the local psychological institute.

Although Bronfenbrenner may have presented the contrasts somewhat too sharply in my opinion, he at the same time makes it abundantly clear that there are variations within the Soviet Union also. Not only are there differences in emphasis, as he points out, between Moscow and Leningrad, but within the same city opinions as to the scope and nature of psychological research are by no means unanimous. Struck by the exotic appearance, during my stay in Moscow, of many visitors from the outlying republics, I suggested to my colleagues that the Soviet Union might be a veritable paradise for students of culture and personality. One psychologist agreed, and regretted that so little had been done. When I made the same point to another, however, the reaction was very negative. First he said that these people are all changing and becoming industrialized so rapidly that there was no point in carrying out such investigations; my response was, all the more reason for studying them in a hurry! Then he added a second objection, which he himself termed "political"; he did not think that the people of the other republics would take kindly to being studied, as if they were curious specimens of humanity, by the "superior" Russians. For the sake of political harmony in the Soviet Union, it would be better *not* to stress the ethnic variations. A third psychologist agreed with this view.

Two observations suggest themselves. The first is that the earlier Soviet emphasis on cultural pluralism seems to be losing out to the view that homogeneity, as the result of industrialization, is on the way. Regional folkways, dances, music, artistic products, still get some attention, but are definitely subordinated to the goals of technology. The second observation is to the effect that political considerations may be more important in determining the problems with which Soviet psychologists deal, than in determining how they handle those problems, once they have chosen to work on them. In any case, statements about *all* Soviet psychology are almost as difficult to make with any certainty as would be similar generalizations about *all* American psychology.

To my questions about social psychology and its place in Soviet science, the usual answer was that social factors are considered to be so fundamental to the understanding of *all* behavior, that there is no need for a special discipline or branch which is so labeled; it is "built-in," so to speak. This is at least partly true; some of Leontiev's work on perception stresses aspects of experience which seem to him to come close to our emphasis on social factors. (On the other hand, the work on mental defects, asphasia, and other disorders, in the case of Luria and others, is much more anatomically, and less socially, oriented than corresponding American research.) There are a number of observational studies of groups, and the relation of the individual to his collective (in Smirnov's laboratory), frequently related to pedagogical problems (as in Kostiuk's Institute in Kiev). There is practically nothing, however, of what might be called *experimental* social psychology as far as I could judge, except in the indirect manner mentioned above. Attitude and opinion research is almost entirely lacking, but some beginnings have been made, and there are prospects that it may develop further, probably with very definite restrictions as to the topics which may be explored in this manner. The approach to delinquency appears to put the blame *inside* the individual, and not in the (presumably excellent) society.

There is apparently something of a paradox in a situation which, on the one hand, stresses at all times the importance of the "collective," and on the other shows so little interest in what Americans know as *social* psychology. There is some indication, however, that the paradox may be in the process of resolution. Interest in social psychology appears to be increasing, and I was asked many questions about recent developments in this field. A number of Soviet psychologists had at least a modest acquaintance with the relevant literature, and even had some of that literature on their own bookshelves. They also broached the question as to the possibility that one or more American social psychologists might be interested in giving a series of lectures in the Soviet Union. I share with Bronfenbrenner the prediction that in the near future social psychology will occupy a more prominent and respectable place in Soviet psychology.

CHAPTER IV

Soviet Mental Health Facilities and Psychology

HENRY P. DAVID AND TEMA S. DAVID[1]

During the summer of 1960 we had a unique opportunity to visit mental health facilities in the Soviet Union and discuss practices and programs in that country.

We drove into the Soviet Union in our own car, crossing the Polish-Russian border at Brest, and proceding via Minsk, Smolensk, Moscow, Kalinin, Novgorod, and Leningrad. Most of the time we were without official guide or interpreter, traveling a pre-arranged route, but free to go as we wished within cities. There were many opportunities to meet colleagues in the mental health professions, all of whom were gracious hosts and seemed as interested as we in exchanging information on common problems.

It has often been said that there are no experts on the Soviet Union, only degrees of ignorance. And so, our notes must be clearly labeled for what they are: impressions from a two week's whirlwind visit to a vast country so very different from our own that it becomes exceedingly difficult at times to make any sort of judgment.

While in Moscow, the State Committee for Cultural Relations with Foreign Countries arranged a trip to Kashenko Mental Hospital, one of the largest Soviet psychiatric centers, with 2,500 beds and a staff of 2,300. Of 160 physicians, 91 are qualified psychiatrists, most of them women. Patient care is in the hands of nurses; there are no psychiatric aides. Everything considered, the patient-staff ratio appeared more favorable at Kashenko than in New Jersey State hospitals (with whose facilities we are most familiar).

Admissions to Kashenko are about 10-12,000 per year, of whom approximately 90 per cent are readmissions. We were told that within

[1] We wish to acknowledge the generous support of the Social Science Research Council, whose travel grant underwrote a portion of our expenses, and the editorial encouragement of the *New Jersey Welfare Reporter,* in whose pages these comments first appeared.

a year's time about 80 per cent of the patients go home, 1.7 per cent die, and 18.3 per cent remain in the hospital. As in New Jersey, emphasis is on early release with limited concern about the readmission rate.

In a sense, the mental hospital's setting was similar to that found in a general hospital. Patients were in pajamas and the staff in white. Doors were locked; instead of bars the curtained windows had special safety glass. The building was old and might well be considered substandard in New Jersey. However, the atmosphere was warm, cheerful, and home-like, with nurses and physicians obviously caring about the patients. Accommodations for children were especially attractive, including school rooms, a small zoo, and a garden tended by the patients.

The total hospital budget was about 40 million rubles, or about $10 million at the 1960 official rate and $4 million at the 1960 tourist rate. Per diem costs, at the tourist rate, are about $4.10, including $.80 for food. (New Jersey's per diem is $.83; the Veterans Administration per diem is $11.43.) Put another way, the cost of maintaining a patient in a Soviet mental hospital is about one and a half times the average income of Soviet workers. Patients are not required to participate in housekeeping chores or in the physical maintenance of the institution. All staff members, from director on down, receive a 15 per cent bonus for working with mental patients and 30 per cent if assigned to the children's unit. Nurses work on a 12 hours on and 48 hours off schedule, and enjoy an annual paid vacation of 36 working days (48 days on the children's service). Nursing is a coveted profession and there is no recruitment problem.

In Leningrad, we visited the Bekhterev Institute of Neurology and Psychiatry, a facility comparable to the National Institute of Mental Health Clinical Center in Bethesda. There are numerous in- and out-patient sections, with admission largely determined by teaching and research interests. Typical of the excellent staffing pattern is the 45-bed children's unit, with its chief physician and four full time assistants plus 12 nurses (five on each shift). Working hours, bonus pay, vacation schedule, etc., are identical with that noted in Moscow. There were an even number of boys and girls, ages seven to sixteen, and our hosts expressed surprise when told that in New Jersey we need about four times as many facilities for boys as for girls. Again, the atmosphere was warm and cheerful, and everyone we met seemed genuinely fond of the children.

In discussing Soviet mental health facilities with various hosts throughout our travels, we gained the impression that the overall picture is one of excellent care but limited resources to meet the country's needs. General hospitals have priority over mental hospitals. We were informed that for the 208 million Soviet population, there are currently about 130,000 beds and 4,500 psychiatrists, which is a rough ratio of about 1 psychiatrist per 28 patients. (For 175 million Americans there are about 750,000 state hospital beds and 3,000 psychiatrists, or 1 per 250 patients.) It may be more meaningful to note that the U.S.S.R. has more physicians than the United States, but only half the number of psychiatrists. We were told the number is rising. The largest Soviet mental hospital has 3,000 beds, and, as in New Jersey, current emphasis is on smaller units.

About 70 per cent of all psychiatrists are women, most of whom received six years of medical school training after graduating from high school, followed by two or three years as general physicians and a year's training in adult and child psychiatry. It was surprising to learn that the medical school curriculum apparently has no courses in psychological theory. The Soviet Ministry of Health is responsible for the hiring and training of all physicians; and personnel are assigned on the basis of regional needs and priorities. Beginning State salaries for professionals are about the same as those for skilled factory workers.

Within the facilities we visited, the basic orientation in psychiatry was organic. The view was widely expressed that the primary cause of most mental illness, especially schizophrenia, was probably organic and that, in time, research would provide the evidence. It was also postulated that organic changes may occur without psychotic components, which suggests that organicity may not be the sole basis for psychoses, and that environmental stresses function as a trigger mechanism. Neuroses are attributed largely to a faulty environment (school, family, etc.) and so the environment is changed. There appears to be less reluctance in the Soviet Union to hospitalize neurotic patients, but hospital authorities can refuse admission if they disagree with the diagnosis.

In discussing psychotherapy, we quickly learned that Freudian notions are still officially taboo; however, a type of brief, supportive "re-educational counselling" is employed in efforts to alleviate neurotic symptoms. While the possibility of psychogenic disorders is acknowledged, there are only infrequent attempts to delve into childhood experiences or family influences. Although Freud was not unknown in the Soviet Union, and a Psychoanalytic Society did exist in the 1930's, psychoanalysis is presently considered unscientific, non-experimental, idealistic, and a potential source of political reaction. While there seems to be general agreement that the problems explored by Freud are important, it is usually held that unconscious motivation should be considered in Pavlovian terms. Emphasis is focused on external influences and social environment, not on instinctual drives and anxieties. It should be noted, however, that Freud's volumes, in several translations and editions, are available in the Lenin Library and in psychological centers, and English-language publications are reviewed in Soviet journals. We were told that courses on psychotherapy are given to physicians in the main hospitals of each of the Soviet republics, and that pertinent books are received in training and research centers.

It should be recalled that Pavlov's views, pointing to a physiological rather than psychological basis of disorders, are particularly acceptable to Marxian materialism because they stress the physiological and rational (which fits the Marxian notion of man responsible for his behavior). Freud, on the other hand, emphasized the psychological and irrational. Soviet psychiatry thus endeavors to localize events in the brain, not in the mind. It is frequently held that behind every human action there is a definite physiological occurrence, effecting a state of excitation or inhibition in the brain. Therapy consists largely of drugs, insulin, sleep, and conservative use of electric shock. Pavlov, incidentally, was a Professor of Psychopharmacology before he obtained fame as a psychologist.

We saw little evidence of anything approaching a team concept. Qualified physicians seem plentiful in supply and they do all therapy. Clinical psychologists generally limit their activities to testing for organic involvement, and related research. There were no trained psychiatric social workers, in the American sense. We were told that there is less need for social workers in the institution since State agencies are responsible for housing, employment, rehabilitation, etc., and see to it that the individual's and the family's needs are met, both on hospitalization and on return of the patient. If a child is a ward of the State or placed in a special school, official agencies assume all responsibility.

The most recently established research section of the Bekhterev Institute is concerned with alcoholism, long a social phenomenon in Russian history. We were told that it has lessened somewhat since the Revolution, but there is no attempt to play down its severity. Although there is no Soviet counterpart of Alcoholics Anonymous, much interest was expressed in American efforts to cope with this common problem.

One of our objectives was to explore Soviet facilities for emotionally disturbed children. This term has no equivalent in Russian and it was difficult to convey to our hosts, psychiatrists or psychologists, just what we had in mind.[2] We only began to be understood when we indicated what some of our problems were in New Jersey and asked how similar cases might be approached in the Soviet Union. It appears that when little Ivan gets into trouble in school, the situation is handled by committee. There is a Mothers' Committee in school, a Tenants' Committee in the housing project, a Workers' Committee at the factory, etc. What is bothering Ivan is seemingly of less concern than how to stop him from bothering others and upsetting school routine. There is no organized system of child guidance clinics. A youngster who does not readily fit into an accepted social pattern is considered either an educational or medical problem. If educational, the school and the committees focus on "re-education," and teachers are expected to handle the problem. If considered medical, the child is referred to his local polyclinic where all of his medical records since birth are filed. (There is no choice of agency or physician.) A psychiatrist may then prescribe physical treatment, including drugs, or send the youngster to a hospital or boarding school. Unfortunately, we had no opportunity to explore the Soviet system of child rearing, the effects of crammed housing quarters, sexual mores, etc., all of which may have to be considered in attempts to understand little Ivan's emotional problem.

When we inquired about juvenile delinquency, we again made little progress until we discussed New Jersey problems and asked how similar children might be helped in the Soviet Union. It seems that juvenile delinquency is now reluctantly accepted as a fact of Soviet life, a by-product of increased industrialization and better times. But, there is an equal insistence that the problem is not as severe as in the West. It had been hoped that the Soviet system of collectives, Young Pioneers, Komsomols, etc., would keep youngsters well-organized and reduce the stimuli for delinquent behavior. Yet, one of the chief justifications for the educational reforms and the work-study program seems to be that it will discourage "hooliganism, stylism, and delinquency." Research on juvenile delinquents and their families has been initiated in the Pedagogical Institute, and appears to be directed both toward an understanding of the individual and toward an effort to learn how social group pressures can be employed more effectively. We were frequently told that horror comics and films are not permitted in the Soviet Union.

Assuming that, in fact, the U.S.S.R. does have a lower rate of juvenile delinquency than most other industrial countries, the real

---

[2] [The Russian term for "emotionally disturbed children" is "nervous children."—EDITOR.]

question may well be how much of this is due to up-bringing, as reflected in the individual character, and how much to contemporary conditions, such as organized social pressure or lack of stimuli, or both. There was general agreement that shifting family values and instabilities may be involved and that juvenile delinquency could provide a unique opportunity for cross-cultural research on a problem plaguing all societies. Later we learned that despite their interest there may be little hope of actually obtaining the cooperation of Soviet colleagues in social research. Such problems are considered the responsibility of society (the State and the Party), and not the province of psychology. Thus there is little social psychology in the traditional sense; those concerned with social issues tend to work not in psychology, but in the Academy of Philosophy and its subsection on Social History and Dialectical Materialism. The evaluation of group functions, the collective, and Soviet social experiments is considered the prerogative of the Communist Party.

During our stay in Moscow, Professor A. R. Luria escorted us on a brief tour through the very impressive Moscow University (where we later visited A. N. Sokolov's well-equipped laboratory) and also arranged an interview with the Head of the Section on Mental Retardation of the Institute of Defectology, one of eight institutes organized under the auspices of the Academy of Pedagogical Science. (Another is the Institute of Psychology, headed by Professor A. A. Smirnov, whom we also visited.) Professor A. N. Leontiev directs the Psychology Department of the Academy of Pedagogical Science. Professor Luria is a member of the Presidium of the Academy, teaches at Moscow University, and has a good deal to do with directing the work of the Institute for Defectology. He has described his experimental approach and theories in numerous publications over the past 40 years.

At the Institute of Defectology (center for the scientific study of handicapped children), much emphasis is placed on hearing tests. We were told that approximately 30 per cent of allegedly mentally retarded children in fact suffer from deafness and are not actually retarded. Luria has observed that only one-half of one per cent of any age group falls into the defective category: "All other children can handle the curriculum." Those who cannot be rehabilitated or trained are institutionalized. (As in most States, there appears to be a shortage of beds.) During our visit to the Institute, we learned, among other things, that Soviet colleagues do not agree with our distinction between "educable" and "trainable" and that they, too, have difficulty differentiating between mentally retarded and schizophrenic children (although both handicaps are considered organic in origin). Schools for the retarded are headed by teachers trained in defectology; classes have about 12 to 15 students. There is a shortage of teachers and evening seminars have been developed to provide additional training. "Difficult" retarded children are considered medical problems and are housed in special institutions. Unfortunately, there was no opportunity to visit any of these centers.

Much has been said and written about Soviet psychology and its adherence to Pavlovian concepts of higher nervous activity and Marxist philosophy of dialectical materialism. On his 1960 visit to this country, Professor Luria defined Soviet psychology as the "science of voluntary behavior in man." Current research focuses on Pavlov's second signal system, involving aspects of physiology, conditioning, and speech in relation to problem solving. Much of the work done in Soviet psychological laboratories would be labelled physiological in the United States. However, "speech" is not regarded as purely motor or verbal; it includes culturally derived meanings and concepts. Although Russian psychology also emphasizes the importance of social interaction in man's historical development, we did not learn of any empirical studies in this field. As noted earlier, social psychology is usually considered the prerogative of the Party.

The Soviet Psychological Society has 1,800 members (compared to a membership of over 18,000 in the American Psychological Association). Basic undergraduate training requires about five years, with heavy emphasis on biological sciences, but little concern with statistics. A graduate student may work for several years in a university or institute laboratory, and after completing a thesis, attain the rank of Candidate, considered equivalent to a Ph.D. According to Professor Luria, about 250 Candidate degrees are awarded annually (100 in Moscow, 100 in Leningrad, and 50 elsewhere). A Doctor of Science degree may be awarded later for independent scientific research and is considered equivalent to our Associate Professor rank. We were told that 70 per cent of the graduate students read English and that major interest is in brain-neurological and educational-developmental areas. A Candidate receives about 2,500 rubles per month, or 250 dollars at the 1960 tourist rate and 625 dollars at the official rate.

The Institute of Psychology of the Academy of Pedagogical Science was established in 1912 and its current Director, Professor A. A. Smirnov, was one of the first students. It now has a staff of 118, including 72 scientific workers. There are laboratories in the traditional areas of experimental psychology plus growing interest in child development, teaching methods, and aspects of work. About 15 per cent of all Soviet graduate students in psychology are at the Institute.

Current journals published by the American Psychological Association were on display in the Institute Library, and recently published American books were among new acquisitions listed on the bulletin board. Perusal of the catalog suggested an excellent collection of pre-1935 English-language publications, followed by a considerable gap until post-World War II editions. Freud's works were available in Russian, German, and English.

The Soviet psychological laboratories we visited were often located in old and cramped quarters reminiscent of our basement shops in American universities. They were, however, usually well-equipped, especially with conditioning and EEG recording apparatus. As Yvonne Brackbill later told us, about half of the human subjects are children, and there is frequently a waiting list of children whose parents want them to live for a while in pediatric research centers. Emphasis is on the experimental method, with an avowed goal of eventually applying research findings to practical field situations.

At the American Psychological Association 1960 Convention Roundtable, other visitors to the Soviet Union indicated their esteem for the work reported. Professsor Neal Miller noted that the term "conditioning" is used synonymously with "learning" at all levels of complication, from classical conditioning to naturally learned responses, such as a rabbit eating a carrot thrust at him. It was also observed that despite the high level of Soviet mathematics, much psychological research is in the Helmholtzian tradition of replicating studies, using a minimum of statistics. A good deal of work is reported in the *Pavlov Journal of Higher Nervous Activity* (authors are paid for articles), now available in English translation. Particularly noteworthy was the substantial financial support for researchers and their assistants, which permits long-term planning and provides cohesion for a productive group. Since the State is the sole employer and salary levels are fairly standard throughout the U.S.S.R., there apparently is little shopping for better positions once a satisfactory setting has been attained.

Soviet clinical psychology also follows a Pavlovian orientation, which means that major interest is usually focused on studies of pathological changes in the higher nervous processes believed to lie behind disturbances in psychic activities. Dean of Soviet clinical psychologists is Madame B. V. Zeigarnik, well-known in the United States for her earlier work with Lewin. She teaches psychopathology at the University of Moscow and heads the Clinical Psychology Laboratory at the Institute of Psychiatry, affiliated with the Academy of Medical Science. She was away while we were in Moscow, but we were told that her main interests are in evaluating pathological thinking and emotion in childhood schizophrenia. There are about 70 clinical psychologists in Soviet psychiatric centers. Many of them are concerned with "personality," which is considered to have a biological basis, with development depending on social environmental factors. Different types of temperament are believed to be products of different types of higher nervous activity, measured by physiological indices of brain processes.

Psychological tests were severely criticized in 1931, and condemned in a 1936 Communist Party resolution as unscientific, detrimental to public education, and "in conflict both with dialectical materialism and the practical experience of Soviet society." The I.Q. concept was rejected on the grounds that it allegedly reflects only innate intelligence and inherited abilities. We were told that one of the Russian objections to standard American tests is that "different children can achieve the same results in quite different ways." It is held that tests yield limited information about the process of problem solving considered so important for training.

There are indications that some form of psychological assessment is used. Yvonne Brackbill,[3] for instance, was told on her visit to the Institute for Defectology that children suspected of mental retardation are asked to classify pictures, draw proper conclusions, match colors and forms, and describe a story shown in pictures. While there are no published norms, psychological examiners are expected to make clinical judgments on the basis of their experience.

Projective techniques are known and we were told that the Rorschach is used as a diagnostic aid in the evaluation of brain function. However, there is little interest in psychodynamics. As one Soviet psychologist put it, "We are not so much interested in probing man's depths as in understanding the heights he can attain."

Soviet colleagues asked many questions about our work in New Jersey and about psychological testing. We usually replied that the tests of 1960 were not those of 1936, and that considerable effort was continually going into research studies designed to improve reliability and validity of new devices helpful in education and industry, areas of general interest for the current Soviet seven-year plan. Many Soviet psychologists were exceedingly well-informed about American experimental studies. This is in part due to the journal, *Problems of Psychology,* which began publication in 1955. A recent issue reported on major psychological conferences held outside the Soviet Union, surveyed foreign literature received in Moscow's scientific libraries, and published an annotated bibliography of new acquisi-

---

[3] See Chapter V.

95

tions in psychology from abroad. An English language edition is published in Great Britain by Pergamon Press, under the sponsorship of the British Psychological Society.

Soviet mental health facilities and psychology are inevitably related to Soviet life. And, perhaps the outstanding fact of Soviet life is that it is planned. There appear to be fairly clear notions of desirable behavior, and a large network of institutional machinery has been created to attain these goals. Parent education, nursing schools, young pioneer programs, and other vast organizations that touch the varied life stages of most Soviet citizens have identical objectives and tend to operate on the same principles, supported by press, TV, and related mass media. It was especially interesting for us to observe the extent to which Soviet colleagues participate in this planning. For example, psychological research is instrumental to better pedagogical work, and psychologists in responsible positions in the Academy of Pedagogical Science play major roles in determining teaching methods.

As has been noted by visiting social scientists, another striking aspect of Soviet life is the uniformity throughout the whole society or collective. Norms are apparently generally accepted and there is much social pressure toward conformity. Thus any person can anticipate with some accuracy what others will notice and accept or reject. It may well be that this circumstance is at least partially responsible for the puritanism in Russian behavior and attitudes (especially toward sex) that was reported to us by several local observers. It should be added that the standards themselves, e.g. hard work, devotion to duty, cleanliness, orderliness, no public manifestations of sexual interest, are not considered uniquely Russian or communist; rather, it is held that such standards must be adhered to if one wishes to avoid public censure and maintain his standing as an accepted member of the collective.

Soviet colleagues believe that since an individual is so largely a product of his social environment, it is up to all those with some responsibility for his development to assure a correct social environment with the right stimuli to shape the right habits. In terms of Pavlovian learning theory, the right habits are continuously reinforced throughout life by the example of others and through group pressures. Thus in Soviet mental health practice, there is little interest in probing for psychodynamics or fostering insight. Rather, the Soviet approach seems intent on strengthening the positive, that is, those aspects of the person that are unimpaired, diverting a strong motive into constructive channels and maintaining the social role of the collective, the State.

In reflecting on our trip, and comparing it with previous European travels in other years, it seemed to us that our Soviet experience in many ways was the most intellectually exhausting yet stimulating venture we have ever undertaken. No book or TV series can possibly portray the dynamism of Soviet life. It must be seen and personally experienced in all its paradoxical perplexities. We concluded that while there may be a gulf in our theoretical approaches, there is commonality in our empirical search for a better way to resolve human problems. Today, more than ever, there are impelling reasons for exchanging students, specialists, and tourists, and thus perhaps enhancing understanding between East and West.

SUGGESTED READING LIST

Boguslavsky, G. W., Psychological research in Soviet education. *Science,* 125, 915-918, 1957, *Psychol. Abstr.*, 5833, 1957.

Bondarenko, P. P. and Rabinovich, M. Kh., Scientific inference on the problems of the ideological struggle with contemporary Freudism. *Vop. Filos.,* 13, 164-170, 1959. *Psychol. Abstr.*. 2383, 1960.

Cammer, Leonard M., Conditioning and psychiatric theory. *Amer. J. Orthopsychiat.,* 31, 810-819, 1961.

Chauncey, Henry, Some notes on education and psychology in the Soviet Union. *Amer. Psychologist.,* 14, 307-312, 1959.

David, Henry P., Report on Bonn and Moscow, *J. Proj. Techn.,* 25, 282-286, 1961.

Fedotov, D., The Soviet view of psychoanalysis, *Monthly Review,* Dec. 1957.

Field, Mark, Approaches to mental illness in Soviet society: some comparisons and conjectures. *Soc. Prob.,* 7, 277-297, 1960.

Kerbikov, O. V., The teaching of psychiatry in the U.S.S.R. Geneva: *WHO Pub. Health Pap.,* No. 9, 159-167, 1961

Klein, R. H., A visit to the P. P. Kashenko Mental Hospital, *World Ment. Health,* 10, 182-191, 1958, Mental Hospitals, 1958.

Kline, Nathan S., The organization of psychiatric care and psychiatric research in the U.S.S.R., *Annals, N.Y. Acad. of Sci.,* 81, 149-224, 1960.

Klumbner, George M., Child psychiatry facilities in Moscow, Russia. *Amer. J. Psychiat.,* 116, 1087-1090, 1960.

Kubie, Lawrence S., Pavlov, Freud, & Soviet Psychiatry. *Behav. Sci.,* 4, 29-34, 1959.

Lebedinski, M. S., Psychotherapy in the Soviet Union. *Gp. Psychother.,* 13, 170-172, 1960.

Luria, A. R., Psychopathological research in the U.S.S.R. In Simon, B. (Ed.) *Psychology in the Soviet Union,* Stanford, Cal. Stanford Univ. Press, 279-287, 1957.

Murray, Henry A., May, Mark A., and Cantril, Hadley, Some glimpses of Soviet psychology. *Amer. Psychologist,* 14, 303-307, 1959.

O'Connor, N., Russian psychology, 1959. *Bull. Brit. Psychol.,* 502, 1960.

O'Connor, N. (Ed.), Recent Soviet psychology, N. Y.: Pergamon Press, 1960.

Piaget, Jean, Some impressions of a visit to Soviet psychologists. *Newsletter, International Union of Scientific Psychology*, 1, 13-16, 1956. *Amer. Psychologist*, 11, 343-345, 1956.

Popov, E. A., On the application of I. P. Pavlov's theory to the field of psychiatry. *Zh. Nerropat. Psikhiat.*, 57, 673-680, 1957. *Psychol. Abstr.*, 2332, 1960.

Razran, Gregory, Recent Russian psychology: 1950-1956, *Contemp. Psychol.*, 2, 93-101, 1957.

Razran, Gregory, Psychology in Communist countries other than the U.S.S.R., *Amer. Psychologist*, 13, 177-178, 1958.

Razran, Gregory, Soviet psychology and psychophysiology. *Beh. Sci.*, 1959, 4, 35-48.

Razran, Gregory, The observable unconscious and the inferable conscious in current Soviet psychophysiology: interoceptive conditioning, semantic conditioning, and the orienting reflex. *Psychol. Rev.*, 68, 81-147, 1961.

Simon, Brian (Ed.), Psychology in the Soviet Union. Stanford, Cal.: Stanford Univ. Press, 1957.

Smirnov, A. A., The tasks of psychology in the light of the decisions of XXI Congress of the Communist Party of the Soviet Union. Vop. Psikhol., 5(5), 7-28, 1959. *Psychol. Abstr.*, 6828, 1960.

Tizard, Jack, Children in the U.S.S.R.: work on mental and physical handicaps. *Lancet*, No. 7060, Dec. 20, 1958.

Winn, Ralph B. (Ed.), Soviet psychology, NY: Philosophical Libr., 1961.

Winn, Ralph B. (Ed.), Psychotherapy in the Soviet Union. NY: Philosophical Libr., 1961.

Wortis, Joseph, A psychiatric study tour of the U.S.S.R. *J. Ment. Sci.*, 107, 119-156, 1961.

Ziferstein, Isidore, Dynamic psychotherapy in the Soviet Union. *Gp. Psychother.*, 14, 221-233, 1961.

CHAPTER V

Research and Clinical Work with Children

YVONNE BRACKBILL[1]

The year 1901 marked the publication in Saint Petersburg of a monograph by A. P. Nechaev entitled, *Contemporary experimental psychology in relation to questions of academic education.* It was followed by a second monograph (Nechaev, 1901b) and by a series of shorter articles on visual memory, associations, and the value of the scientific method (Kaufman *et al.,* 1903; Korolkova, 1904; Byshevskii *et al.,* 1904; Livshits, 1908). This was the beginning of Russian research on the behavior of children. The work of Bekhterev's students, it was born of pedagogical problems and nurtured in an experimental tradition.

It has been sixty years since Nechaev's publication, but the original endowment of biology and pedagogy to behavioral research still accounts for the salient features of today's major studies— experimentation, a proximity to practical application, a physiological frame of reference. Meanwhile, the number of studies of child behavior has greatly increased. Indeed, at present, a higher proportion of developmental behavioral research cannot be found in any other country.

[1] To credit but a single author is somewhat presumptuous, for many people have contributed a great deal to this chapter. The Human Ecology Fund and the American Psychological Association made my second trip to the Soviet Union possible through the generosity of their financial and professional support. My colleagues who contributed the material in this chapter are to be especially commended for their kind hospitality, their tolerance of first-year Russian, their patience under the fire of endless questioning, and their thoughtful comments on this manuscript. Patricia Sheppard, Illustrations Department, The Johns Hopkins University, provided all the drawings and one-half the total encouragement needed to round out the text.

All transliterations appearing in this chapter have been made according to the rules adopted by the Library of Congress.

This manuscript was prepared during the tenure of a U.S.P.H.S. research fellowship at The Johns Hopkins University. The author is now at the University of Colorado Medical School.

The purpose of this chapter is to describe some of this research and research-related applications—work that, as of 1960, had just been completed or was still in progress. The chapter is quite inadequate in the extent of its coverage, a predicament for which the author can think of a great many excuses, but will mercifully refrain from offering. Instead, as a measure of compensation, each account includes all the factual detail that was extractable, and each is presented here as objectively as could reasonably be expected from a presented here as objectively as could reasonably be expected from a reporter unfree of biases for and against certain methods, designs, and topics of research.

The major topics of the chapter include:

RESEARCH WITH INFANTS
    Physiological Development
    Development of Sensory and Response Systems
    Complex Processes
RESEARCH WITH PRESCHOOL AND SCHOOL AGE CHILDREN
    Personality
    Cognitive Development
    Learning and Problem Solving
CLINICAL WORK
    Mental Deficiency
    The Deaf-Blind
    Neurosis and Psychosis

The chapter is followed by an appendix: Illustrations and Notes Relating to Instrumentation in Research with Children.

RESEARCH WITH INFANTS

PHYSIOLOGICAL DEVELOPMENT

The Medical Pediatric Institute of Leningrad[2] functions not only as a research institute, but also as a clinical and teaching center. (During the academic year 1959-1960, 2400 medical students were enrolled there.) The Chair of Hospital Pediatrics is occupied by A. F. Tur, who also directs the Departments of Physiology and Premature Infants. Research within this Department centers on questions of basic physiological development in infancy, including individual differences in the physiological development of newborns and the physiology of prematures. One continuing project, for example, has been concerned with the effects of various kinds of milk on metabolism, general physical development, resistance to disease,

---

[2] Litovskaia ul., 2, Leningrad K-100. This institution is also known as the Leningrad Pediatric Medical Institute.

and ease of recovery from disease. The kinds of milk studied have included mothers' milk, breast fed to the infant; mothers' milk collected, bottled, and fed to the infant after increasing periods of delay since time of collection; and formulas whose ingredients approximate mothers' milk in various ways.

As a laboratory for the study of infant development, the Physiology Department maintains a residential nursery for 30 normal infants, who are between birth and three years of age. The infants are housed and cared for in small, like-age groups. The program for their upbringing emphasizes verbal stimulation by nurses; attention to and respect of developing individual differences in preference for activities, dress, etc.; and exposure to new and stimulating environmental objects (e.g. specially designed toys and play furniture). The most prominent aspect in the program for upbringing is its stress on physical development: diet, sleep, and, most particularly, the daily massage and exercises in which the child is involved from age 60 days forward. Table 1 and Figure 1 show the overall plan of massage and exercise, the descriptive name of each, and photographs illustrating some of these procedures. Massage and exercise are important parts of the daily routine. Every day the same nurse massages or exercises "her" child, and talks to him throughout. In addition to the physical and verbal stimulation, there is, as can be seen in the photographs of Figure 1, considerable non-verbal social stimulation as well as physical contact between nurse and child during the lengthy exercise period.

Another distinctive practice within the residential nursery— referred to as "hardening" or "strengthening"—was described by Professor Tur as follows:

The physiological clinic not only conducts massage and gymnastics for infants, but also systematically tries to strengthen them by air treatments, water treatments, and, in summer, by sun baths.

From the age of one month, infants take air baths. At first, the baths are two minutes long, but gradually they are lengthened to 10-15 minutes, for one-year-old infants, and to 30 minutes for three-year-old infants. The temperature of the room where the air baths are taken is 71.6°F. for infants under one year and from 64.4° to 68°F. for those between one and three years. During the summer, air baths are taken in the garden in the shade at the above temperatures. Air baths are never given directly after meals nor on an empty stomach. The infant having an air bath is quite naked, and should not necessarily be lying down, but may play quiet games.

The clinic uses fresh air in other ways to strengthen the infants; in winter they take walks up to four hours a day; in summer they are out of doors the whole day. They also sleep outdoors in the daytime at all seasons. In winter the infants sleep in special sleeping bags, if the temperature outdoors is not lower

TABLE 1

SCHEDULE OF MASSAGE AND GYMNASTIC EXERCISES FOR CHILDREN IN THE FIRST YEAR OF LIFE

AGE IN MONTHS <1 1 2 3 4 5 6 7 8 9 10 11	TYPE OF MASSAGE OR EXERCISE
	1 Arm massage
	2 Leg massage
	3 Stomach and abdominal massage
	4 Back massage
	5 Foot massage
	6 Reflex crawling
	7 Reflexive straightening of spine into position on the side
	8 Foot exercise
	9 Thoracic massage
	10 Swimmers' position
	11 Turning by the arms from supine to prone position
	12 Coachman's movements of the arms
	13 Stamping
	14 Suspension by the legs
	15 Flexing and extending the arms
	16 "Flying", prone position
	17 Pulled to sitting position by both hands
	18 Flexing and extending the legs together and alternately
	19 "Flying", supine position
	20 Supine position: raising extended legs to vertical position
	21 Exercise for the biceps
	22 Upright, tensed arch
	23 Turning by the legs from supine to prone position
	24 Circling movements of the arms
	25 Creeping
	26 Side, tensed arch
	27 Circling motion in the hip joint
	28 Slight lift of shoulder from prone position
	29 Bridge
	30 Wheelbarrow
	31 Climbing
	32 Pulled to sitting position by one hand
	33 Squatting
	34 Pulling the body to upright position from inclined position

than 14°F. At lower daytime temperatures or in a strong wind they sleep indoors with the windows open.

The water strengthening treatment is both local and general. Local water strengthening means a daily sponging or douche of the feet with cool water once or twice a day, beginning at age one month. The temperature of the water is gradually decreased to that of tap water. This type of strengthening is a good prophylaxis for infants against colds, rheumatic illnesses, and aggravation of all chronic diseases connected with chilling.

A general water treatment for infants from six to twelve months of age is general sponging. At first, the temperature of the water is 96.8°F.; every two or three days it is lowered by 1.8°F. until it reaches 77°F. After the age of one year, infants receive showers instead of general sponging. The temperature of the water is also gradually lowered every two to three days by 1.8°F.—from 86° to 77°F. In the summer time showers are taken out of doors.

Before receiving sun baths the infants are carefully examined. If there are no contraindications, they are given sun baths from the age of six to twelve months at an air temperature of from 71.6°F. to 73.4°F. The sun baths are taken at about 10 a.m. or after 3 p.m. The first sun baths are about two minutes long. Their duration is increased very gradually to 14 minutes, for the younger infants, and to 30 minutes for infants up to three years.

The physiological gymnastics and massage and the thorough strengthening of infants favor their harmonious development and provide a good prophylaxis against disease.

DEVELOPMENT OF SENSORY AND RESPONSE SYSTEMS

This section describes work currently underway in the laboratories of N. M. Shchelovanov and N. I. Kasatkin. Shchelovanov, who has been doing research in this area for nearly half a century, established the laboratory that is now under Professor Tur's direction. In the middle of his career, Shchelovanov moved to Moscow and assumed directorship of the Institute of Pediatrics' Laboratory of Higher Nervous Activity of Children.[3] This Laboratory is one of the smaller laboratories of the Institute. It has a total staff of 48, 12 of whom are scientists. There are 25 beds in its residential nursery. The Laboratory—and indeed, the Institute—which has for many years made its home not far from the center of Moscow, at Solianka 14, will soon move to much larger quarters in a new building on the new Moscow University campus. Then there will be room for 65 beds in the residential nursery and, of course, a proportionately larger staff.

The types of research currently underway in the Laboratory include studies of motion and speech development, emotional responses, the orienting response, polyeffector comparisons in conditioning, intersensory connections (particularly visual-auditory), and EEG correlates of conditioning.

M. I. Kistiakovskaia, who directs the laboratory's pedagogical work, is using both experimental and clinical methods to study the development of motor movements, particularly emotional-expressive movements. Under investigation are social and non-social stimuli, while dependent measures include behavorial responses, e.g. smiling, and physiological responses, e.g. visceral reactions.

Research on visual orientation is being carried out by A. M. Fonarev. Generally speaking, "orientation" is operationally equivalent to both "attention" and "pursuit" or "following." Using a soundproof, lightproof crib housing shown in an earlier publication (Brackbill, 1960, Figure 1, and reproduced in the Appendix), Fonarev

---

[3] There are 22 Institutes of Pediatrics within the Academy of Medical Sciences of the U.S.S.R., and the Moscow Institute acts as the focal point of inter-communication and coordination for them. The director of this Institute is O. D. Sokolova-Ponomareva.

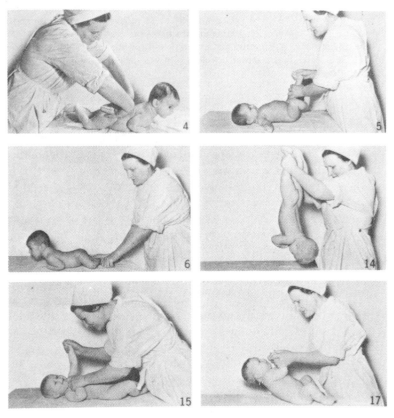

Figure 1. Massages and exercises for infants and toddlers, Medical Pediatric Institute, Leningrad. The number in the lower right hand corner of each of the first nine photographs refers to the number given that massage or exercise in Table 1. The last three

gets a continuous photographic record of Ss' eye coordination and eye movement by corneal-reflected light. Photographs can be taken in the dark or under varying degrees of complexity of stimulation. (Notice that the crib housing allows simultaneous use of two cameras. For investigations of orienting, one camera can be used for initial eye-head position, and the other for final eye-head position—the second camera being physically coordinate with the final position of the stimulus light.)

Fonarev has found that eye coordination in the dark condition begins shortly after birth, but that the coordination disappears upon stimulation with light. The age at which coordination during stimulation is finally achieved depends upon the complexity of the stimulus and the difficulty of the response required of the infant. At two

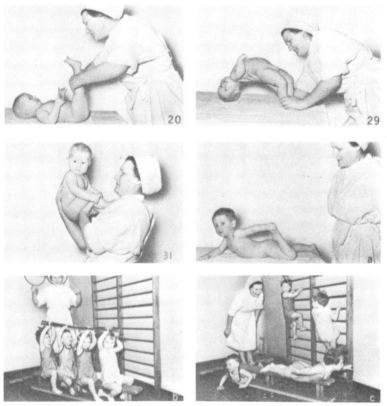

Figure 1 (continued)
photographs (a, b, c) show toddlers doing advanced exercises. (Photographs courtesy
A. F. Tur.)

months, the infant should be able to maintain coordination while
orienting to (following) a simple light. Convergence on a complex
stimulus does not usually occur until the age of six months.

Conditioned orientation is achieved, of course, much earlier than
visual coordination. If conditioning is begun at age nine days, then
it should be complete in another ten days. 15 to 20 trials are given
per day, with random length intertrial intervals ranging from 30 to
60 seconds. A complex tone is typically used as CS.

N. S. Mirzoiants is interested in parietal and occipital functions of
the developing cortex. She is now working on the first studies of a
series that will ultimately include EEG correlates of conditioning.
At present she is investigating simultaneously conditioned visual and
tactile discriminations. Her methodology will be described in some
detail.

Figure 2. Professor N. M. Shchelovanov and colleagues.
(Author at right.)

Establishing Visual Discrimination. A diffuse, colored light, e.g. green, is used as CS+. The interest is not in color per se, but in choosing an experimental stimulus that is maximally distinct from normal background stimulation. Milk is the UCS, and anticipatory sucking, the CR. (For a method of recording sucking, see Figure 8, Figure 9, and also Brackbill, 1960, p. 229.) *E* holds the bottle of milk. A sheet hangs from the ceiling of the crib housing; its free end makes a perpendicular contact with *S*'s face below the eyes and above the mouth. Thus all that *S* can see of the procedure is the CS.

Subjects are started on the experimental procedure as soon as they arrive from the nursing home, at 10 to 15 days of age, and after they have been pretested to ensure that they do not show an unconditioned sensitivity to the CS. While the experiment is in progress, sessions are scheduled just prior to normal feeding times. One session a day is devoted to the visual conditioning procedure. Each session consists of 12 to 14 trials.

On the first experimental day, the CS and UCS are presented simultaneously for 10 seconds. From Day 2 forward, the onset of CS precedes by three seconds the onset of UCS. In order to avoid conditioning to time, length of intertrial interval is randomized within a range of 30 to 40 seconds. Under such a procedure, the first CR appears in about 10 days, a semi-stable CR in about 25 days, and a fully stable response in about 45 days. By "stable CR" is meant one that is of invariable occurrence and maximum amplitude for a constant intensity value of the CS.

Next, discrimination training is introduced. A red light may be used as CS −. Mirzoiants has found that three or four of the total 12 to 14 trials per session provide the optimal proportion of CS − trials. A smaller proportion of CS − trials to total trials prolongs pre-criterion training unnecessarily, while a larger proportion brings the CR dangerously close to extinction. The first discrimination should appear by the first part of the third month of age, and a stable discrimination follows shortly thereafter. The distinctive behavioral stages that typically appear during the process of establishing conditioned discrimination are outlined in Table 2.

TABLE 2

The General Sequence of Stimulus and Response Events During the Course of Conditioning to a Simple Discrimination

---

1. Conditioning to a criterion of stable responding on CS +.
2. Introduction of CS −. At this point the amplitude and frequency of response to CS + are subject to some interference.
3. Discrimination training is continued, using a randomized sequence of CS + and CS − trials. If the number of trials to CS − is kept below 50% of the total number of trials, the intensity and frequency of responses to CS + increases again. However, at this stage, CS − also elicits the response.
4. In the final stage, the response to CS − gradually extinguishes to the point of perfect discrimination.

Establishing Tactile Discrimination. Tactile and visual conditioning are begun at the same age, and the general procedure for tactile conditioning is the same as that just described for the visual CR and visual discrimination. The ages at which various stages of tactile conditioning can be attained are shown in Table 3. For the tactile discrimination, the CS + is a light stroke administered to the sole of the left foot by a camel's hair brush. The CS − is a brush stroke to the right foot. The apparatus for delivering this stimulation, invented by Kasatkin, is sketched in Figure 3. The UCS is an air puff; a device used to deliver air is illustrated in Figure 4 (and in Brackbill, 1960, Figure 2).

107

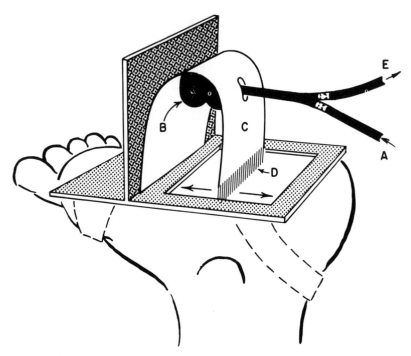

Figure 3. An apparatus designed by N. I. Kasatkin for tactile stimulation. A. Air input. B. Rubber balloon. Because of a circumferential constriction, the balloon expands more in length than in width when it is inflated. C. Metal spring, pushed outward when balloon is inflated. D. Camel's hair brush. E. Air outlet, providing pneumographic record of stimulation. Although the apparatus as shown is strapped to the sole of the foot, its use is not restricted to that part of the body.

The CR is, of course, the eye blink. To measure the frequency or amplitude of blinking, or both, the apparatus most suitable for use with children is a light weight, carbon amplifying mechanism designed by Fonarev.[4]

In Figure 4, notice that S's head is not fixed, but is free to turn to the right or left. Since this is the case, what prevents S from learning to turn his head to the right or left and to keep it there in order to avoid the air jet? Occasionally this does happen, but the problem is easily overcome for two reasons. First, if the infant acquires an avoidance response, the response tends to be consistent and stereo-

---

[4] On the question of recording the frequency of conditioned eye blinks, I should like to point out that, with infants S's, the remarkable accentuation and qualitatively different appearance of the conditioned eye blink from the unconditioned eye blink would permit highly reliable recording of response frequency by untrained human observers bereft of gadgetry.

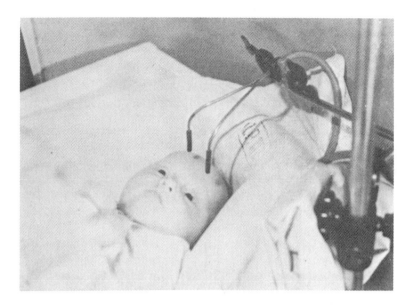

Figure 4. A crib attachment for the delivery of air to elicit blinking in infants. (An apparatus suitable for use with toddlers and older children is shown in the Appendix.) (Photograph courtesy N. I. Kasatkin.)

typed; he turns his head *either* to the right or to the left. Then, since the apparatus is extremely flexible, it is a simple matter to change the position of the air delivery tubes.

Each *S* is run twice a day: once under the visual conditioning procedure and once under tactile conditioning. EEG is recorded under both conditions. The morning-afternoon sequence of these two procedures is alternated daily. Mirzoiants pointed out that contamination between the two CRs, blinking and sucking, happens very rarely. If it occurs at all, it occurs during the very earliest stages of conditioning. (I have also seen it occur during the final stages of extinction.)

THE IMPORTANCE OF THE CONDITIONAL STIMULUS
IN CLASSICAL CONDITIONING

The description of Mirzoiants' procedure referred to the conditioned connection under investigation in terms of the conditional stimulus used and not in terms of the response being conditioned. Thus Mirzoiants is investigating a tactile discrimination, not a conditioned eye blink discrimination; and a visual discrimination, not, a discriminated sucking response. One has only to glance at the index of any volume of the *Journal of Experimental Psychology* to realize

109

that the Soviet emphasis on conditional stimulus is quite different from the emphasis on response that is characteristic of research in the United States. Since this important difference seems not to have been aired before, it will be worth-while to point out its general relevance, if only to the area of infant conditioning, before proceeding with descriptions of particular investigations in that area.

Soviet physiologists maintain that in conditioning—at least in classical conditioning—there is only one really influential member of the triad, CS—UCS—CR, and that is the first member. The basic parameters of conditioning, as well as the age at which conditioned connections can first be established, are not affected by the type of UCS or R used in conditioning. This is quite apart from the fact that methodological considerations may lead an experimenter to choose one type of UCS in preference to another.

To rephrase this more concretely: The age at which a simple conditioned connection can be developed *is* a function of the type of CS used. It is *not* a function of the type of UCS—R combination used; it does not matter whether one uses milk and sucking as UCS and R, or air puff and eye blink, or moving light and orienting (head turning and visual pursuit), or stroke to the sole of the foot and Babinski.

Table 3 shows the developmental sequence in which conditioned responses may be established during infancy, according to the sensory type of conditional stimulus used.

There has not been enough systematic work on the extinction of conditioned connections in infants to allow construction of a companion table to Table 3—one that showed differential resistance to extinction as a function of type of CS. However, most investigators would agree that, other things equal, a kinaesthetic-proprioceptive connection is the most difficult to extinguish.

There are two types of conditional stimuli that do not appear in Table 3, and that certainly merit some comment. The first of these is the passage of time. Whatever its physiological basis, time perception becomes an effective CS by an early age, probably by eight days of age. The use of randomized intertrial intervals to avoid conditioning to time has already been mentioned as a standard feature of conditioning procedures. A more direct illustration can be found in a recent study by M. V. Krachkovskaia (1959) of the naturally conditioned but experimentally manipulable rise in leukocyte count that occurs just prior to time of feeding in neonates fed on a regular schedule. Like any other conditioned response, the "anticipatory"

TABLE 3

Developmental Sequence of Conditionability as a Function of Type of Conditional Stimulus*

Ages appear as days (d) or months (m).† The figures for this table were made available by N. I. Kasatkin and other scientists of the Institute of Evolutionary Physiology, Leningrad, and the Institute of Pediatrics, Moscow. Cells containing more than one entry indicate a difference of opinion, and in those cases Professor Kasatkin's figure appears in parentheses.‡

Type of Conditional Stimulus

		Vestibular	Auditory	Tactile	Olfactory	Taste	Visual
Simple CR	Example, CS	Change of body position (Up, down, or sideways)	complex tone§	brush against sole of foot (See Fig. 3)	oil of roses or lavender§	5% sugar solution	diffuse light (colored most discriminable)§
	First appearance	8d	(15d) 24d	28d	28d	35d	40d
	semi-stable response	15d	40d	45d	45d	45d	2m
	fully stable response	(20-24d) 1m	(35d) 2m	2m	2m	2.5m	3m
Simple Discrimination	Example, discrim. stimulus	up-down from sideways	1 octave higher or lower than CS+	right foot from left	roses from lavender	1% from 5% solutions	red from green or blue
	First appearance	1m	2m	2m	2m	2.5m	3m
	semi-stable discrim.	1.5m	2.5m	2.5m	2.5m	3m	3.5m
	fully stable discrim.	2m	3m	3m	3m	3m	3.5m

111

leukocyte rise can be extinguished and reconditioned to a new feeding schedule or to a new formula.

The second conditional stimulus that does not appear in Table 3 is skin temperature change, or more precisely, change in the temperature of a small area of the skin. Pavlov said of skin temperature change that it is a very weak CS for dogs, and the same statement

---

* For experimenters who prefer operant terminology, Sidney Bijou has suggested that an alternate title for this table might be: Developmental timetable of SD discriminability.

† Figures are for normal, full term infants. Conditionability is retarded in cases of birth trauma, amount of retardation corresponding to severity of trauma. (See Kasatkin, 1957, and Dashkovskaia, 1953.) Conditionability is also retarded according to degree of prematurity, although the relationship is by no means a one-day-to-one-day function; that is, one may not use date of conception as an index of conditionability. With an auditory CS, Kasatkin has conditioned one and two months prematures whose "conception ages" at the time of conditioning were less than 280 days. (Kasatkin, 1957.)

‡ Professor Kasatkin and his colleagues caution that their figures are approximate. I would like to add, however, that if any cell entry is in error, the error is a conservative one. Through a succession of technical and experimental refinements, positive results have been obtained for ever younger Ss. Indeed, at the present time, there are more liberal figures available for many of the cells of this Table (e.g. Dashkovskaia, 1953), and after the new figures have been sufficiently replicated, they should replace the present cell entries, just as these cell entries have replaced earlier ones (Kasatkin, 1951). But in any event, most investigators would probably agree that whatever the absolute values of past or future changes, the rank ordering of conditional stimuli (from vestibular to visual) has not changed and is not likely to .

§ Kasatkin has provided further operational details of several frequently used CS procedures. They are as follows:

Auditory stimulation. Sixty db. above threshold is an optimal value for sound intensity. Unless it is the focus of study, frequency per se is not so important a consideration for infant study as is complexity: the stimulus tone must have more than one frequency component and be perceived as acoustically complex.

Olfactory stimulation. The stimulus solution can be sprayed through an atomizer, as in studies of adult olfaction. However, instead of introducing end pieces into the nostrils, it is better to use a cup fitted over the infant's nose. A second method provides less precise control over stimulation, but is useful in the event that experimental conditions for some reason or another preclude use of the atomizer. A narrow piece of heavy paper or light weight cardboard is saturated with an oily solution of the stimulus substance. One end of the paper is mounted on the narrow end of a stopper. For storage, the paper is kept in a test tube, the open end of which is plugged by the stopper. For use, the scented paper is passed at a standard distance in front of S's nose.

Visual stimulation. Kasatkin uses an apparatus similar to that shown in the earlier publication (Brackbill, 1960, Figure 2), but adds a diffusing reflector to its lower horizontal edge; the reflecting surface makes a 45° angle to the upright face of the apparatus. Behind the colored filters are 75 watt white lamps. A distance of one meter separates the diffusing reflector and S's face.

appears to be true for infants. Even with Ss as old as six months, it fails in approximately 50 per cent of the cases to elicit a fully stable CR. A fully stable discrimination is rarer yet, even when widely differing values of CS+ and CS— are used. Furthermore, a CR based on temperature change appears to be easily inhibited, as when S's attention is caught by some visual aspect of the apparatus just prior to the onset of CS. It is also easily over-generalized, so that in some cases and at some times—not always predictable—the CR will be elicited by the sight of E, the apparatus, or some other invariable concommitant of the conditioning situation.[5]

To return to a description of work from the laboratory of Professor Shchelovanov:[6] E. I. Makarova has found that the level of arterial blood pressure during infancy appears to be an index not only of the child's physiological development but also of his emotional tone. It was previously held that arterial blood pressure level depended on the child's height and weight. Makarova found that the dependency is more complex: the heavy, inactive child may have a lower level of arterial blood pressure than the child who weighs relatively less and who is active and lively. (Variation within the normal limits of weight is being considered here.) Arterial blood pressure is measured by means of sound, oscillographic, piezo-electric, or photoelectric methods.

Makarova's work was extended to questions concerning the physiology of the vestibular sense. She has found that stimulation of the vestibules by rotation depresses blood pressure level in children under six months of age, but raises it in older children. This change of reaction—from parasympathetic to sympathetic—reflects the emergence of a cortical mechanism for regulating vestibular-somatic reactions. In addition, the individual differences that appear in vestibular-motor reflexes serve as useful indices of CNS typological characteristics.

As participant in a Chinese-Soviet collaborative study, Makarova is also studying the motor and vegetative components of conditioned feeding and defense responses. A polyeffector comparison of conditioned responses is being used to clarify the relative rates of development of the two sets of variables under study.

---

[5] See Usoltsev and Terekhova, 1958.

[6] The description of the work of Makarova, Nechaeva, and Liamina was written by Professor Shchelovanov (personal communication, April, 1961) and freely translated by the author. Professor Shchelovanov has also generously contributed several comments that have been incorporated in appropriate parts of this section.

I. P. Nechaeva is investigating the functional aspects of auditory development during infancy. By means of classical conditioning techniques, she has established the limits of sound discriminability for the first months of life. (That is to say, she has done a parametric study of difference limens for sound frequency as a function of increasing age.) She has also been studying the formation of connections between auditory and visual sensations—associational connections, irradiation of excitation, and second order conditioned connections.

G. M. Liamina is principally concerned with the development of speech during the first three years, and is studying both the external or environmental factors as well as the internal factors (or peculiarities of development) that retard and that accelerate language development. Among the results to have emerged from this study to date, it appears that for children between one and two years of age the lack of coordinated intersensory connections between speech and other aspects of activity, results in considerable response competition. When, for example, infants of 20 to 22 months are playing with toys or are fully engaged in some kind of gross motor movement, the occurrence of speech as a concomitant activity is relatively rare. But gradually, starting about the end of the second year, the infant shows an increased ability to make complex responses, i.e. to combine familiar actions and motions with words. With an understanding of the factors that slow down or speed up the acquisition of speech, one may devise a program for optimal development of speech in the residential nursery as well as for children living at home. Liamina is currently working on problems of speech development during the third year of life, with particular attention to the acquisition of correct pronunciation of words.

THE RESIDENTIAL NURSERY

The Institute as a whole has an "in-patient" capacity of 200 beds, of which 50 are for normal children. Half this number, or 25, spend their first three years of life together in the Laboratory of Higher Nervous Activity of Children. The children are divided into two groups: infants (birth to about one year) and toddlers (one to three years). By virtue of this age split, the infants usually number eight or nine. They spend some of their time in laboratory rooms, their napping time outdoors in a shaded grove, weather permitting (Figure 5), and the rest of their time in a large nursery room. The furnishings of this room are different from typical U.S. design and manufacture. All the furniture and play equipment are of unusually sturdy, hardwood construction. Among other advantages, this makes it possible to

Figure 5. Research subjects resting in the garden of their home, the Institute of Pediatrics, Moscow. A mother visiting her own child keeps an eye on his companions.

elevate everything from playpens to cribs, so that nurses are not required to bend down to their charges or to lift them from a stooped position. Another distinctive feature is the spaciousness of the two nursery playpens. One playpen, of the conventional Spartan architecture, measures approximately 5 x 10 feet. Its size allows a measure of ecological sanctuary and an introduction to group living. The second is even larger, measuring approximately 5 x 12 feet. Its design is sketched in Figure 6. There are no high chairs for feeding, but rather a large and sturdy table with openings for what might be called "drawer-chairs." These are chairs with long runners for arms. After a child is placed in such a chair, the runners are slid into the horizontal drawer guides of the table, just as one might shut a drawer. Thus it is physically impossible for an infant either to fall or slide from his chair or to upset any part of the apparatus by thrashing about wildly. Another piece of functionally designed apparatus, a walker, is sketched in Figure 7. It is popular with the infants and apparently effective in stimulating their walking and running. (It is also effective in keeping nursing staff attentive and nimble of foot.) The infants learn with a surprising degree of skill to extricate the contraption, when it is caught under pieces of furniture, by walking backwards with it, and even manage now and then to turn the wheels to some extent.

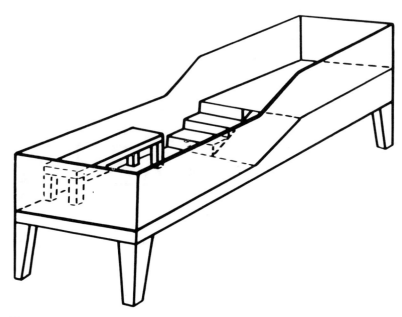

Figure 6. A playpen, measuring approximately 5 x 12 feet, in the nursery of the Institute of Pediatrics, Moscow.

Even more unusual than its furnishings is the nursery's program for verbal and motor stimulation of the children. This is regarded by the staff as a matter of great importance and something that merits their sustained effort. As a part of the overall plan, every nurse has specific duties that she performs with each of the infants. As an example of "verbal duties," the task for Nurse A might be to ask each infant in turn, Where is the cat?, Where is the window?, Show me your ear., Give me your hand., and so on. In each case, the child's answer is followed by appropriate reinforcement. When the mother visits—and she is urged to visit often—she has access to the nurses' lists of stimulants and is encouraged to further the verbal and motor training herself.

Attention to verbal and motor development is carried over into the toddler group. But in addition, a new goal is added to their program of upbringing. Staff efforts are now also focussed on the child's development of self-help. (Some readers might prefer to call this the development of initiative or mature behavior.) The one- to three-year-olds are shown how to pick up their toys before midday dinner, how to feed themselves, how to get along sociably with their three table companions at dinner, how to prepare themselves for a nap after

Figure 7. A walker, designed to assist in the transition from crawl to toddle; nursery, Institute of Pediatrics, Moscow.

dinner. It should be emphasized that the "do-it-yourself" approach is a reflection of policy, not lack of personnel. Although the nurse/child ratio is constantly shifting throughout the day, it is at a maximum for such daily events as meals and nap preparations. That is to say, there are several attendants who have other duties quite outside the nursery, but who leave these duties to join the regular nursing staff during the periods when the children are most likely to need close supervision. This is because the staff sees their main function as one of encouragement and teaching rather than service. It may take only one minute for a nurse to pick up a child's toys for him, as opposed to 15 minutes for the nurse to persuade him to do it himself; but the choice is always the latter, because the goal is to teach the child and not to get the job done.

Preparations for after-dinner nap provide an even better illustration of the self-help policy. The toddlers bed down in shifts, starting with a very small group of the youngest. So, for example, the first group to enter the dormitory may be the three youngest toddlers and as many nurses. The nurse puts out a foot warmer rug, a small chair, and pajamas. The child proceeds to undress, lay his clothes neatly over the back of the chair, put on the pajamas, and climb into bed. Naturally, this procedure may go rather slowly for a 16 month old infant. Still, the child is never hurried, nor is he helped unless help is necessary.

For an extensive account of all aspects of the Institute's child rearing program, see Shchelovanov & Aksarina (1960).

Source and Laboratory Apportionment of *Ss*. In the past, the residential nursery population has come mainly from illegitimate births to mothers who either want to give the child up for adoption or who want to keep the child while continuing to work, and who feel that the nursery is the best caretaking alternative available during the child's infancy. However, the summa cum laude characteristics of the nursery graduates have brought about an increase in the nursery's prestige and desirability, with the result that its facilities are now being sought by a wider population, e.g. married students attending the University.

After a mother, or the parents, decides to enroll her infant in the nursery, she is also asked to agree upon some definite length of time (up to three years) during which she will leave the child in the nursery. This permits the scientific personnel to plan the child's research future with some certainty. Her agreement carries the force of a promise or obligation but it is not legally binding; she may remove the child at any time.

The infant is taken directly from nursing home to nursery. There, he will probably contribute his services to more than one research project before he leaves. But during any given period of time he is most likely the main, if not exclusive, province of one investigator. This is particularly necessary for the time consuming conditioning studies. With all 25 beds filled, the maximum number of principal *Ss* per investigator per year is about four.

RESEARCH IN THE INSTITUTE OF EVOLUTIONARY PHYSIOLOGY

N. I. Kasatkin is Director of the Laboratory of Development of Higher Nervous Activity of Infants, Institute of Evolutionary Physiology named after I. M. Sechenov,[7] Academy of Sciences. He is also an associate member of the Academy of Medical Sciences. Professor Kasatkin—whose first publications were in English, by the way (Kasatkin & Levikova, 1935a, b)—was a member of the scientific group at Professor Shchelovanov's laboratory before he moved to Leningrad a few years ago. As in Shchelovanov's laboratory, the

[7] Staropargolovskii Prospekt, 52; Leningrad.

interests of Kasatkin's co-workers span all aspects of sensory development. Some of the projects either recently completed or currently underway are the following.

A. V. Zonova has just finished a study of color vision between birth and six months. Her results are particularly relevant to methodological questions of measurement. Two methods of measuring color discrimination were used: the Bronshtein "adaptation" method and the standard classical conditioning method. By the first method, the infant sucks milk from a nipple that remains continuously in his mouth. The sucking movements are registered by a Marey capsule strapped under his chin (see Figure 8) and are thus transmitted to

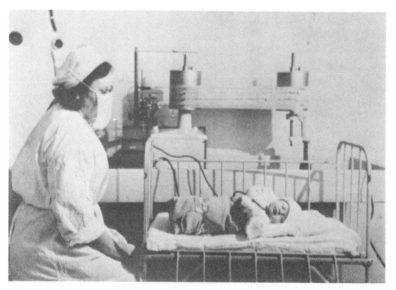

Figure 8. An arrangement for the plethysmographic recording of sucking. The pickup or sensitive part of the plethysmograph is called a "Marey capsule." (Photograph courtesy N. I. Kasatkin.)

a kymograph or other recording device. Immediately following the onset of a stimulus, the infant typically stops sucking for several seconds (section a, Figure 9). The experimenter continues to present this stimulus until S adapts to it, i.e. until he continues sucking despite its onset (section c, Figure 9). At this point, a second stimulus is presented; if S stops sucking, it is taken as evidence that he can discriminate between the two stimuli (section d, Figure 9).

The stimuli actually used for both adaptation and conditioning measures were red, green, and blue lights. They were presented by

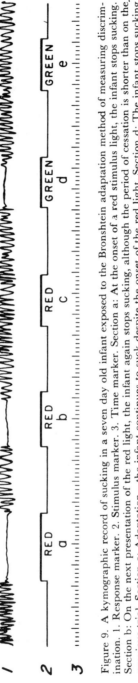

Age, seven days

Figure 9. A kymographic record of sucking in a seven day old infant exposed to the Bronshtein adaptation method of measuring discrimination. 1. Response marker. 2. Stimulus marker. 3. Time marker. Section a: At the onset of a red stimulus light, the infant stops sucking. Section b: On the next presentation of the red light, the infant again stops sucking, although the period of cessation is shorter than on the previous trial. Section c: Adaptation—the infant continues to suck despite the onset of the red light. Section d: The infant stops sucking when a green light is presented; therefore it is concluded that he has discriminated between the green and red stimuli. (Original record courtesy A. V. Zonova.)

120

means of interchangeable, colored glass filters covering a white light situated 50 cm. above *S's* head.

The adaptation method was used, in a cross-sectional design, on infants between the ages of 1.5 hours and six months. Table 4 shows numbers of *Ss* and results in terms of per cent of *Ss* showing typical (criterion) response. The conditioning method, likewise cross-sectional, was used with 24 infants between the ages of one and six months.

TABLE 4

Percent of *Ss* at Five Age Levels for Whom a Typical Response Was Recorded (as Illustrated in Figure 9) Under the Bronshtein Method of Testing Discrimination

Age	N	% *Ss* showing typical response
1.5 hours—17 days	180	34.7
1-2 months	8	46.3
2-3 months	8	49.3
3-4 months	8	50.7
4-6 months	8	51.3

The eye blink response served as CR. A fully stable discrimination was obtained by age 55 days for all *Ss*. (Fifty-five days represents an earlier figure than is shown for attainment of a stable visual discrimination in Table 3. Regarding this discrepancy, see footnote 3, Table 3.)

It would appear that for the study of discrimination, classical conditioning is the more sensitive and reliable of the two methods, as operationally defined in this study. In one sense, this is an unfortunate finding, since the adaptation method is certainly the less complex, less time consuming method. But there is still the possibility that an operational change in one or more of the parameters of the adaptation method could have a favorable influence on its sensitivity. Higher intensity stimulation might be a first nomination, and another possible candidate would be drive level at the beginning of the session as well as caloric intake during the procedure, e.g. water vs. milk vs. formula.

I. A. Vakhrameeva has been experimenting with the use of motor movements as a proprioceptive conditional stimulus. Air puff and eye blink serve as UCS and CR. At the same time the air puff is delivered, E bends S's forearm to the point that it makes a 90° angle with S's body. A stable CR is reached after 12 to 15 reinforcements, the number of these depending upon the age of the S. The age range under investigation is two months to one year. Note that a muscular movement is more typically encountered as a *response* rather than conditional *stimulus*, and that unless S is kept swaddled between sessions, the "presentation" of CS comes under *his* control.

T. T. Karakulina is interested in developmental changes in elicitation of the sucking reflex, and has mapped the limits of the facial areas within which tactile stimulation will elicit spontaneous sucking in the neonate. She finds that the first feeding produces the greatest change in reflexogenic area. Before the infant is ever fed, stimulation of any one of the seven points shown in Figure 10 will elicit sucking. After the first feeding and until three days of age the limits of stimulability telescope to the region around the mouth (points 1-4). Then, from four to seven days of age, the area of sensitization re-expands to include cheeks as well as mouth (points 1-6), while a touch on the forehead (point 7) elicits blinking.[8]

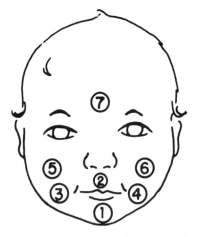

Figure 10. Reflexogenic areas for sucking studied by T. T. Karakulina. (see text.)

T. G. Antonova and A. N. Shepovalnikov have been studying visceral responsiveness in exploratory investigations that will hopefully be followed by full scale studies of interoceptive conditioning. Antonova has studied inter- and intra-individual differences during sleep and awake periods in fontanelle pulse rate (see Figure 11),

[8] These results differ in some respects from those obtained by Degtiar, 1952.

respiration, and sucking under non-stimulating conditions and under conditions of visual, auditory, olfactory, and tactile stimulation. Using much the same sets of conditions, Shepovalnikov has begun to study change of biopotential over the first 60 days of life. (For a brief review of studies on the conditioning of visceral responses in infants, see Kasatkin, 1957.)

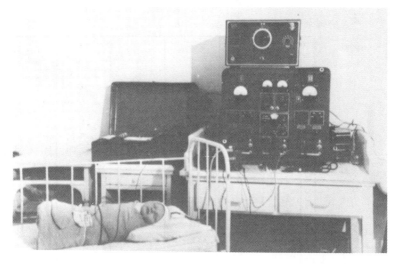

Figure 11. An arrangement for the plethysmographic recording of fontanelle pulse. (Photograph courtesy N. I. Kasatkin.)

COMPLEX PROCESSES

The traditional work with infants that has been discussed up to this point would be exemplified in Table 5 by the paradigms shown in rows A-C. The work in Professor M. M. Koltsova's Laboratory of the Physiology of Higher Nervous Activity of Children (Institute of Physiology named after Pavlov)[9] provides examples of research that illustrate the remaining models. In Table 5, all of the concrete examples beginning with row D were intended to serve two purposes. One purpose was to illustrate the abstractions of columns 1 and 2, and the other purpose was to illustrate a specific set of operations used in actual experiments from this Laboratory.

Row D, Table 5: Conditioned connections based on stimulus relations. The concrete example given in row D leaves little to be said about the design of this experiment. For stage I, a large group of Ss

---

[9] Makarova Embankment 6-a, Leningrad V-164. This Institute is part of the Academy of Sciences.

TABLE 5

TYPE OF CONNECTION	DIAGRAM	CONCRETE EXAMPLE
FIRST SIGNAL SYSTEM		
A. Conditioned response		
B. Conditioned discrimination		
C. Conditioned generalization		
D. Conditioned connections based on stimulus relations (example)	Stage I / Stage II / Stage III / Etc	I 120 bpm—60 bpm—120 bpm—60 bpm—etc II 60 bpm—30 bpm—60 bpm—30 bpm—etc III 200 bpm—120 bpm—etc. OR 30 bpm—15 bpm—etc
E. Sequential conditioned connections (or stereotype) (example)	A) / B)	(CS₁) LIGHT—PURE TONE—WHISTLE ... 120 bpm—BELL—60 bpm—WHISTLE
SECOND SIGNAL SYSTEM		
H. Third degree integration (or conditioned connections example to class 2 name)	OBJECT NAME / CLASS I NAME / NAME, OBJ₁ / NAME, OBJ₂	(A) "BALL" VIS. AUD. TCT. KIN CS CS CS CS
G. Second degree integration (or conditioned connections example to class 1 name)	CLASS 2 NAME / CLASS I NAME	(A) "BALL" ... "BALL" (ANOTHER) "BALL"
F. First degree integration (or conditioned connections example to object name)		"TOY" / "BALL" / "DOLL"

124

(age range, one to two years) was trained to a criterion of perfect discrimination on 120 bpm + and 60 bpm − An average of 50 reinforcements was required to reach criterion. Following this, all Ss were conditioned to the same criterion for stage II, requiring a mean of 12 reinforcements. For stage III, both alternatives, A and B, were used, so that one-half of the Ss were run under the condition, 200 bpm + and 120 bpm −, while the remaining Ss were run under the condition, 30 bpm + and 15 bpm − At this stage, acquisition was immediate, i.e. the discrimination criterion was reached with two reinforcements. The experiment was replicated on a second large group of Ss, age two to three years. The results were the same in all respects except, of course, that fewer reinforced trials were needed to reach criterion in stages I and II. The experiment has also been replicated with tones of differing cps values as conditional stimuli.

With reference to the change from stages I and II to stage III in the magnitude of the difference between CS+ and CS−, notice that the stimulus relation being conditioned here is not 1 : ½, but larger : smaller.

The similarity of these results to the Harlow-instigated work on learning sets hardly needs comment, except for the coining of an appropriately similar term. Conditioning sets?

Row E, Table 5: Sequential conditioned connections. Two experiments have investigated the role of associational connections in behavioral integration (response chaining). The results of both point to associational connections as chief catalyst in the process of converting responses into behavior.

The first experiment made use of the three conditional stimuli shown in example A, row E. There were two experimental groups. Subjects in group I were exposed to an invariable CS sequence during training, i.e. CS_1 was always followed by CS_2, and CS_2 was always followed by CS_3.[10] Conditioning criterion was the elicitation of maximum intensity CRs in a complete sequence (CR_1, CR_2, CR_3) upon presentation of CS_1 alone. (Number of reinforcements per CS required to reach criterion averaged 25 for younger Ss and 20 for the replication group of older Ss.)

---

[10] During acquisition, the duration of the CS was ten seconds. Five seconds after its onset, the UCS was presented, and its duration was five seconds. Inter-CS interval was 15 seconds. The experiment was tried initially with an inter-CS interval of 60 seconds. Because results were not affected by interval length, and because the longer interval proved excessively tiring for younger Ss, the shorter inter-CS interval was adopted.

Subjects in group II were run under a randomized CS sequence. They were matched with group I for number of reinforcements. In this case, test trials with any CS elicited *only* the one response with which that particular CS had been connected.

For Ss of group I (invariable sequence treatment), test trials on CS_2 and CS_3 provided equally interesting results. In rare cases upon presentation of CS_2 alone and in occasional cases upon presentation of CS_3 alone, more than one CR was elicited. However, when this did occur, the multiple responses tended (1) to be elicited in "improper" order and (2) to be contaminated. In most Ss, test trials on CS_2 or CS_3 elicited only CR_2 or only CR_3. Both the less and the more frequently occurring results indicate that during the course of and because of invariable sequence conditioning, those conditional stimuli that are presented after the first one lose their "individuality" —their individual effectiveness—as conditional stimuli. On a theoretical level, it would seem that the observed behavioral phenomena must be reflected in relatively more complex cortical effects than in the case of simple S-R connections.

On the practical level of child training, Koltsova suggests on the basis of these results, that a consistent ordering of events will speed the appearance of independent, self-propelled behavior and will minimize any tendency for links in the behavioral chain to disappear or to become displaced. For example, suppose a mother adheres to the same routine each night in putting her child to bed. She first says, "It is time to go to bed." This signal is then followed by the undressing, then washing, then teeth brushing, then toileting, then bedding down, then kissing good night. Under such an invariable sequence, the signal "it is time to go to bed" should, in a minimum of time, acquire strong chaining power so that all the desired responses in the bedtime sequence will be performed automatically and without omissions.

The first stage of the second experiment is illustrated by example B, row E. Since the complete design is somewhat more complicated than those previously discussed, it will be helpful to outline the entire procedure.

stage I (Σ N)   120 - - bell - - 60 - - whistle
                                           bpm   bpm
                                             +   +   —   +
stage II.
  treatment A: change   level 1 (N/4)   bell - - 120 - - 60 - - whistle
  of CS sequence.   bpm   bpm
                                             +   +   —   +

126

	bell - -	60 - -	120 - -	whistle
		bpm	bpm	
	+	−	+	+

treatment B: change of response	120 - -	bell - -	60 - -	whistle
(reversal); CS sequence	bpm		bpm	
unchanged. (N/2)	+	−	+	−

In this experiment, the same CR (eye blink) was conditioned to each instance of CS +. At stage I, all Ss were conditioned to criterion. The total group was then divided into sub-groups for stage II procedure, as indicated in the outline. The dependent variable was the number of reinforcements necessary to reach the same criterion in stage II. Subjects under both levels of treatment A showed severe response disruption, younger Ss requiring an average of 288 reinforced trials (three weeks at 16 trials per day), and older Ss requiring an average of 192 trials to reach criterion. Only 64 trials to criterion were required on the average by Ss run under treatment B. Apparently, links in the behavioral (and associational) chain are tolerant of reversals, but not of reordering. The entire experiment was replicated using words as conditional stimuli, with similar results.

Rows F, G, and H: The conditioning of hierarchically ordered responses as the basis of generalization. The experimental procedure for Ss of group I is outlined in row F, Table 5. Tactual, visual, auditory, and kinaesthetic-proprioceptive conditioned connections were established first to a particular concrete object, a black ball, and then to the spoken word, "ball." The result of this procedure was that both the object and the object name elicited the same conditioned responses. In addition to the usual conditioning criterion of attaining a fully stable CR, S was required to choose correctly the black ball from a variety of objects upon E's instruction, "Give me the ball." (The selection of Ss for the experiment was based upon their inability to respond correctly to these instructions or any other commands involving the word "ball" prior to training.) An extinction procedure followed acquisition. At this first level of language mediated generalization, the extinction of any one of the conditioned connections based on the concrete object also generalized to the object name, so that neither the ball object nor the word "ball" would elicit a response.

For group II (row G, Table 5), conditioned connections were established to two different appearing ball objects, to the object name, and to the generic term or class 1 name, "ball." For group III (row H, Table 5), the class 2 name, "toy," was added to the conditioning procedure. In both instances, extinction of any one of the conditioned connections to the object did not generalize to either class 1 or class 2 names. These signals showed as much effectiveness as conditional stimuli after extinction as they had before extinction.

For two additional groups of Ss, one step of the hierarchy was omitted. The two experimental conditions are outlined in Figure 12. For group IV, omission of the basic sensory-effector CRs constituted the missing step. The E simply showed S successive instances of ball objects and said "ball" upon each presentation (Figure 12-a). When, at the end of "training," E presented S with a variety of ball and non-ball objects, and said "Give me the ball," S showed little discrimination in his choices. He handed E ball and non-ball objects alike, appearing to respond chiefly to the "give me" aspect of the instructions.

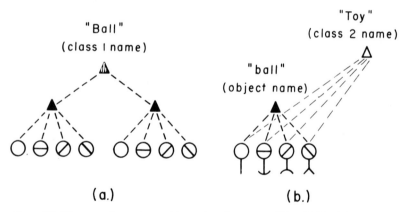

Figure 12. Diagram of experimental procedure for groups IV and V in M. M. Koltsova's study of the conditioning of hierarchically ordered responses as the basis of generalization. (See text.)

Group V was exposed during training to a conditioning hierarchy that included sensory-effector conditioned connections, object name, and class 2 name. Conditioning to class 1 name was omitted (Figure 12-b). The result in this case was that the class 2 name, "toy," became nothing more than a signal equivalent to the object name, "ball." That is to say, the instructions, "Give me the toy" and "Give me the ball" elicited the same response from S; in either event, he chose from the display of ball and non-ball objects only the particular ball that had been used during conditioning (Koltsova, 1960).

The Importance of Kinaesthetic-proprioceptive Stimuli in the Acquisition of Auditory Discriminations

From Table 3 it can be seen that kinaesthetic- proprioceptive conditioned responses are the first to be developed; they are also the most difficult to extinguish. The results of the following two experiments[11] indicate that kinaesthetic-proprioceptive responses are basic to the process of forming other discriminations—at least during the period of infancy.

Both experiments were concerned with the discrimination of speech sounds. Part I of the first experiment used as conditional stimuli the Russian vowels a and y (/a/ and /u/). (If one ranked all paired combinations of non-iotated Russian vowels on a continuum of auditory discriminability, this pair would rank as the first or most discriminable pair.) Subjects for the experiment were children between the ages of three months and three years. Subjects from each age level were randomly assigned to three experimental groups, corresponding to three different methods of presenting the conditional stimuli:

(1) Tape recorded presentation of pure tone vowels. The vowels, as pronounced by E, were tape recorded and passed through a series of acoustical filters designed to eliminate overtones.

(2) Tape recorded presentation of full tone vowels. The vowels were pronounced by E, recorded, and used without any modification of the tape.

(3) "Live" presentation of vowels. E pronounced the vowels while facing S.

The results of this part of the experiment showed uniform failure to establish conditioned discriminations in any Ss at any infant age level. The most advanced stage recorded in the process was the elicitation of CR by both CS + and CS − (see Table 2, stage 3).

The procedure in the second part of the experiment was the same in all respects as that used in the first part, except that the conditional stimuli were consonant sounds. In this case, fully stable conditioned discriminations were developed only in those Ss who could themselves articulate the consonant sounds used as conditional stimuli.

The difference between the two sets of results poses a paradox if

---

[11] See also the experiment by Koltsova reported in Brackbill, 1960, p. 230.

129

one considers that vowel sounds are more clear and distinct than are consonant sounds. On this basis, one would expect vowels to be discriminated more easily than consonants. On the other hand, the articulation of consonants requires muscular movements of the face, mouth, and throat to a much greater extent than does the articulation of vowels. And apparently, this mediating effect of the kinaes-thetic-proprioceptive responses is much more important than is auditory distinctiveness to the process of establishing a conditioned auditory discrimination.

(For the precise measurement of subtle motor responses, Koltsova uses an electromyograph, the circuit diagram of which appears in the Appendix.)

In the second experiment, the conditional stimuli were again vowel sounds, but the conditioning method was changed so as to incorporate kinaesthetic-proprioceptive responses as an intrinsic part of the (instrumental conditioning) procedure. Upon hearing the CS + signal, S reached for a piece of candy. He was not to reach for it on non-reinforced trials. (On CS − trials, no candies were present, their delivery being under E's control.) Three experimental groups differed in terms of the length of reach required to pick up the candy. Subjects of group I had only to move one hand to get the candy; Ss in group II moved one arm in order to pick it up; and for Ss of group III it was necessary to move the entire body in order to reach it. As expected, the number of trials taken to establish a discrimination decreased in inverse proportion to the amount of motor involvement required of S.

RESEARCH WITH PRESCHOOL AND SCHOOL AGE CHILDREN

PERSONALITY

E. I. Kulchitskaia, Institute of Psychology, Kiev,[12] has recently completed two studies on the development of the feeling of shame in preschool age children. The first study consisted of observations made in naturalistic situations. The Ss were 80 children between the ages of three and seven years, or 20 Ss at each age level. There were four standard situations in which each S was observed. The child was faced with the same task in each situation: to recite poems he had learned in his nursery school class. The S's reaction to his own mistakes during recitation was the observational measure of chief interest. The characteristics of the audience confronting S differed in each situation:

[12] Lenina 10, Kiev.

1. *S* recited in the presence of *E* (who was familiar to *S*).
2. *S* recited in front of his teacher and two or three peers.
3. *S* recited in front of two or three peers; during the recitation, *S*'s best friend was brought into the room.
4. *S* recited in the presence of a stranger.

The second study was experimental in nature. Subject selection for the second study was based on a series of behavioral situations so structured that each child could respond either in a socially approved (compliant, "good," or "honest") fashion or in a socially disapproved (non-compliant, "bad," or "dishonest") way. Only the children who responded in a socially disapproved way became the actual subjects of this study. These were the situations:

1. The child was left alone in a room full of toys, and was instructed not to touch them. The *E,* unobserved, observed the child from an adjoining room. The criterion for subject selection, i.e. the disapproved behavior, was the child's touching the toys.

2. The child was blindfolded and given the task of locating a well concealed object. Other children were present, and the situation was presented to all as a game. The disapproved behavior was the child's finding the object.

3. The *E* was provided with the titles of all poems that each child, at some previous time, had mastered in nursery school class. The *E* asked the child to indicate which of these poems he remembered perfectly, and recorded the child's answers. On the following day, *E* asked the child to recite one or more of the poems he claimed to know. The criterion response in this case was the child's incorrect or incomplete recitation, or his inability to recite at all.

4. The child was shown a new and interesting toy, and was told that he might play with it. Then, a second child was brought into the experimental room. Failure to share the toy constituted the disapproved behavior.

Two more situations were used for the oldest children only, as follows:

5. The child was asked to enter a dark room and bring out a book.

6. The child was shown how to make a toy, and then was asked to make one for younger children. A short time later, *E* asked if the work had been finished.

Again, only the children who responded with the disapproved behavior in each of these situations constituted the actual sample. For one-half of these *S*s, the disapproved behavior was immediately followed by a reprimand from *E*. No treatment was accorded the remaining or control *S*s. In all cases, the dependent variable was the

131

appearance or non-appearance of reactions indicating feelings of shame, as judged by *E* and the teacher. Table 6 incorporates a portion of Kulchitskaia's results. (The same investigator is currently studying the development of feelings of pride in young children.)

TABLE 6

Proportion of *S*s Displaying Feelings of Shame, According to Experimental Condition, Experimental Situation, and Age

	Type of Disapproved Behavior			
Age Group and Experimental Condition	1. Touched forbidden toys.	2. Located object when "blindfolded."	3. Unable to recite "known" poems.	4. Failed to share toy.
3 years; reprimanded by *E*	.90	.80	.80	.60
3 years; no reprimand	.30	.20	.10	.00
4 years; no reprimand	.60	.50	.30	.20

In the same Institute, A. I. Zhavoronko is directing a study of peer relations within a boarding school, as well as the influence of these relations upon individual personality development. The 90 *S*s are fifth, sixth, and seventh grade children (N = 30 at each grade level). Most of the children are orphans. The particular emphasis of the study is on the redirection of behavior through situational manipulation and the use of social reinforcement. The behavioral variables under study are (a) the development and course of friendships, (b) leadership, (c) dependence-independence relations, and (d) cooperation. Zhavoronko's collaborator, T.V. Rubtsova, has recently completed an investigation of the influence of radio, television, and literature on the behavior and moral development of children of the same age.

Stimulated by the observation that eagerness in young volunteers was not a good predictor of ability to maintain high rates of performance, L. S. Slavina, Institute of Psychology, Moscow,[13] recently finished an experimental investigation of responsibility. The *S*s were 119 children between the ages of seven and ten years. Two subject

---

[13] Mokhovaia 9, Moscow K-9. The Institute of Psychology is part of the Academy of Pedagogical Sciences.

selection procedures preceded the actual experiment. In the first of these, the child was left alone for five minutes in a room where there were two options available: playing with toys or constructing something with paper, glue, and scissors. This second option had been found to be of considerably less interest value, on the average, than the first. Any child who chose paper construction work during this five minute period was discarded. Those children who, instead, played with the toys progressed to the second subject selection procedure.

For that phase, E took S back to the experimental room, told him that paper toys were badly needed for nursery school children, and added that S might either construct such a needed toy or play with the available toys—but not both, since he would only be able to remain in the experimental room for a short time. From this procedure, only children who chose to make a paper toy for the needy nursery children were accepted as Ss. The children who elected to play with the toys were discarded.

By virtue of both selection procedures, Ss selected for the experiment proper were (a) more or less uniformly nondisposed toward paper construction work in a free play situation, but (b) motivated toward such work by a social appeal. One might label these Ss, children with a social conscience.

However, Slavina's thesis was that high motivation to be socially responsible is a necessary but not sufficient condition for the trait we call responsibility; it instigates but does not maintain performance. The further requirement is a *habit* of responsibility, and it was to the end of "habit training" that the experimental treatment directed itself.

The experiment proper covered five successive days. Each day Ss were given enough material for 12 paper toys that they were to construct at home and to return, finished, to E the next day. Training consisted in having the experimental Ss devise a plan as to the time, place, and manner in which they would construct their toys—the plan being submitted beforehand to E. No commitments of any kind were required of the control Ss.

The principal dependent measure was the number of paper toys finished and returned to E. Out of a possible 60 toys, the experimental group finished and returned an average of 54, while the control group averaged 36. Both groups returned a decreasing number of finished toys each day throughout the five day period, but the rate of decrease was faster for the untrained or control group. In analysing the results separately by age levels, it appeared that with increasing age, (a) the number of finished and returned toys increased, and (b) the experimental-control difference decreased. The results for the youngest children (first grade, seven years) are shown in Figure 13.

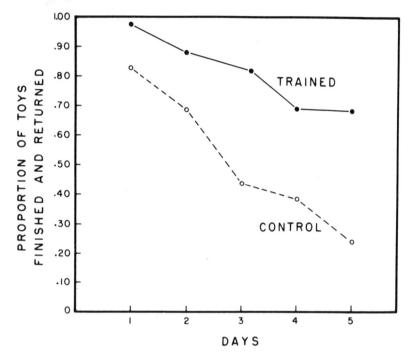

Figure 13. One part of the results of L. S. Slavina's study of the development of responsibility. The data are the proportions of finished paper toys returned on the five successive experimental days. Each proportion is based on the total possible return for that day. Results are for the youngest age group of the experiment (first graders, seven years of age.)

As a sequel to this experiment, Slavina has been studying the interaction effects of initial motivation (experimental instructions) and negative verbal reinforcement (criticism) on attempts to improve performance. Children are given the materials necessary to make paper mats and flags. They receive one of the following four types of instruction, the essentials of which are as follows:

1. You may make these if you want to.
2. Make these for yourself; you will need them for the coming festival.
3. Make these for your mother, for mother's day.
4. Make these for a younger child who needs them.

When S has finished his production, E tells him that it is not really very good. As predicted, differences in attempts to improve accord with the intended disposition of the handicraft. Children run under the last two instruction conditions usually attempt a second construction with the intent of improving upon the first, while Ss run under the first two conditions counter E's criticism by pointing out that they themselves are the recipients of their work and that they are satisfied with it.

Finally, mention should be made of the experimental studies of personality by Bozhovich that were reviewed briefly in an earlier publication (Brackbill, 1960).

Cognitive Development

Creativity or creative imagination is the topic of a current investigation by L. K. Balachkaia, Institute of Psychology, Kiev. Subjects for this four-year, longitudinal study are drawn from two age levels: children who at the outset of the study were of first year school age, and another group of first year preschool age. The data for the study come from observations made during free play and also from standardly presented assessment materials—sets of verbal and visual tasks. The complete battery includes two types of tasks, a basic set administered every year in unmodified form, and tasks of age-bound applicability administered one or more times at the appropriate age levels. A principal criterion in selecting tasks was to sample the dimension of structure, so that the tasks range, in terms of stimulus content, from the highly structured to the highly unstructured. The general characteristics of the basic tasks may be described as follows. Verbally presented tasks:

1. Incomplete stories. Subjects must (a) tell how the story will end, (b) act out the ending.

2. Picture stories. The E reads to S (a) several words that are unconnected but are suitable cornerstones for a story, or (b) a complete story. Then S is asked to tell how he would draw a picture of the story. Subsequently, S is asked to draw the picture.

Visually presented tasks:

1. Picture description. The pictures vary in number of details, degree of ambiguity, etc.

2. Incomplete pictures. Each set of pictures consists of a series of line drawings of an object, and each successive drawing of this object includes more lines, i.e. is more complete and, hence, recognizable. Starting with the least complete drawing of each set, S is shown one

135

picture at a time and asked to guess the identity of the stimulus object.

3. Description of ink blots. The stimulus cards include both symmetrical and non-symmetrical, black and colored blots.

The general results to date for the main variables of the study are briefly as follows. Type of task: Imaginative productivity is higher for visual than for verbal tasks. Degree of structure: The responses of older *S*s to unstructured tasks show more creativity than their responses to structured tasks. The reverse is true for younger *S*s. Age: The younger the *S*, the more unimaginative the response, except for tasks involving animals or those based on fairy tales.

From the more specific points of inquiry, Balachkaia cites these results as most striking. The responses of younger children appear to reflect almost exclusively the most salient features of their stimulus environment. For example, when confronted by visual tasks, young *S*s concern themselves with foreground objects and tend to ignore background. Analogously, their responses to the verbal tasks are framed in terms of the present, with little reference to past or future.

Also during these early years, if any imaginative production is elaborated at all, it almost always comes to light within the free play situation, so that creativity gives the appearance of being tied to activities and movements. And, in contrast to the preference of older *S*s, younger *S*s prefer to play or act out their stories rather than to tell them.

While the play of younger *S*s is more imaginative than that of older *S*s, its content is also more wildly unrealistic. The task responses of younger *S*s are also less bound by reality; e.g. it makes little difference at younger ages whether the hero of a story is "good" or "bad." But the older the *S,* the stronger his negative reaction to a "bad" hero. The increasing constraints of reality also appear in age shifts in story preference. At the time older children are beginning to take an interest in magic and science fiction-like tales, the younger children still prefer simple animal stories since, according to Balachkaia, the line separating reality from magic and unreality is not yet clearly established for them.

Pertinent to the subject of age changes surrounding play activities are the earlier studies of D. B. Elkonin and L. I. Bozhovich, both of the Institute of Psychology, Moscow. Using as the theoretical background for his study Vygotskii's ideas concerning the role of speech in determining form and content of the child's play, Elkonin renamed objects and proposed that his *S*s play with them according to their newly assigned functional roles. This maneuver was accepted easily by children of three and four years, but older Ss were both unwilling and, to an increasing extent, unable to play under these conditions.

Bozhovich compared learning efficiency under play conditions and under typical academic conditions. She found that three- to five-year-olds learned the experimental material faster when it was presented as an intrinsic part of the play activities. But the older Ss (six to seven years) who had already painstakingly sifted out fantasy from reality, did not find play and learning a comfortable recombination, with the result that their learning efficiency decreased when the learning took place under play conditions.

In the area of language development, I. E. Sinitsa, Institute of Psychology, Kiev, is directing a project concerned with psychological aspects of mastering the Ukrainian language. In one of his current studies he is comparing the rates of development of written vs. spoken Ukrainian in fifth, sixth, and seventh graders. In the first part of the study, the sources of data are written and orally presented stories elaborated from both assigned and free themes. The dependent measures are frequency of usage and frequency of correct usage of the parts of speech and of various syntactical constructions. (So far, it appears that there is no marked difference between writing and speech in the frequency of using any part of speech or type of construction.)

In the second part of this study, the same measures are extracted from an alternating series of written and orally presented stories. After S chooses a theme, he uses it first in an oral presentation. Then, he is asked to write the story as he has just told it. Next, he is asked to retell the same story and to improve upon his first verbal performance. Finally, he is asked to rewrite the story and to improve upon his first composition. In each case, the oral presentation is tape recorded without S's knowledge.

The development of concepts of number and measurement has recently undergone a critical appraisal by P. Ia. Galperin, Chair of Psychology,[14] University of Moscow. Galperin took issue with the traditionally held view that educational instruction in basic arithmetical operations (counting, adding, subtracting) must come before the teaching of measurement. According to that view, in the natural sequence of cognitive development, the attainment of numerical concepts precedes the attainment of concepts relating to measurement. According to Galperin, we have mistaken cause for

---

[14] Faculty of Philosophy, University of Moscow, Mokhovaia 11, Moscow K-9.

effect, for the child's normal development is in quite the opposite sequence—from measurement to numbers. Even further, Galperin hypothesized that if education honored the actual sequence of developmental events, the child would learn both measurement and numbers more easily and thoroughly.[15]

For an experimental investigation of his hypothesis, Galperin used a pretest-training-posttest design. His *S*s were six-year-old kindergartners. Experimental and control *S*s were first administered 20 tests measuring ability with numbers and concepts of quantity. The tests duplicated exactly or approximately those used by Piaget, and the test responses were highly similar to those reported by him for six-year-old Swiss children.

Following the pretest, the control group of *S*s was exposed only to the usual kindergarten curriculum: they learned to count to 10 and to add the quantity *one* to any number from one through nine. The training procedure for the experimental group (N = 60) began by introducing the children to measurement rather than to numbers. First, the children were taken to shops where they watched people measure the length of various articles offered for sale. Then back in their classrooms, the *S*s were given unmarked paper measures of different lengths and were shown how to go about measuring objects by themselves. The length of any object, e.g. a table, was taken as equivalent to all the (uncounted) measures that *S* had to use in order to cover the distance between two ends of the object. As the next step in training, *S*s were asked to re-measure the same objects but were provided with fewer measures than they needed to cover the full length of any object. When the children protested that there were not enough measures, *E* pointed out that it was possible to put a little marker at the end of the last measure and to use that measure again. And so the training procedure progressed—through manipulation of objects, measures, and markers—until the *S*s had mastered the concepts *more, less,* and *equal.*

At this point, numbers were finally introduced. First, *E* defined *one* as that fractional length of an object covered by a measure of a particular length. Then, in succession, the *S*s were taught (a) to count and write the numbers 0, 1, 2, 3, and 4—each number being paired in presentation with an appropriate quantity of markers; (b) to add and subtract, using these five numbers; and (c) to count, add, and subtract the numbers 6, 7, 8, 9, and 10.

At the conclusion of training, the original 20 tests were readministered to the experimental group, to the control group, and also to a

---

[15] See Chapter II.

group of fourth graders. Any pretest-posttest difference for the control group was eclipsed by the gains shown for Ss of the experimental group, 55 of whom made no posttest errors at all. The experimental group also bettered the performance of the traditionally educated fourth grade pupils.

LEARNING AND PROBLEM SOLVING

Of the many research issues currently under investigation in this general area, there are four topics that are considered by psychologists and educators alike to be of prime importance and that are frequently found to be the principal variables of psychological and educational investigations. The research problems are these:

1. The relation between theory and practice, or between academically acquired knowledge of a subject and skill in applying it. Most of this research has been concerned with some part of or elaboration on the question: which training sequence is more efficient for learning, retention, and transfer—abstraction followed by application, or vice versa?

2. The relative effects of active participation as opposed to passive learning on the acquisition, retention, or transfer of various types of learning material.

3. The effect on learning, retention, or transfer of the degree to which the learning situation is structured for the learner, i.e. the degree to which it approximates trial-and-error learning at one end of the continuum or "guided" learning at the other.

4. The effectiveness of learning to learn: The learning of methods of learning as preliminary and basic to the learning of content.

These variables—at least the first three—are not clearly separable in conceptual or operational terms, so that a single study is often relevant to more than one experimental question. The following investigations are illustrative of current research in learning and problem solving.

As the first step in a program of research into the learning of the English language, G. G. Saburova, Institute of Psychology, Moscow, has recently begun an investigation of the ability to converse in English as a function of the particular abstraction—application sequence used during learning. In one experimental group, Ss must first learn an abstract grammatical rule or family of rules, such as those governing the formation and use of the present continuous tense. After this, they are given a set of conversational exercises to which the abstract rule must be applied. Subjects in the second experimental group must try to do one-half the set of exercises before the grammatical rule is explained. Following the explanation, they receive the remaining exercises. Subjects in group III are given no instruction, but only the conversational exercises.

The dependent variables in this experiment include the total number of correct responses, the frequency of various types of errors, and the number of correct restatements of the grammatical rules. During the academic year 1959-1960 the Ss were fifth grade children (11 years of age) none of whom had had any prior instruction in English. During the academic year 1960-1961 the study will be replicated on a sample of pre-school children.

An earlier study—similar in purpose, though different in experimental material—was done by E. M. Kudriavtseva, also of the Institute of Psychology, Moscow. Kudriavtseva was interested in the extent to which knowledge of botany is utilized in horticultural activities (chiefly cultivation) and in botanical classification based on pictures of plants, dried specimens, and growing plants. A standardized questionnaire or interview form was used to measure the children's knowledge of botany. An example of the questions used and of the children's responses is shown in Table 7. Subjects were drawn from both rural and urban schools, in order to assess the effects of differences in background familiarity with plants on botanical knowledge and on horticultural skill. Age was the second basis for selection of Ss; the data were obtained from several classes

TABLE 7

Children's Responses to the Question:
What Conditions Are Necessary in Order for Plants to Live?
Entries Show the Percent of Pupils by Grade and Place
of Residence Who Mentioned Each Condition.
N = 30 at Each Grade Level.

Moscow school children	first grade	second grade	third grade	fourth grade
Earth	53	53	53	77
Water	67	93	100	100
Sun	0	13	27	40
Air	0	0	20	47
Rural school children				
Earth	75	80	80	100
Water	80	100	100	100
Sun	0	40	60	80
Air	0	0	10	30

at each grade level from first through sixth (seven through twelve years of age).

In the same Institute, T. V. Kudriavtsev has initiated a study of the transfer effects between technical knowledge and technical skills. The kinds of tasks under study include both real and artificial problems, e.g. practical problems involving machines that are actually used in industry and hypothetical problems in physical balance. The experiment utilizes a pretest-training- posttest design. Two equivalent sets of tasks are used for the pretest and posttest. During the training phase, one experimental group is required to use a theoretical approach first in their attempts to solve the problems, while the other experimental group first approaches the tasks with a manipulatory or trial-and-error approach to solution. The Ss in this experiment are between 16 and 18 years of age.

The next three experiments to be described are more relevant to the second and third research questions: active participation vs. passive learning, and degree of structure of the learning situation. The first experiment is a study of vocabulary retention by Sinitsa, whose programmatic investigation of language development was mentioned earlier. In this study, children drawn from the fifth, sixth, and seventh grades were given reading exercises somewhat beyond their ability levels and were asked to list all the words they did not understand. For one group of Ss, E defined all the unfamiliar words, adding basic synonyms as well as illustrations in context. The other group of Ss was required to ferret out these definitions by themselves by studying the contexts within which the words were used. They were free to ask questions of E in order to confirm or modify their inferred definitions, but they were not allowed to use a dictionary.

Recall was measured after an interval of three days, three weeks, or six months—one third of the total group being tested at each recall period. Each S was asked to write a composition on a theme similar to that of the original text, and was told that he was free to use the previously studied vocabulary words or not, as he chose. The dependent variables were the number of new words used and the frequency with which they were used correctly. The recall data obtained after a six-month retention interval showed that 40 per cent of the new vocabulary words had been used correctly by those Ss who had learned them under the first condition (passive learning), while 70 per cent of the new words had been used correctly by Ss run under the second condition (active, trial-and-error learning).

E. A. Milerian, Institute of Psychology, Kiev, used the same variables—extent of activity and structure in learning—in an investigation of their effects on the transfer of technical design skills and technical construction skills. Milerian used as a training task the design and construction of a simple electrical device. There were five possible circuit designs for this device, and quality of construction could be rated independently of design. For the transfer task a similar problem was used, and the measures were the number of workable circuit variants and rated quality of construction.

The training phase of the experiment included five experimental groups, matched for ability. The essential points of procedure for the five conditions were as follows. (In all cases Ss were first told what functions the apparatus had to fulfill. Also, note that the operational definition of "active participation" includes "group participation.")

1. The Ss were given one completely drawn circuit diagram along with detailed information on the best procedure for constructing the apparatus.

2. The Ss were asked to figure out all circuit possibilities, to choose the best one, and to construct the apparatus on the basis of this choice.

3. The Ss were given one circuit diagram, and then discussed as a group all the possible ways of building the apparatus on the basis of that circuit. The apparatus was then built according to the group's decision as to the best method of construction.

4. The Ss were asked to figure out all possible circuits. Then, as a group, they discussed all the possible ways of constructing the device given every possible circuit design. Actual construction followed the group's decision as to the best circuit and the best mode of construction.

5. (a) The Ss were given one circuit diagram and information about one way in which the device could be built. They constructed a model accordingly. (b) The circuit and the finished product were then discussed and criticized by the group of Ss. Their discussion covered all remaining circuit alternatives as well as all other possibilities in regard to construction. Finally, if the Ss so decided, the device was rebuilt.

Milerian calls the last training condition his "two-phase" method. He found, as he predicted, that Ss run under this condition showed the greatest amount of transfer of both design and construction skills. Milerian feels that the greater effectiveness of the two-phase method is due to the fact that a tangible product is achieved quickly, thus increasing the Ss' interest and motivation to improve their performance.

The second major finding of this study was that, in general, design skills were more easily transferred to new problems than were construction skills. Figure 14 shows a subject at work in one of Milerian's laboratory rooms in the Institute.

Figure 14. A subject at work on a construction problem in E. A. Milerian's laboratory, Institute of Psychology, Kiev. (Photograph courtesy E. A. Milerian.)

The psychological aspects of learning mathematics has been a continuing research interest of A. V. Skripchenko, Institute of Psychology, Kiev. His current study in this area concerns the relative effectiveness of three different training methods for ability to solve algebraic equations. By the first method, modelled after traditional pedagogical practices, *E* demonstrates the solution to a problem and then helps the students as they attempt to solve other equations of the same type. Under the second condition, *E* states the general rule for problem solution; the *S*s must try, without *E*'s assistance, to apply the rule to the solution of the test problems. Neither instruction nor assistance is given to *S*s run under the third condition. They must try to solve the equations as best they can and then, by a process of induction, to formulate the general rule for solution. The principal dependent measure in this experiment will be the number of correct solutions. It is Skripchenko's hypothesis that the third training method will be most effective, i.e. will yield the largest number of correct solutions, and that the first method will prove to be the least effective.

143

Professors P. Ia. Galperin, University of Moscow, and D. B. Elkonin, Institute of Psychology, Moscow, are both devoting considerable research effort to the study of the feasibility of teaching children generally applicable methods of learning and problem solving, with the idea that the child should ultimately be able to learn any new material with minimum assistance and maximum efficiency.

Galperin has been exploring the parameters of this research question by varying sample characteristics (age, academic achievement level, and readiness) and by varying the characteristics of the experimental material, concepts drawn from geometry, grammar, algebra, arithmetic, and physics. In all cases, the essential points of his experimental procedure are these:

A. The first and most important step is to analyze the concept to be learned into its essential components. That is, it must be dissected in terms of the necessary and sufficient criteria governing its application to any given instance. As an example, consider the geometrical concept of perpendicularity. The criteria that must be fulfilled if a given case is to be labelled perpendicular are that (1) there must be two straight lines (or surfaces), (2) the lines must intersect, and (3) the angle of intersection must be 90°. These criteria are printed on a card that S keeps in front of him.

B. The S is presented with a pack of cards on each of which appears one training item, i.e. one particular case that either is or is not an instance of the concept. He is asked to decide for each item in turn whether or not the first criterion applies. Then he must reconsider each item in reference to the second criterion—and so on.

C. The E removes the card on which the criteria are listed; S must be able to recall each of them correctly. The card is not returned.

D. Using a new set of training items, S repeats the procedure outlined above (stage B).

E. Finally, the S must use all criteria in combination to identify correctly each instance of the concept that occurs in the training material or in new test material.

In the first year of his experimental teaching project (see Brackbill, 1960, p. 232) Elkonin emphasized teaching first graders to analyze the general strategy of arriving at an answer or conclusion, and to analyze resultant errors in terms of their methodological antecedents. Elkonin also attempted, in teaching Ss to analyze new tasks by themselves, to have them identify in their analyses those components of the new task that they had already mastered in connection with previously learned tasks, i.e. to make a deliberate appraisal of the possibilities for positive transfer.

For example, upon entering the first grade, both experimental and control classes learned to make paper chains, woven paper mats, and woven paper baskets with handles, in that order. The experimental group, however, was required to make a "job analysis" before starting to work on the paper chains, and what might be called a "job and transfer analysis" before they began the second and third constructions. Specifically, the experimental Ss were asked to analyze the first task—before starting it—into its component skills, e.g. using a ruler to mark off paper strips of equal width, drawing straight lines with a pencil and straightedge, cutting with scissors, gluing, and so on. The second task had to be analyzed in terms of its operational requirements, and in addition, these operations had to be compared to the operations of the first task in order to sort out those operations that were the same across tasks from those that were new and still had to be learned.

Elkonin reports that an experimental-control difference was quite apparent by the end of the third construction. The control group turned out constructions of poorer quality and needed considerably more assistance from the teacher in order to finish their work. Similar results were found in studies using beginners' reading material and arithmetic. For example, after both groups had been taught to add numbers up to 10 during training, a transfer test, involving the addition of numbers between 11 and 100, showed almost no overlap between the experimental and control groups.

CLINICAL WORK

MENTAL DEFICIENCY

M. S. Pevzner, Institute of Defectology,[16] has devoted many years to the study and clinical application of diagnostic procedures in oligophrenia. Dr. Pevzner would define the term oligophrenia as any residual or non-progressive form of deficiency that is of exogenous etiology (prenatal, perinatal, or early postnatal damage) and that represents an organic abnormality. The organic component is regarded as a derangement of the outer layers of the cortex; in Pavlovian terms of physiological function, the most important feature of the derangement is inertness of nervous processes.

The types of oligophrenia may be classified as follows:

1. Simple oligophrenia, characterized by inertness of the nervous system.

---

[16] Pogodinskaia 8, Moscow. This Institute is part of the Academy of Pedagogical Sciences.

2. Simple oligophrenia complicated by hydrocephaly. CNS inertness is accompanied in this case by a lack of balance between inhibitory and excitatory states. Such children are easily disposed to fatigue.

3. Oligophrenia in combination with a particular local dysfunction, such as a visual-perceptual disorder, a motor disorder, or an aphasic speech disorder.

4. Oligophrenia in combination with a special systemic disorder, particularly a frontal lobe dysfunction. Personality defects characterize the child's behavior.

A longitudinal study of children from each diagnostic classification has been in progress for ten years at the Institute of Defectology.

The diagnosis of oligophrenia begins with a developmental history and a medical examination, including an EEG and an examination of sensory organs. In addition, any or all of the following forms of psychological assessment may be used: exclusion of the dissimilar member of four stimuli; classification of pictures into categories, as indicated by the examiner; telling a story about what is going on in a picture; arrangement of pictures into their proper temporal sequence, i.e. picture arrangement; drawing correct conclusions from a story told by the examiner, i.e. comprehension; and personality assessment based on observation of behavior. Clinical judgment rather than formally standardized norms is used in evaluating the results of these assessment methods.

In the differential diagnosis of oligophrenia from environmentally retarded development, the clinician looks for distinctive neurological and EEG signs, a more stable developmental history in oligophrenia, and in the case of the non-oligophrenic child, an indication of greater potential for improvement under the guidance and encouragement of a special teacher.

In the same Institute, Zh. I. Shif directs the Department of the Psychology of Deaf and Mentally Retarded Children—a department established by Vygotskii in 1936. The Department could appropriately be described as an applied research laboratory; its investigations seek to discover more profitable methods and directions in training oligophrenic children. Here, for example, are some of the training techniques the Departmental staff is recommending on the basis of their recent research. (1) General *methods* of memorizing should be taught to retardates prior to teaching them any substantive material. (2) Training in perceptual accuracy must precede the learning of cognitive material. (3) Active trial-and-error methods should be avoided during the initial stages of learning in order to minimize error perseveration. (4) Learning conditions should be systematically varied rather than held constant in order to maximize retention of the learned material.

It should be mentioned that there are both residential and extended-day schools for oligophrenics, who, like normal children, are legally required to attend school for eight years. In Moscow, there is also a "parents' university" where mothers and fathers may receive special instruction on the care and training of their oligophrenic children.

In A. M. Goldberg's Department of Special Psychology, Institute of Psychology, Kiev, two staff members are also concerned with the assessment of abilities and the training of retardates. Stadnenko is studying abilities through picture description and understanding, while Manzhula is seeking to identify the conditions that lead to maximum transfer of agricultural knowledge to agricultural practice.

THE DEAF-BLIND

Also in the Institute of Defectology is a separate Department for Deaf-Blind Children. Its Director, Professor Sokolianskii,* is assisted by A. I. Meshcheriakov. This laboratory is the successor to a much larger research and training center built several years before the Second World War in the Ukraine. (The center and its occupants were destroyed during the war.) The Department's present quarters are scheduled to be replaced by two new schools, one in Moscow and one at the original site, in Kharkov. At present, there are five children receiving residential training in Moscow, and the same number who are treated on a consulting basis in Leningrad.

A minimum age for acceptance in the training program is three years; five years of age is preferred, since total training time is inversely related to the age at which training is begun.

At the time of referral, the typical deaf-blind child does little more than vegetate. He does not crawl or walk, lacks normal emotional responses, is incontinent, has no system of communication. Furthermore, he is not interested in touching or handling objects; this is perhaps the most significant developmental shortcoming, since touch and kinaesthesia are the principal means by which he may interact with his environment. His response to non-food objects is most frequently to push them aside, although sometimes they evoke a stronger negative reaction. Even the usual orienting response to tactile stimulation is absent.[17]

* Professor Sokolianskii died Nov., 1960.

[17] All of this would suggest that the need for sensory stimulation—as inferred from reactions to sensory deprivation—is perhaps an acquired rather than inborn need.

However, the child does eat, and it is on his need for food that an entire system of learned responses is built. His teacher begins to build conditioned generalizations and feeding contingencies by capitalizing on those objects most directly connected with eating. As a first step, simply handling the spoon is sufficient to bring food reinforcement. Then, one by one, the handling of other objects is chained into the response sequence—plate, cup, napkin, etc. Thus the feeding situation becomes more and more complex, and a small tactual world develops around the child.

Professor Sokolianskii calls this part of his program the period of "primary humanizing." Its completion takes about five years for a child accepted at three years of age. By the end of it, the child has learned to sit on a chair, to walk, to emote, to be continent.

Toward the latter part of this period, through the consistent and judicious application of reinforcement, the child has also begun to use gestures to communicate his immediate desires. The gestures, of course, are quite limited in number and idiosyncratic in form. The first post-humanized phase of training is to condition or shape these uncommon signals into the common gestures that constitute the formal digital system for the Cyrillic alphabet. The primary goal is not that the child learn all the letters of the digital alphabet as quickly as possible, but rather that he learn the sequence of gestures for object labels that have letters in common. As soon as the child realizes that some of the gestures by which he summons different objects are identical, one formidable obstruction to rapid progress disappears. He has hit upon the possibility of the gesture as an abstraction, of label as distinct from object.

When all digital letters have been mastered, the child learns to identify each with its Braille equivalent. Only after this point does his teacher stress the building of a vocabulary—heretofore purposely restricted in size and degree of abstraction. Within two to three years of concentrated effort, according to Meshcheriakov, the deaf-blind child can acquire a vocabulary larger than that of a deaf child of the same age, and in some cases, equal to that of a normal child.

NEUROSIS AND PSYCHOSIS

In the Children's Department, First Municipal Psychoneurologic Clinical Hospital, Moscow (under the directorship of G. E. Sukhareva), patients are grouped according to sex and type of illness. The disorders for which the children are admitted are psychosis, epilepsy, and neurosis (or "beginning psychotic forms"). The Department—actually a separate hospital in itself—can accommodate 240 children. Referrals with a diagnosis of psychosis or epilepsy are taken

148

immediately, but there is a waiting list for children diagnosed as neurotic. The immediate source of referral and diagnosis is the Moscow Central Dispensary in Child Psychiatry; this agency in turn receives its referrals from the many polyclinics for children situated throughout the city. Length of hospitalization is generally not over two to three months, since only cases judged as showing some potential for improvement are referred to this hospital. (There are country institutions for children with highly unfavorable prognoses.) Most of the children are discharged to their own homes, where their treatment is continued on an out-patient basis at the nearest polyclinic. During the child's stay in the hospital, his parents come to visit him and also to confer with his doctor and "teacher" (psychiatric assistant).

The kinds of treatments available here may be grouped into two categories: medical-psychiatric and occupational-pedagogical. The first category includes the use of medicines (largely insulin, chlorpromazine, reserpine, sulfazine, and anti-convulsants), physical therapy, hydrotherapy, and psychotherapy (hypnosis and rational therapy). Professor Sukhareva feels that a not inconsiderable success has been achieved with the introduction of chlorpromazine, especially in the relief of anxiety at time of intake and, after the child returns home, for the maintenance of gains made during hospitalization.

Rational therapy is quite a different species from Western varieties. Its distinguishing principles appear to be first, that the patient bears a greater responsibility for his own treatment, and second, that problems are handled in terms of overt behavior rather than inferred, unconscious motives. To illustrate, when the patient arrives at the hospital, his doctor talks with him, endeavoring first to find out if the child understands that he is ill and that he has been hospitalized because of the illness. If the child shows some understanding and if he is not unduly disturbed by the change in his surroundings, his doctor goes on to explain that he (the patient) has come to the hospital in order to be cured of his illness, that it is the function of his doctor and his teacher to help him get well, but that *his* help is also essential to the process. He must, as it were, be therapist as well as patient. If the child does not realize that he is ill, or if he is anxious and upset when admitted, or both, chlorpromazine and rest precede this initial discussion with his doctor. (See Sukhareva, 1959.)

An individual program is then planned for each child to accord with his particular behavorial aberrations. If, for example, his chief problem is hyperactivity, he is given special "assignments" in which

149

he must strive to be quiet and to remain calm for increasing periods of time. If he is destructive, he is assigned small tasks of a constructive nature. Encouragement and rewards are administered by his doctor and teacher.

Reinforcement also comes from other sources. Each day, for example, the child meets with a group of his peers to discuss, commend, or criticize each other's behavior. The size of the group is generally not over 15 members, and each member takes a daily turn as group leader.[18]

Occupational-Pedagogical Therapy. All of the patients are of school age (seven years and older), and all school-age children—patients or not—are required to attend school. Therefore, each weekday morning is occupied with academic work, albeit somewhat modified for psychotic pupils. School is followed by dinner, and dinner, by a nap. Then comes the occupational therapy time of the day—the afternoon, to be spent working in one of the gardens or in the "zoo." Situated well outside the city proper, the hospital grounds are quite extensive, accommodating a large kitchen garden, an even larger flower garden, and orchards. The resident adult gardeners proudly claim that their role is limited to supervision and help—that the children themselves do all the bedding and cultivating.

Wandering about the garden areas are the hospital pets—a donkey, a monkey, dogs, cats, and domestic fowl. Foxes and other animals not so amenable to domestication, are housed in cages in various parts of the garden. The largest cage is a well-stocked aviary. The care of these animals also falls to the children, who groom them, feed and water them, and bestow affection on them. The children also record their daily contributions in each animal's dossier, which is kept in a garden house along with a small horticultural and zoological library, biological exhibits, and various supplies.

In Leningrad, the Psychoneurologic Hospital for Children[19] (directed by S. S. Mnukhin) accommodates 200 children between the ages of four and fifteen years. The major parts of the patient population are epileptic and neurotic; the remainder are psychotic and oligophrenic. To some degree, the relatively low incidence of psychosis reflects a difference in the frequency of use of that diagnos-

---

[18] In the Soviet Union, meetings held to evaluate one's behavior and that of others are not unique to children's groups or to medical settings, but are customary events for many stable groups of whatever function and membership composition. For a factual, detailed and illuminating account of sub-group and full group meetings within a children's institution, see Makarenko (1953).

[19] Fermskoe Shosse 36.

tic category. Mnukhin feels that the diagnosis is used elsewhere too freely.

Professor Mnukhin is also of the opinion that psychotherapy is more of an art than a science, and that success depends largely on the skill of the teacher. He therefore concentrates on the careful selection of Hospital personnel, leaving the rest up to their individual efforts.

The medical programs are more systematic, particularly the programs of medical therapy in oligophrenia and epilepsy and of research into the etiology of these diseases.

In treating oligophrenia, the Hospital has experimented with the use of glutamic acid, thyroid extracts, and a recently contrived X-ray method of German origin, but without notable success in any instance.

For the treatment of epilepsy, Professor Mnukhin has tried a variety of anti-convulsants (e.g. Myolin and Trematin), dehydration (using magnesium sulfate and glucose), and Penfield's surgical intervention. None of these has been wholly satisfactory.

In psychotic states, both chlorpromazine and insulin have been used. Mnukhin prefers the latter. Young children receive sub-comatose insulin therapy. Older children are given full shock treatment, i.e. a dose of between 67 and 200 units every day for 30 days or until side effects contraindicate further use of the drug.

Neurotic children are considered the most difficult to treat. The therapeutic program in this case includes education, parent education, hydrotherapy, work therapy, and chlorpromazine (in two month treatment cycles).

The average length of hospitalization varies according to diagnostic category. It is about three to four months for epileptic and neurotic patients, and less than that for oligophrenic patients. Length of stay for psychotic children varies, since there are usually a few chronic cases awaiting placement in country institutions.

APPENDIX

ILLUSTRATIONS AND NOTES RELATING TO
INSTRUMENTATION IN RESEARCH WITH INFANTS

In this Appendix, instruments that relate to the elicitation or measurement of one particular response are grouped together. Thus Figures 1.0 - 1.4 illustrate three different pieces of equipment for stimulus presentation and measurement of the orienting response. Figures 2.0 - 2.2 show apparatus for stimulus presentation and measurement of the blinking response. Figures 3.0 - 3.2 illustrate a device for the measurement of muscle movement.

Figure 1.0

Figure 1.0 Experimental crib and crib housing in the Laboratory of Higher Nervous Activity of Children, Institute of Pediatrics, Moscow. Among its several uses, this experimental arrangement is suited to the study of orienting. To obtain a record of the response one camera may be moved up into position and run continuously during the experimental session. A kymographic record of head movement may also be obtained from the stabilimeter under the crib's head rest. The UCS may be either a moving light or a flickering light. The first of these constitutes the more difficult problem in instrumentation, and it has been solved for this apparatus as follows: Mounted on the crib headboard is a narrow, six-inch long cylinder that encloses a low intensity lamp at its base end. When the lamp is switched on, a small, round spot of light is projected onto the interior wall or ceiling of the crib housing. The light is attached to the crib by a universal joint, so that it may be moved in any degree of arc. As a UCS for orienting, the light may be moved approximately 90° —from top center of the dome ceiling to the right or to the left of S's head. On-off and degree-of-arc controls for the light are outside the housing.

If an auditory stimulus, for example, were to serve as CS, a small speaker could be placed on the platform on which the crib rests. If a frequency discrimination were to be developed, one might place the speaker directly behind the head. If a discrimination based on localization were to be developed, one might use two speakers, placing them on opposite sides of the head. (Original photograph courtesy N. M. Shchelovanov; reproduced from Brackbill, 1960, with permission of the American Psychological Association.)

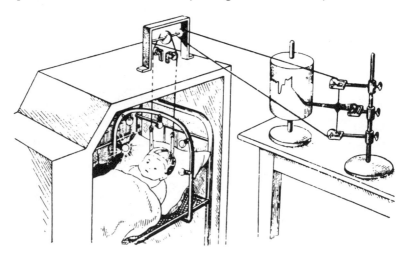

Figure 1.1

Figure 1.1 A simply constructed and inexpensive device invented by Kasatkin, Mirzoiants, and Khokhitva (1953) for eliciting and measuring orienting. Here the infant writes his own kymographic record, as it were, for any head movement to the side displaces the kymograph pen, and the extent to which it is displaced is directly proportional to the extent of head movement from the median position. Source of UCS is an arch studded with ordinary light bulbs. These may be switched on and off in sequence, from top to side, or the side-most light may be made to flicker. (From Kasatkin, Mirzoiants, and Khokhitva, 1953.)

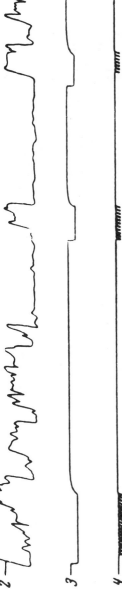

Figure 1.2

Figure 1.2 A segment of kymographic record obtained with the apparatus shown in Figure 1.1. This record shows the second and third experimental trials for a 74 day old infant; a conditioned orienting response has just made its first appearance. (1) Stabilimeter. (2) Head movement; a turn of the head to the right moved the pen upward. (3) CS, a tone of 810 cps. (4) UCS or reinforcement, a blinking light (from the lamp at the end of the arch to the infant's right). (5) Time in seconds. (From Kasatkin, Mirzoiants, and Khokhitva, 1953.)

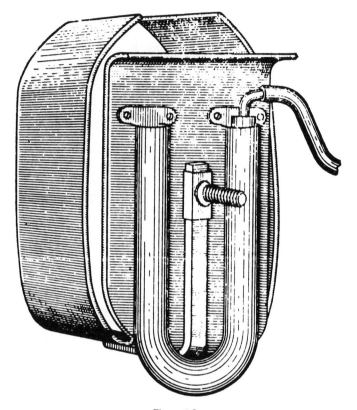

Figure 1.3

Figure 1.3 A device for recording the orienting response; invented by Papoushek, Institute for the Protection of Mother and Child, Prague. The infant's head rests on the platform, which rotates when the head is turned. A pneumographic record of head movements is obtained through a water manometer attached to the back of the head rest platform. (From Papoushek, 1959.)

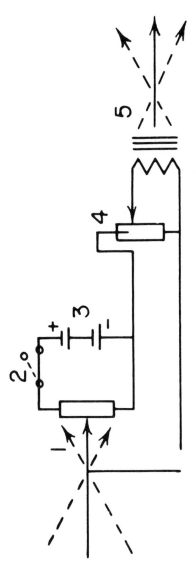

Figure 1.4

Figure 1.4 The circuit of an electrical system for recording head movements. This system may be used in place of the manometer-pneumograph recording method illustrated in Figure 1.3. (1) Potentiometer and pickup for rotation of head rest platform. (2) Switch. (3) Battery. (4) Potentiometer for regulating scale calibration. (5) Voltage change recording system. (From Papoushek, 1959.)

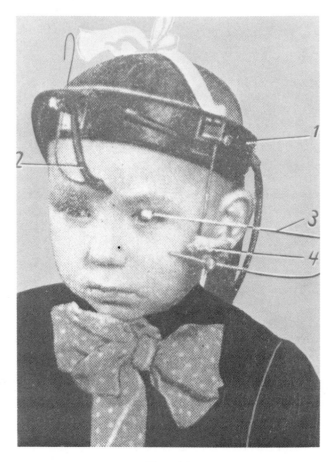

Figure 2.0

Figure 2.0 An apparatus for delivering air to the eye and for recording blinking. Designed by Korotkin, the apparatus is shown *in situ* on an infant subject in the Laboratory of the Physiology of Higher Nervous Activity of Children, Institute of Physiology, Leningrad. (1) Headband, from which all parts of the apparatus are suspended. The weight of the headband is distributed over the top of the head as well as around the head by tying together two ribbons—attached to the headband at one end—into a "hairbow." (2) Rubber tube, from which air is ejected into the eye. (3) Movable bamboo piece, fixed by adhesive tape to the upper eyelid. (4) Pneumographic device ("Marey capsule") that transmits the movements of the bamboo pickup. (From Koltsova, 1958.)

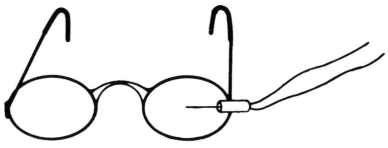

Figure 2.1

Figure 2.1 An eyeglass frame device for recording blinking; modified by Koltsova from an original design by Fonarev (1955). This device has replaced the apparatus previously used by Koltsova to record blinking (parts 3 and 4, Figure 2.0). The modified apparatus is lighter and permits greater freedom of movement on the part of the subject. The frames and pickup are adjusted so that the eyelash will brush the pickup when the eyelid closes. The pickup is an insulated piece of copper wire .5 mm. in diameter. Its transmitting end enters a plexiglass cylinder filled with powdered carbon. To prevent leakage of the powdered carbon, the diameter of the aperture through which the wire enters the side of the cylinder cannot exceed .57 mm. The inside diameter of the cylinder is 3 mm., and the thickness of its walls, .5 mm. Two tin foil covered stoppers plug the ends of the cylinder; they are attached to each other by a spring, the pull of which keeps them in position and in constant contact with the powdered carbon.

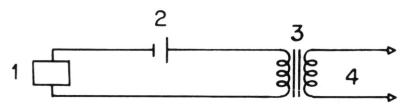

Figure 2.2

Figure 2.2 Circuit diagram for the eye blink recording apparatus illustrated in Figure 2.1. (1) Pickup and carbon-filled cylinder. (2) Battery. (3) Transformer (ratio, 1:30). (4) Leads to oscillograph or kymograph. Record consists of eye blink frequency and amplitude. The latter is proportionate to the amount of pressure of the eyelashes against the pickup. (From Fonarev, 1955.)

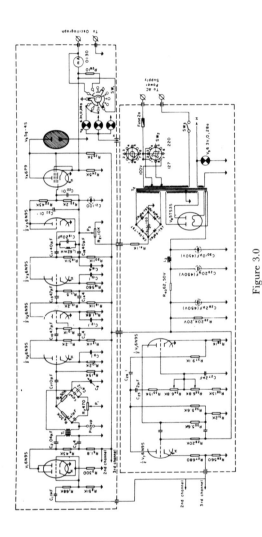

Figure 3.0

Figure 3.0 Circuit diagram for an electromyograph of the type used by Koltsova for studies of (motor) response meditation in infants. V = tube. CR = diode. P = potentiometer. H = heater. L = inductance. SW = switch. T = transformer. C = condenser. R = resistor. (Redrawn and translated from Shteingart, 1959. Further details concerning this apparatus may be found in the text of the Pergamon Press translation of the original article, *Pavlov J. high. nerv. Act*, 1959, pp. 685-690. However, the reader will find the diagram translation of Figure 3.0 to be more accurate than the corresponding Pergamon Press translation, p. 687. The author is grateful to Thorstein Larsen and C. Harvey Palmer, Jr., Electrical Engineering Department, The Johns Hopkins University, for their kind assistance in fathoming this circuit.)

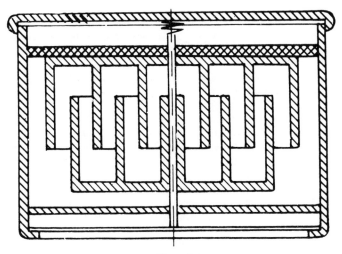

Figure 3.1

Figure 3.1 Diagram of pickup for the electromyograph circuit shown in Figure 3.0.

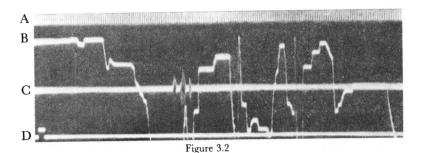

Figure 3.2

Figure 3.2 Electromyogram from the mylohyoid muscle of a child with speech disturbances. The child was asked to pronounce the word *stol* (table). (a) Time in tenths of a second. (b) Electromyogram. (c) Oscillogram. (d) Stimulus marker.

REFERENCES

Note: References that are not at the time of writing publicly available in English have been transliterated and translated. References that are available in English are given only in translation.

Brackbill, Y. Experimental research with children in the Soviet Union: report of a visit. *Amer. Psychol.*, 1960, 15, 226-233.

Byshevskii, N. O., Kirst, A. N., and Navrotskii, N. Ia. Nabliudeniia Nad razvitiem zritelnoi pamiati u Kadet of 11 do 15 letnego vozrasta vkliuchitelno. (Observations on the development of visual memory in cadets from 11 to 15 years of age.) *Vestnik psikhologii, krimin. antropolog. i gipnotizma (Herald of Psychology, criminal Anthropology, and Hypnotism)*, 1904, No. 9, 667-669.

Dashkovskaia, V. S. The first conditioned reactions in newborn infants under normal and in certain pathological conditions. Reprinted in: *The Central Nervous System and Behavior*, translations from the Russian medical literature collected for participants of the third Macy conference on the central nervous system and behavior, Princeton, N. J., Feb. 21-24, 1960, 126-146. Prepared and distributed by the Russian scientific translation program, National Institutes of Health. Library of Congress Catalog card number: 5960785. (The article originally appeared in *Zh. vyssh. nerv. Deiatel.*, 1953, 3, 247-259.)

Degtiar, E. N. Nekotorye bezuslovnye reaktsii rebenka pervykh mesiatsev zhizni. (Some unconditioned responses of children in the first months of life). *Trudy Instituta Fiziologii (Transactions of the Institute of Physiology)*, 1952, 1, 259-265.

Fonarev, A. M. Metodika registratsii migatelnykh refleksov u grudnykh detei (A method of recording blinking responses in infants). *Fiziologicheskii Zhurnal SSSR (Physiological Journal of the U.S.S.R.)*, 1955, 41, 101-102.

Fonarev, A. M. (Pribor dlia elektricheskoi registratsii mikrodvizhenii iazyka pri skrytoi artikuliatsii (An apparatus for the electrical recording of micromovements of the tongue in covert articulation). *Izvestiia Akad. Ped. Nauk RSFSR (Proceedings of the Academy of Pedagogical Sciences of the R.S.F.S.R.)*, 1956, No. 81, 99-101.

Kasatkin, N. I. *Ocherk razvitiia vysshei nervnoi deiatelnosti u rebenka rannego vozrasta. (A report on the development of higher nervous activity in the young child).* Moscow: Gosudarstvennoe Izdatelstvo Meditsinskoi Literatury (State Publishing House of Medical Literature. MEDGIZ), 1951.

Kasatkin, N. I. Rannii ontogenez reflektornoi deiatelnosti rebenka (The early ontogenesis of reflex activity in the child). *Zh. vyssh. nerv. Deiatel. (J. high. nerv. Act.)*, 1957, 7, 805-818.

Kasatkin, N. I. and Levikova, A. M. On the development of early conditioned reflexes and differentiations of auditory stimuli in infants. *J. exp. Psychol.*, 1935a, 18, 1-19.

Kasatkin, N. I. and Levikova, A. M. The formation of visual conditioned reflexes and their differentiation in infants. *J. gen. Psychol.*, 1935b, 12, 416-435.

Kasatkin, N. I., Mirzoiants, N. S. and Khokhitva, A. P. Ob orientirovochnykh uslovnykh refleksakh u detei pervogo goda zhizni (Conditioned orienting responses in children in the first year of life). *Zh. vyssh. nerv. Deiatel. (J. high. nerv. Act.)*, 1953, 3, 192-202.

Kaufman, M. L., Nechaev, A. P. and Tychino, N. N. Nabliudeniia nad razvitiem zritelnoi pamiati i kharakterom preobladaiushchikh assotisiatsii u detei doshkolnogo vozrasta. (Observations on the development of visual memory and the character of predominant associations in preschool children.) *Russkaia shkola (Russian School)*, 1903, Jan.

Koltsova, M. M. *(O formirovanii vysshei nervnoi deiatelnosti rebenka (The formation of higher nervous activity in children)*. Leningrad: Gosudarstvennoe Izdatelstvo Meditsinskoi Literatury (State Publishing House of Medical Literature. MEDGIZ), 1958.

Koltsova, M. M. Development of system as the basis of the process of generalization. *Pavlov J. high. nerv. Act.*[20] (Pergamon Press translation), 1960, 10, 179-184.

Korolkova, N. Eksperimentalnye dannye k voprosu ob assotsiatsiiakh. (Experimental data relating to the question of associations.) *Vestnik psikhologii, krimin. antropolog. i gipnotizma (Herald of Psychology, criminal Anthropology, and Hypnotism)*, 1904, No. 5, 333-342.

Krachkovskaia, M. V. Reflex changes in the leukocyte count of newborn infants in relation to food intake. *Pavlov J. high. nerv. Act.* (Pergamon Press translation), 1959, 9, 193-199.

Livshits, K. P. K voprosu o primenenii obektivnykh metodov issledovaniia pri izuchenii psikhiki rebenka. (On the question of using objective methods of research for the study of the mentality of the child.) *Obozrenie psikhiatrii, neurologii i eksperim. psikholog. (Review of Psychiatry, Neurology, and experimental Psychology)*, 1908, No. 9, 570.

Makarenko, A. S. *Learning to Live* (originally titled, *Flags on the Battlements*). Moscow: Foreign Languages Publishing House, 1953.

Makarenko, A. S. *Kniga dlia Roditelei (A Book for Parents)*. Detrozovodsk: National Publishing House of the Karelian Autonomous Soviet Republic, 1958.

Makarenko, A. S. *Pedagogicheskaia Poema (A Pedagogical Poem)*. Leningrad: Newspaper, Periodical, and Book Publishing House, 1949.

Nechaev, A. P. *Sovremennaia eksperimentalnaia psikhologiia v ee otnoshenii k voprosam shkolnogo obucheniia. (Contemporary experimental psychology in relation to questions of academic education.)* Saint Peterburg, 1901a.

Nechaev, A. P. *Nabliudeniia nad razvitiem interesov i pamiati v shkolnom vozraste. (Observations on the development of interests and memory during school years.)* Saint Petersburg, 1901B.

Papoushek, G. A method of studying conditioned food reflexes in young children up to the age of six months. *Pavlov J. high. nerv. Act.* (Pergamon Press translation), 1959, 9, 136-140.

Shchelovanov, N. M., and Aksarina, N. M. *Vospitanie detei rannego vozrasta v detskikh uchprezhdeniiakh. (The bringing up of young children in institutions for children.)* (4th ed.) Moscow: Gosudarstvennoe Izdatelstvo Meditsinskoi Literatury (State Publishing House of Medical Literature. MEDGIZ), 1960.

Shteingart, K. M. New methods for the investigation of motor reflexes in man.

---

[20] In Russian, this journal is titled, *Zh. vyssh. nerv. Deiatel. im. I. P. Pavlova,* and is literally translated, *J. high. nerv. Act. named after I. P. Pavlov.* The English translation of the journal, recently started by Pergamon Press, is titled, *Pavlov J. high. nerv. Act.*

Pavlov. J. high. nerv. Act. (Pergamon Press translation), 1959, 9, 685-690. See also original article, Novaia metodika izucheniia dvigatelnykh refleksov u cheloveka, *Zh. vyssh. nerv. Deiatel. (J. high. nerv. Act.),* 1959, 9, 782-787.

Sukhareva, G. E. *Klinicheskie lektsii po psikhiatrii detskogo vozrasta (Clinical lectures on child psychiatry),* v. 2, Moscow: Gosudarstvennoe Izdatelstvo Meditsinskoi Literatury (State Publishing House of Medical Literature, MEDGIZ), 1959.

Usoltsev, A. N. and Terekhova, N. T. Functional peculiarities of the skin-temperature analyser in children during the first six months of life. *Pavlov J. high. nerv. Act.* (Pergamon Press translation), 1958, 8, 174-184.

Zaporozhets, A. V. *Razvitie proizvolnykh dvizhenii (The development of voluntary movements).* Moscow: Izdat. Akad. Ped. Nauk R.S.F.S.R.(Publishing House of the Academy of Pedagogical Sciences of the R.S.F.S.R.), 1960.

CHAPTER VI

Observations on Soviet Educational and Industrial Psychology

EDWIN A. FLEISHMAN

This chapter summarizes some observations on Soviet education, educational psychology and industrial psychology made during my visits to psychological laboratories and schools in Moscow, Leningrad and Tbilisi, during the period of May 13 to June 6, 1960. This chapter does not represent a definitive statement or review of Soviet psychology in those areas. As other contributors to this volume have pointed out, such short visits can only hope to scratch the surface. Furthermore, it was impossible for any of us to visit all of the centers doing important work. Even when we were enabled to visit these centers, considerable time was wasted finding the relevant sources and then arranging appointments within the limited time available. In addition, there is the language translation problem which, although it is not critical, does slow one down and confuses some of the discussion. However, all of us found the experience useful and informative. Although the main purpose of this volume is to illustrate some small part of the developing picture of Soviet psychology, it also serves to provide future visitors with sources and suggestions which may make their own visits more fruitful. These visits involved much exposure to psychophysiology and Pavlovian learning research, but it has been left to others to cover those areas in this volume.

INDUSTRIAL PSYCHOLOGY

LABORATORY OF LABOR PSYCHOLOGY, MOSCOW

The Laboratory of Labor Psychology is located in the Institute of Psychology, 9 Mokhovaya Street, in the center of Moscow (a few blocks from Red Square). The Director of the laboratory, Professor D. A. Oshanin, was ill and Dr. V. V. Chebisheva was temporarily in charge. After giving a general orientation in Soviet "labor psychology," she introduced several assistants who discussed their laboratory research. The principal professional people present, besides Dr. Chebisheva, were Drs. V. Suvorova, O. A. Konopkin, and L. V. Filonov.

There are three general lines of research bearing on industrial psychology. The first is concerned with industrial labor activity and emphasizes problems of work methods, analysis of tasks, structuring of skills, problems of monotony, etc. The second emphasizes "occupational and industrial teaching." A third area mentioned concerns the "preparation of children for occupations."

The first area was defined as "psychological characteristics of work activity in production." This is investigated at several levels, such as in manual assembly jobs, in conveyor line jobs, in maintenance jobs (trouble-shooting?), and in laboratory field studies in plants.

One series of such studies concerned the problems of "tempo" at work. There are considerable and consistent individual differences in the pace at which people work. What is the basis of "tempo" and what is the relation between "tempo" and skill? Dr. Chebisheva investigated the development of tempo during a vocational training course. Observations of students at work, laboratory tests on experimental tasks with these children, and data from teachers' reports confirmed stable individual differences in "general tempo." No differences were found associated with general development or physical characteristics of the student. An important factor seemed to be that some students were more self-critical and made greater demands on themselves. Another factor was their grasp of the entire cycle of work "as a whole." Slower pupils had poorer habits of planning and organization, and did not have a good grasp of how the separate stages of work were related. It was also found that the tempo to which a student adjusted early carried over into later performance. The importance of "improving" tempo as early as possible in the course of training is indicated. Also, they believe a great deal of emphasis should be placed on giving the worker an "organized conception" of the task.

Another problem mentioned was the crucial role of "set-up men" (as distinguished from "production workers") in industry. Set-up men maintain the machines and change its operation for new jobs. The researchers were interested in the unique aspects of this job as a basis for improving training in this area. Their main method of analysis seems to be to compare the "best" workers with "poor" workers. A primary finding was that "mental solving of problems" was the main aspect of the job. Yet, the usual training was found to be "on the job" training. A program is under way to determine if

166

special occupational schools would be best. This is done for several industries (e.g. the ball bearing industry has its own occupational schools). Text books have been developed; and the course is combined with practical experience. The psychologist works with experienced set-up men in determining how to make the training more systematic and how to present the principles of training. The training emphasizes "how to isolate relevant problems," "how to plan," "how to trouble shoot for damage," and "how to identify reasons for faulty products." These studies have led investigators to conclude that such elements are common to various occupational groupings involving set-up men, mechanics, electricians, etc. General principles about teaching these elements are now being formulated to apply to school children in their occupational training.

A recurring point in these discussions is emphasis on training people "to think," to intellectualize their jobs, as it were. One aspect in training school children is getting them to develop habits of planning and "checking one's work," as well as teaching them the importance of thinking about standards, goals, and the relationship of one's work to the total operation. In fact, an extensive program has just begun to compare "common sense" training in vocational courses with the "best methods." Emphasis is placed on stimulating activity of the pupil, "relieving him of a passive attitude," exploring methods other than lectures, and having him formulate his own objectives.

There is much planned in the improvement of vocational and polytechnical education. These plans include examining the content, method, and organization of training for different age levels; the formation of effective skills and habits; and providing guide lines for schools on how best to develop technical interests and abilities, "technical thinking," initiative, and creativity. The development of a "communist attitude" toward work was also stressed.

Tempo and Monotony

Other work has been carried out on the relationship between "tempo" and monotony. This work is carried out with the help of a miniature conveyor belt set up in a basement laboratory. Various assembly tasks are presented to subjects and the pace of the belt can be varied. The general finding: tempo influences the degree of monotony experienced. Within the limits investigated, with fewer short pauses, either between sub-units or between total operations, monotony was greater. When asked the meaning of these statements, the researchers replied that this work was just beginning and it is difficult to generalize yet.

In another experiment, a group was instructed to "Work faster than you usually do." After a time, in this kind of practice, it was found that the "normal tempo" had increased. This was done mainly with "tapping type" tests (electrically recorded taps on a metal plate), but confirmation of this finding has been obtained in industry.

In the laboratory with the conveyor belt, experiments are frequently run using micromotion film. One finding is that some workers are highly variable in how they perform the same task on the line, while other workers are "more standardized." It is also found that too fast a tempo may break down the structure of the skill. Thus the question arises, can principles be worked out regarding the relationships between optimum tempo and the structure of different tasks?

Two types of tasks were compared under different tempos. One task was a "hierarchical task," in which the subject composed rings on a stick. (These had to be arranged in a certain order or they would not fit.) The second task required "more planning ahead," since the rings had to be in a given order, but it was a haphazard order which had to be kept in mind. It appeared that there was an optimal tempo for each kind of task at which the variability in performance was lowest. A tempo either slower or faster than this optimum produced greater variability. The performance measure used was a ratio of time to errors. As for the two types of operations, variability was lower in the hierarchical task (where conditions themselves established the order) and larger where the subjects had to keep the order in mind.

This finding, that as "thinking increases, variability increases," is consistent with a second experiment, in which two tasks were compared. One was a procedural task in which the order of the operations was specified; the second required the solution of problems. The first task seemed to be principally a choice reaction time task involving pushbuttons, and visual and auditory signals; the second involved light *sequences* related to particular buttons. Tempo was also varied, but no conclusion on this was presented.

The variability measure was the best measure of monotony, since it seems most sensitive to their experimental manipulations. (This measure has lately been advocated by Bartlett, Broadbent and other researchers at Cambridge.)

Other research on skills was also in progress. For example, Dr. Filonov was investigating the influence of the "amount of information provided" on decision time. He was also looking into the problem of the effective coding of information needed to improve differentiation of stimulus cues and the effect of these variations on choice reaction time.

Analysis and Structuring of Skilled Acts

One line of research has dealt directly with the analysis and structuring of skilled acts, where these are primarily perceptual-motor (my term). The point was made that the process of acquiring habits of simultaneously performing several activities is more complex than learning a sequence of actions. (A device described was similar to one used in the author's laboratory.) For this, the subject has to monitor and regulate three indicators simultaneously, as in aircraft piloting. Four stages in the habit were established: (1) mastery of each control action separately, (2) successive execution, (3) incomplete combination of action (fixating on one and simultaneously executing another), and (4) skill in executing all three elements simultaneously.

A more intensive analysis was focused on the different methods used by the subjects in mastering this task. This led to the conclusion that initial emphasis on proficiency in performing the component movements, apart from the required coordinations, was ineffective. In such cases retraining was necessary to get combined action in later stages. Successive addition of components is not effective either. The best approach seems to be to practice on the coordinated task, with emphasis on guidance procedures at this stage. (These conclusions agreed with the present author's own findings, in which a much different approach is used.)

Positive and Negative Transfer of Skills

Dr. Suvorova described some of her experiments on positive and negative transfer of skills. In one experiment, skilled lathe operators were given a task on a lathe with either one component missing or one added. Both simplification and complication led to decreased speed and more errors, not only in the new component, but also in the old components.

In another experiment (by Borkova) beginners learned to type on a standard keyboard and then on a different keyboard. There were wide individual differences in original and transfer performance. Those who learned the first task readily, also learned the second faster. Those who mastered the first task slowly had a harder time with the second. (It was difficult to tell if they had controlled for performance level before switching tasks.) The researchers found that the "slow" learners and relearners emphasized more speed and less precision early, whereas the fast learners emphasized slower speed and more precision early.

In an exchange of reprints, it developed there was some interest in the author's radio telegraphy studies. One study of theirs, carried out during the war, focused on the use of visual control in auditory code learning. The problem was to assist code senders in sticking to the required time relations of dots, dashes and pauses (despite individual "sending" styles). Three groups were compared: one had exercises under aural control by his instructor only, another controlled their rhythm by listening to a mechanical recording of the proper rhythm, and the third had aural control plus visual control with the opportunity to compare printed lengths of dots and dashes with those from the mechanical transmitter. The results showed the last method to be best.

Procedures of Vocational Training in Schools

As indicated earlier, a great deal of work concerns procedures of vocational training in schools. The relative balance of verbal explanation and demonstration required to produce optimum results in task learning was investigated. The results indicated that, after verbal explanation, the work produced was of a higher quality but required more time. Conversely, the demonstration method produced more rapid performance, but the work was of lower quality. The use of both methods produced better quality and more speed than was the case where either method was used alone. Observation revealed that subjects exposed to demonstrations differed in their method of work from subjects instructed orally. Those exposed to demonstration imitated the instructor; after oral instruction they reverted to their own method. A rationale for the use of different methods in vocational training is being sought.

The importance of "self-evaluation" in productive work is emphasized. When it is lacking, students often allow their work to fall below standards. Studies have investigated factors in "self-checking" training in trade schools. Laboratory tasks were given to students and their instructors and photographic, micromotion techniques, and other instrumentation recorded all their working movements (duration, rhythm, tempo, pressure of tools on the work surface). Changes in organization of time on each movement also were recorded. A list of differences between pupils and instructors included insufficient planning, failure to organize their time properly, lack of proficiency in using instruments to get proper feedback (author's term) from their actions, and rigidity in performing certain actions when they were no longer useful. These suggest needed training emphasis. (There seems to be a certain circularity in their use of these concepts. Thus the term "self-checking" is coined to account for lack of proficiency, then the factors investigated indicate lack of self-checking.)

The sessions with this group were extremely interesting. While it was difficult to follow the details of many experiments, the flavor of their work is reflected in the preceding comments. They spend a good deal of effort observing what they call "leading" or expert workers and comparing their activities with less efficient workers. In fact, many conclusions rest on these comparisons. The experiments do not seem highly controlled, by our standards, and our usual statistical tests are seldom applied. They rely more on replication. There seems to be a great deal of freedom to investigate whatever they like, but it is clear that they are in touch with the practical needs of the time. Also, it appears that vocational schools make specific requests for assistance in certain training problems.

Their view of labor psychology is narrower than ours, consisting mainly of training, "engineering psychology," and the study of methods and conditions of work. However, these problems are approached on a broad front, in the laboratory, in the factory, and in the schools.

I described the topics which are of interest to American industrial psychologists (which included social industrial psychology, motivation, group dynamics, leadership, organizational behavior, etc.) and asked about their interest in such topics. At this point, my interpreter assumed more of a role in the conversation, stating, "The whole basis of the communist society makes the investigation of such topics unnecessary." My hosts replied, "some topics are of more interest to American psychologists." In the Soviet Union, such topics are of more interest to labor groups, trade unions, and community organizations. The interpreter also pointed out that there are "brigades of communist labor" in various plants, which are responsible for the orientation and guidance of young workers. It is the responsibility of these brigades to see that the young workers are motivated to do their best, not only in their work, but in other forms of "desirable behavior" (e.g. the need to be sober on the job, etc.). Before these young workers can become union members they have to live up to certain standards. General meetings are held periodically to vote on new members and to see if others deserve their titles, etc.

We next pursued the issue of tests and selection and they echoed the view that tests are unscientific and unreliable. Tests, they feel, ignore qualitative differences and methods of solving the problems. It was the challenge of the communist society to develop everyone, regardless of their initial handicaps, and proper emphasis on training and environmental change is the correct approach to use.

When some recent American interests in different organizational structures, participative management, increased delegation down the line, etc., was mentioned they seemed to feel this wasn't their field of competence and showed little interest in discussing these topics. One of the staff evinced an interest in publications on "emotional disturbances of industrial behavior."

LABORATORY OF INDUSTRIAL PSYCHOLOGY, UNIVERSITY OF LENINGRAD
The Director here was Dr. B. F. Lomov. His principal assistants were Drs. A. A. Bodalev and A. G. Kovalev. The laboratory had been functioning only six months and was staffed with eight professional people. The primary concern here was "engineering psychology." Lomov spoke in terms of the "man-machine system" concept. They are interested in human factors, problems among operators and maintenance people in electric power stations, and among "dispatchers" (or controllers) in airports and railroads. In addition, they are concerned with display variables, load variables, procedural variables, as well as with problems of information coding. All of this will sound very familiar to U.S. engineering psychologists and Lomov has been greatly influenced by American developments in these fields. (He was familiar with Fitt's work and knew the Chapanis, Garner, and Morgan volume, but was not familiar with recent books by McCormick or by Chapanis.)

They hope to establish a program around manual remote control devices, with particular emphasis on the role of "feedback" in such devices. When asked about details of this work they said that they were just getting started. Furthermore, they were remodeling the building and all the laboratories were torn up. We were in a very old building and there was debris everywhere from the reconstruction operations.

Feedback
The one program pursued in any detail here concerned "feedback." This particular program viewed the hand as an "organ of perception," and was directed towards determining all they could about the hand as a "system." They felt the best way to describe this was to show a movie of their research. (First, however, the author was asked to give a presentation to their staff. This talk lasted for an hour and a half and dealt with the author's work on perceptual-motor skills. There followed a lively discussion, with much interest evidenced in the apparatus used in these studies. We then adjourned to another building, containing a complete theatre in the basement.) The movie was an expert production job with narration.

The basic methodology of this program requires the subject to make discriminations and identifications of objects using only cues available to the hands. The arms are placed through holes in a screen and objects presented on the other side of the screen. The accuracy of one-handed versus two-handed cues are then compared. Also, with one hand, cues from the different fingers are reduced systematically through the use of stiff "finger sleeves." The subject may be required to trace patterns, where cues are primarily tactual, and then to draw the pattern. In some cases tactual cues are reduced by gloves. He may be handed an object, with tactual and kinesthetic cues available. The object may be two-dimensional or solid; it may be familiar or unfamiliar; it may be symmetrical or asymmetrical; it may be simple or complex. The attempt is made to evaluate the importance of these variations to the "informational capabilities" of the hand.

Studies are made not only in the laboratory but also in work environments, e.g. assembly jobs. The findings are also applied to control coding, e.g. knob shapes. Studies are also made of the cues used by sculptors. (An intensive study, for example, is being conducted with a famous Soviet blind sculptor.) Ultimately, it is hoped to apply the results to problems of training the blind and to methods of presenting information to blind and deaf people at work and in other contexts. Special studies are under way of several Helen Keller type cases, who participate in these experiments. Although of fairly recent origin, it seems to be quite an ambitious program.

Visit to a Tbilisi Factory

After the standard tour of the Institute of Psychology, Georgian Academy of Sciences (it was learned that there was no research in industrial psychology conducted there), Intourist arranged a visit to a tea processing and packing plant. Except for the exterior architecture, it looked much like tea and coffee factories in the United States. The factory, founded in 1940, then had a quota of 90 tons. It now employs 300 people, and has a quota of 7,700 tons. There were conveyor belts, semi-automatic hoppers, a gravity processing system, the usual ovens, etc. There were a large proportion of women workers, although most of the maintenance and heavy work was done by men. The physical layout was uncluttered and clean. There was an attractive dining room and a recreation lounge (including billiard and ping-pong tables). A good deal of shrubbery and lawn was to be seen around the plant areas.

When asked what his biggest problem was the Plant Director replied, "to increase quantity and quality and to decrease price of production"; not a surprising answer. He said the main problem was mechanization, lack of better plant equipment, and shifting to more automated operations. In reply to a question concerning ability dif-

173

ferences on the job, he said that this is not a problem in a socialist state, since all are placed where they fit. When asked wh'at range of productivity there was among individual workers, he replied that some earn 500 rubles a month and others 1500 rubles a month; he added that he hoped they all would earn 1500 rubles. When pressed about individual differences, he replied that special courses will some day enable everyone to produce at a high level. When questioned about labor mobility, he stated that workers can change jobs, although the current policy is for a worker to request a change of position, if he knows of a vacancy somewhere else. Thus a textile worker could apply here if there was an opening. However, some Plant Directors refuse to allow men to leave if they are needed. (Under a new policy, however, workers have the right to leave after 15 days.) On the whole, there appeared to be much more mobility than was expected. There is even competition among industries for the best college graduates, and managers can seek better positions at other plants. Nevertheless, there is always the possibility of a denial of job change if it does not appear "in the interests of the State."

When asked about modern programming methods, the Plant Director replied this was not his problem since, in their economy, it is all planned; the government knows how much needs to be produced. He proudly pointed out that the quota for this factory, in 1959, was 5,600 tons, but they produced 6,000. Thus his whole conception of programming was conditioned by his desire to exceed the goal set by the government economists.

Pay is based on a piece rate system, with 500 rubles a month the minimum guarantee. Supervisors get straight salaries, but there are bonuses for outstanding records. Promotions depend on performance plus completion of courses in evening schools. (Some courses are given in the plant.)

When asked for an organization chart he pointed out they were just completing a reorganization. The object of this, he said, was to decrease the number of people in the administrative sections relative to the number of production workers. (For "before" and "after" charts, see Figure 1.) The number of departments was decreased from 20 to 18. He referred to the new organization as "simplified." Actually, it does seem to provide a slightly "flatter" structure, and has the advantage of giving the director more direct control of the "sorting" department.

SOME GENERAL OBSERVATIONS

It was pointed out that some interesting developments in industrial psychology were taking place at the Institute of Psychology, in

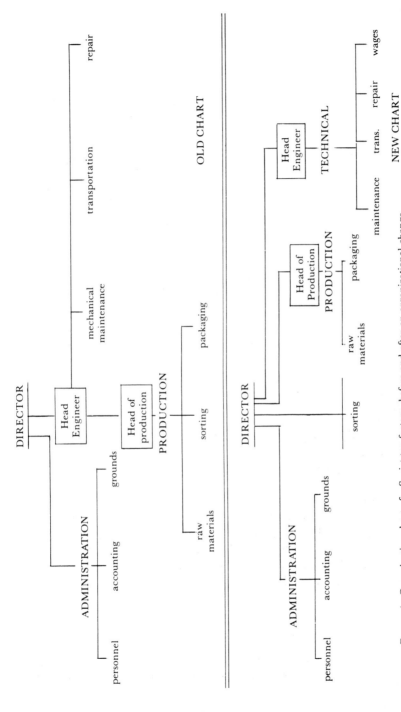

FIGURE 1. Organization chart of a Soviet tea factory, before and after an organizational change.

175

Kiev. However, the itinerary could not be changed in time. Perhaps, the next visitor with these interests can stop there.

Despite the limitations pointed out earlier, it is possible to make the following general observations regarding industrial psychology in the Soviet Union:

1. The Soviet conception of this field is more limited than ours. Research in the areas of "motivation," "group dynamics," "leadership," "attitude change," or "social-industrial psychology" were not observed. This does not mean that there is an absence of interest in these problems. Rather, principles in these areas were regarded either as "givens" in their society or else as outside the realm of scientific psychological study. Of course, one sees in practice many examples of "applied" motivational and social psychological principles (e.g. the stress on group norms and pressure from peer groups, reward systems tied to productivity). In all probability there is much informal feedback concerning the effectiveness of these techniques. However, university and laboratory personnel did not appear interested in these phenomena for scientific study.

2. A large proportion of effort is devoted to training research at various levels. This ranges from laboratory studies on efficient learning of skilled manual movements to operational studies in vocational schools and on-the-job-training. Aside from interest in specific skill training there is interest in training efficient "habits of thinking," which will transfer to a variety of work activities. There is a great deal of interest in understanding the *process* of learning. It is important to note all of this taking place within the "laboratories of labor psychology."

3. There is increasing interest in "engineering" psychology. This is an extension of the continuing interest in work methods, monotony, and environmental factors in productivity.

4. These trends are related to an absence of interest in test development and personnel selection research. Emphasis is directed toward determining the most effective training and techniques for bringing each individual to a high level of productivity. Tests are branded as "unscientific," since "environment plays a major role in performance and since different people can get the same score on a test by using different processes." This, however, does not preclude the use of "examinations" to assess achievement in training.

EDUCATION AND EDUCATIONAL PSYCHOLOGY

The main contacts with educational psychology were through a visit to a Moscow school, a visit to the Laboratory of Educational

176

Psychology, in the Institute of Psychology, Moscow, and a visit to a Pioneer Palace in Leningrad.

VISIT TO A SCHOOL

The school, located near a large apartment development, did not look like one of the newer developments. It was in an old red brick building, not too different from many still in use in the U.S., and was immaculately clean and very attractive. Immediately within the entrance was an enormous statue of Lenin, surrounded by a pond, flowers, and ferns.

During the orientation by the woman Assistant Director (the Director joined us later) it was pointed out that the school ran from grades one to eleven. The eleventh grade is a recent addition to the Russian school curricula. Although there is a trend to separate grades one to eight from grades nine to eleven, some schools, depending on the physical facilities, will continue to have all eleven grades. The Assistant Director stated she prefers it thus, since it eliminates the adjustment period to a new school and new neighborhood. In addition to her administrative duties she also teaches physics; the Director teaches literature.

Curriculum

The required curriculum is spelled out for all schools throughout the U.S.S.R. There are some variations between the Soviet republics, taking cultural differences into account. Within the R.S.F.S.R.[1] the curriculum is highly standardized. (The lack of standardization in the United States is something they can't understand.) The curriculum for education from the sixth grade up (prepared from the author's notes) is shown in Table 1.

School begins at seven years of age. The first four grades have a single teacher (with a special teacher for music and physical education). In the fifth grade there are separate teachers for all subjects. School is compulsory through the eighth grade, whereupon the student chooses either to go on to eleventh grade or to work. If he works, he can attend evening school for work training. They stated, "everyone goes to these evening schools, but it's not compulsory."

---

[1] R.S.F.S.R. refers to Russian Socialist Federated Soviet Republic. This area contains over 50 per cent of the population of the Soviet Union, and includes 76 per cent of its territory. Its territories stretch from the Estonian, Latvian and Finnish borders and the White Russian and Ukrainian lines on the West, to the shores of the Pacific Ocean, and from the Arctic Ocean on the North to the shores of the Black and Caspian seas and the borders of Kayakh S.S.R., Mongolia and Manchuria on the South. Its capital is Moscow.

TABLE 1
Academic Curriculum of the Soviet School
(Standard throughout the R.S.F.S.R.)

Grade	Mathematics	Physics	Chemistry*	Geography*	Astronomy	Literature
6	Geometry, Algebra — hrs. 6	Measures, lengths, weight, force, velocity, levers — hrs. 6		x		
7	Graphic methods, Geometry, Algebra — 6	Electricity, Heat — 6	x	x		x — 6
8	Analytical Geometry, Algebra — 6	Mechanics, (Mathematics coordinated with mathematics course) — 6	x	x		(including MarkTwain) — 6
9	Trigonometry, Solid Geometry, Algebra — 4	Thermo-dynamics — 6	x	x		Old Russian Literature (10th–13th Century), Tolstoy, Pushkin, (18th–19th Century) — 4
10	Trigonometry, Solid Geometry, Algebra — 4	Optics, Electricity — 6	x	x	x or	19th Century, Chekov, Ostrovsky, Turgenev — 4
11	Trigonometry, Solid Geometry, Algebra — 3	"Electrotechnics" — 6	x *Inorganic and organic	*From 4th grade	x	Foreign Literature: Homer, Shakespeare, Moliére, Goethe, Balzac, Cervantes, Longfellow, Steinbeck, London

TABLE 1 (CONTINUED)

Grade	Russian Language*	Foreign Language*	hrs.	History*	hrs.	Art*	Biology	hrs.
6	x	x	4	x	2	x	x	4
7	x	x	4	x	2	x	x	4
8	x	x	4	x	3	x	x	4
9	Composition (Integrated with Literature)	x	4	x (U.S. History)	4	x	x	4
10		x	3	x	3	x		
11		x	2	x	3	x		
	*From 1st grade	*Choice of German, French or English, from 5th grade. First choice is English with French next. No shifting of language permitted		*From 4th grade. Order in Ancient World, European and Foreign countries		*From 1st to 6th grades. Painting and drafting through 11th grade	*From 4th grade. (Biology, Botany, Zoology)	

Physical Education—Grades 1-7 (two hours a week); Grades 8-9 (three hours a week); Grade 10 (two hours a week). Exercises in morning—competitive sports between schools and districts. Swimming pool in district.

Generally no typing or shorthand courses in these schools but one school has it.

Six day week (no homework on weekends).

x means that course is given.

In the fifth grade, labor lessons start. For example, boys may learn carpentry, girls may learn sewing or embroidery. (The school has 15 sewing machines.) In addition, there are duties such as keeping the building clean, looking after plants, and tending the kitchen-garden.

A new development has taken place, starting in the ninth grade. Two days out of the six-day week students go to a plant to work and to be instructed on different jobs. (Students from this school go to an auto plant.) The particular plant attended depends on the location of the school. It was stressed that everyone gets on-the-job training, even exceptional students who plan to go to college later. Although this year only the ninth grade is involved (since it's the first year of the new program), the tenth and eleventh grades will be involved in subsequent years. Pupils receive a certificate, not only from school, but also indicating the industry and type of labor they have qualified for. In answer to questions, it was stressed that this does not obligate anyone to work in that industry since the certificate is for broad occupations (e.g. plumber, carpenter, printer.) Prior to the time when the students reach the ninth grade there are meetings of students, teachers and parents, and skilled workers, who review the possibilities of each occupational area. Applications are filed and considered. Students can change their work program in the plant after the first month, if they are not satisfied.

Student Evaluation

Standard exams are prepared by the Ministry of Education for use all over the U.S.S.R., at the end of the eighth and eleventh grades. It was stated that each teacher can add his questions to these exams. Students are, of course, evaluated at the end of a year by written or oral composition exams. If a student fails he is given a second chance in the autumn. If he fails again he stays in grade. Marks are on a one to five scale, with three the passing grade. Those who receive only ones get gold medals. Marks are given four times a year up to the seventh grade and every two terms thereafter. The particular school visited had 830 pupils, of which about 44 were expected to fail. The eighth grade exam is mainly composition and algebra; the eleventh grade exam covers literature, algebra, geometry, foreign language, history, physics and chemistry.

Visit to Classrooms

During a tour of the school, the Director and her assistant spoke proudly of the projects carried out by the students. A ninth grade science project, for example, consisted of a complete planetarium built by the students. A frame had been put up and covered with dark fabric. Inside were benches and a "projecter," consisting of a light bulb inside a sphere full of pin holes. The mechanism allowed the sphere to rotate and to move along a track as well. The lights were switched off and a show was given in which the "stars" were projected around the curved ceiling and moved in the proper relations to each other. They stated that every pinhole was properly placed from celestial diagrams. There was even a Sputnik projected by a little flash light. It was very impressive. (The instructor, pleased that I liked the project, gave me some reprints of his articles on teaching science in schools, inscribing on them "from a Russian school teacher to an American professor.") Many other projects were also exhibited.

The halls contained many charts, and large photographs of outstanding children in each class. The charts showed each child's grades on "cleanliness, appearance and behavior." Behavior meant more than deportment, but also emphasized "the ways of a good communist child." Children were seen sweeping the floors, much as they would be beating erasers in our schools.

In a second grade arithmetic class, taught by a woman, the children sat, spic and span, with eager faces, on double benches. There was much participation, eagerness, and raising of hands. Most of the hour was spent on two problems. One boy recited the problem: "A plant has produced 800 units in three months; 300 units were produced in the first month and 100 in the second month. How many units were produced in the third month?" The second problem was "Somebody bought pictures for 600 rubles, somebody also spent 200 rubles, and somebody else spent 400 rubles. If each picture cost 20 rubles, how many pictures did they buy?" The procedure used in class went something like this: The teacher would ask, "How do we solve the problem?" She asked around the room. "What kind of problem is it?" "Why do we subtract?" "What do you do next?" "What is the main task of the question?" The children then had to verbalize the whole sequence. (One girl asked a question: "They speak in the problem about rubles, yet why do they ask in the question about things?") The emphasis was on classifying the problem, analyzing its components and relating it to other problems, in order to understand the operations involved. (All this fitted into a discussion with educational psychologists later on.)

The warmth of the teachers was impressive, as well as their devotion to and love of children.

LABORATORY OF EDUCATIONAL PSYCHOLOGY,
INSTITUTE OF PSYCHOLOGY

Dr. D. N. Bogoyavlensky, described the work being conducted at the Laboratory of Educational Psychology. Their main aim, he said, is the study of the thinking process in educational settings. Another aim is to determine how learning principles can best be applied in schools. Cooperative arrangements exist with different schools to examine existing practices and try out new ones. They have made studies in ten grades; different studies are in progress on mathematics, physics, foreign languages and other subjects. Bogoyavlensky also referred to a book he had collaborated on with Menchinskaya entitled, *The Psychology of Mastery of Knowledge at School.*

After discussing some theoretical notions of thinking, he referred to the two processes of analysis and synthesis and stressed their importance in the acquisition of scientific knowledge. One of the problems is that pupils do not engage in deep-enough analysis in acquiring knowledge, but resort to immediately obvious cues and overgeneralizations. He referred to this as the first stage of the thinking process—*faulty or superficial generalization* (the primitive stage). To prevent this phenomenon from occurring certain measures must be taken.

One approach is to teach the individual how to obtain knowledge for himself and not just to receive information and concepts passively. The teacher shouldn't show exactly how to solve the problem, but should get the student to analyze each step. He is to separate essentials from non-essentials, to understand how to avoid initially perceived cues which are not central. In pedagogic science it is important to know how to prevent these things. But how? One attempt in progress is to teach students to discriminate between superficially similar and essentially different things. For example, in an early biology class, fruits are discussed. The students are shown real fruit. The teacher doesn't explain, but says "Why are they all fruit? What unites them?" Common responses are, "They are edible. They are tasteful." "You are wrong—cake is also edible." "They grow on trees." "So do leaves." Then they cut the fruit open and find seeds.

The second stage in the development of the thinking process is "true generalization." Even if the student can identify a concept, one can't be certain he understands it until he can show he knows how to apply it in a new situation. This is essentially the problem of "transfer." Giving students the opportunity to solve problems themselves is still not enough. They must be given opportunities to apply the concepts to entirely new situations. The objective here is to avoid making thinking too standard. He stressed the importance of developing *flexible thinking* as early as possible and in as many fields as possible.

Sometimes rigid thinking is due to the very procedures used by

182

teachers. Often the teacher thinks one and the same type of problem must be repeated over and over to have it sink in. This is too narrow a view. Researchers at the Laboratory of Educational Psychology indicated that if the student is to apply his knowledge to an unusual problem, then better results are achieved by a different approach. Here Bogoyavlensky spoke of experimental and control groups. In the experimental group, flexibility procedures were introduced, in the control group the "usual procedures" were used.

Bogoyavlensky described how this was done in teaching grammar. The students were taught two grammar rules. Presumably, this was done using a large number of exercises. The students actually wrote exercises demonstrating these rules, then proceeded to new material. The new material had in common elements of both rules. The students discussed the two rules simultaneously in terms of differences as well as common aspects. The findings indicated that if the two rules are introduced without previous discussion, they actually interfere with correct performance. However, when the rules are thought through together, the "inhibition" disappears. They are sharply differentiated in dealing with new material. The idea is that abilities and habits are developed to differentiate superficially similar things and to generalize only to appropriate situations.

They have also compared children of different levels of ability. The general finding is that the better students profit most from these procedures. ("The procedures are not universally applicable to all.") The question was posed: Is this contrary to the current communist view that all can master knowledge? His answer was that they are very optimistic that this is possible. The problem is finding the best training method to bring all children up to the best level. He said that individual differences are certainly recognized here but that capitalistic countries have overemphasized them. They have special schools for defectives. For normal students of different abilities, a more individual approach is practiced. That is why they are placing so much emphasis on developing abilities early—to find the correct conditions necessary to bring all individuals to high levels.

After this digression he returned to another objective: "The main thing in school is not knowledge for its own sake, but to develop a means of thinking." Thus in such diverse subjects as mathematics, science, language, and literature the ability to analyze, to generalize correctly, to be flexible, should be stressed. He then used as examples the abilities of "concrete abstraction" (in which the question is raised as to whether the student can notice a quality in an object); and "isolative abstraction" (in which the question is "What do these objects have in common?"). Another objective is to see a subject from different points of view (flexibility). Thus certain ideas can be handled geometrically, algebraically, or linguistically. In this way they hope to develop mental ability independently of the content of the subject matter.

Bogoyavlensky then spent a few minutes discussing the "motivation of learning." (The special Laboratory of Upbringing in Moscow is also concerned with this problem and is investigating the social and family conditions related to the motivation to learn.) His laboratory is concerned with stimulating the "desire to know." In other words, how can the problem be made the student's problem. His main finding here: verbal explanation is not too effective. The important thing is the self-activity of the child. Does the problem provide something for the student to think about? Is he brought up against the problem? The idea is to create difficulties for him. The notion that the student shouldn't make a mistake was ridiculed. (He specifically mentioned Skinner.) He said that reforms are being made in schools as rapidly as possible.

The interesting thing is the repeated use of words like rigidity, creativity, flexibility, and originality, and the stated objectives of finding out how to teach these independent of subject content. It is also apparent that they are involved in "student centered" education. This is carried forth further in the Young Pioneer Palaces, which are discussed on the following pages. The discussion with educational psychologists was verified by observations made in the classrooms the previous day.

PIONEER PALACE VISIT

The Pioneer Palace, in Leningrad, picked for my visit was one of the most elaborate in the Soviet Union. It is one of the Czarist palaces turned over "to the children." This Pioneer Palace was founded in 1937 and had more than 300 rooms. It is mainly open from September to May and over 10,000 children use its facilities. The Pioneer Palaces provide extracurricular activities, serving as a combination Y.M.C.A. and Boy Scout organization. Actually, they are an integral part of the Soviet educational system, under the Ministry of Education. The aim is "to develop further the abilities of Soviet children." Other stated objectives: to "fixate knowledge" and to "motivate further learning." The Director himself took the afternoon off to act as personal guide and to explain the work done there.

There are a hundred different kinds of societies or groups which children can join after regular school hours. These include groups in music, art, books, travel, chess, auto mechanics, mathematics, chemistry, etc. In a sense, we see here the double system of education in effect in the Soviet Union. In the schools there is an emphasis on rigid subject matter, although there is frequent individual project work. In the Pioneer Palace, on the other hand, there is more emphasis on the free child-centered approach. There is considerable integration of Pioneer Palace activities with the schools. It was stressed, however, that this is mainly supportive and that there are a variety of different kinds of contacts. However, considerable effort is expended to convince parents and children that Pioneer Palace activity is worthwhile. (Parents must consent before children can join.) The aim is to attract "average children"; the point was made that these programs are not for superior students only. It was also pointed out that Pioneer Palaces were only one form of after-school activity. There were night concerts, evening programs, special cultural clubs, as well as extra curricular clubs in the schools. The attempt is to get all children involved in some extra activity.

Integration of Pioneer Palace functions with school activities takes several forms. The schools, for instance, are kept informed on the child's status and behavior. Also, the age at which children can join certain groups may depend on when a given subject is taught in school. For example, the chemistry group is for seventh graders up; the project "Life in France" is for 12-year-olds who are studying the French language in school. Also, mass programs of physical exercise and ceremonies connected with traditional holidays are developed in the Pioneer Palaces. Recently, a city-wide competition in mathematics and physics was administered here. The Palaces also serve as a training ground for teachers.

Throughout the discussion one sensed the emphasis on education "as a process of engaging the environment and coming to grips with it," the continual interchange of academic and practical experience. More importantly, the objective seems to be to shape the value system of the society to seek knowledge and to be motivated to seek it as a "good Soviet citizen." There is, of course, a good deal of "moral education" throughout with the emphasis on patriotism, self-discipline, and social consciousness. The value placed on such traits as kindness, politeness, respect for others, etc., was also stressed.

Since it was near the close of the school year, there were very few children around. The building was clean, the rooms well-ordered and the facilities outstanding. For example, there were shops for work in aerodynamics, a transportation section with complete models of city electric transit systems, photography facilities, all kinds of communication equipment (radio, telephone), five electric power laboratories, a lab for house painting techniques, etc. One room was used by a group interested in foreign lands. There were magazines from almost everywhere, but apparently none from the United States. In another area a group interested in mechanics was assembling auto-mobiles. Other exhibits showed scale models of mining equipment, construction machinery, etc., all built by high school age students. The art work and painting were very impressive. The Director, a proud and very warm person, was obviously well-liked and respected by the children and staff.

SOME GENERAL OBSERVATIONS

1. One senses everywhere the central role the Soviet people and their government ascribe to their educational system. There appears to be a tremendous commitment to improved education at all levels. One gets the feeling of a government and people polarized toward educational values which they identify directly with the future plans and hopes of their society.

2. The Academy of Pedagogical Sciences is linked directly to the Supreme Soviet, through the Minister of Education. There is no comparable organization in the United States. Besides the Institute of Psychology previously mentioned, other institutes under the Academy are concerned with theory and history of pedagogy, methods of education, esthetic education, handicapped children, physical education and hygiene, and special problems involved in educating more than 50 nationalities within the Soviet Union. Many educators and educational psychologists are deputies to the Supreme Soviet. The lag between educational research and educational policy is thus very short.

3. The Russians claim there is more emphasis on the individual in their educational system than in ours. They feel they are geared to bring every child up to his potential. Teachers are highly motivated and spend considerable time working with students on an individual basis. A statement heard several times was, "We do not have a class-less society after all. There *is* a ruling class under communism—it is the children."

4. One of the most important things noted was the attempt to find ways of teaching *habits of thinking* which will lead to creativity and a "problem solving" attitude. In this connection, there is a direct tie-in with psychologists doing basic research on the thinking process. In fact, the educational psychologist in the U.S.S.R. is very interested in studying the *process* of thinking. Educational techniques are being researched, but very often these are tied in with some theory or some research on the process of thinking.

5. The amount of political indoctrination is, of course, considerable at all levels. It is a pervasive fact of life. The increasing emphasis on nursery schools earlier and earlier in life, and for longer hours, is of significance here. (See other chapters in this volume.) Often the po-

litical indoctrination is under the heading of "moral character development" or "developing social consciousness," important objectives of Soviet education. An intriguing question is whether the increasing emphasis on flexible thinking, creativity, seeking knowledge for its own sake, etc. will eventually clash with established political doctrine.

6. Education and socio-economic status are more highly correlated in the Soviet Union than in the United States. Rewards are more directly tied to educational level. Workers in factories must go to evening schools to progress. Teachers are well paid. Professors are extremely well paid.

7. There is a continuous effort to introduce difficult subjects and more of them, earlier and earlier in the school curriculum. They are finding, even to their own surprise, that children are able to learn such subjects much earlier than was formerly thought possible.

8. There is a great deal of what we (but not the Russians) would call "progressive education"—student-centered education. The Russians are attempting to have their cake and eat it. The rigid curriculum and the rigorous requirements are there, but there is a great deal of effort to involve the student directly. There is a great deal of emphasis on student projects and interest groups. The Pioneer Palaces and other extra-curricular groups, of course, are an integral part of the system and carry this to an extreme. Museums, historical places, exhibitions are full of children on field trips. Consistent with this is the emphasis on relating theory and abstract principles to practical experiences. One of the main challenges expressed was the need to find ways of combining thoretical knowledge with practice.

9. As indicated earlier there is a great deal of experimentation. The very facts of standardized curricula and state jurisdiction make it easy to do experiments with selected schools.

10. Although "aptitude" tests are frowned upon as non-scientific and "based on false notions of innate abilities," achievement tests are used. There are oral or written "essay type" exams to evaluate course completion and also for admission to universities and institutes. In this latter connection, approximately one out of three get into institutes of higher learning.

This chapter has attempted to convey the flavor of what was seen in Soviet industrial and educational psychology. However, as was stressed earlier, these comments need to be fitted in with those of other psychologists making similar visits. The fact that the different chapters in this volume were written by psychologists travelling separately should not be minimized. The common impressions we received are thus more important and can be accepted, perhaps, with greater confidence.

CHAPTER VII

Aspects of Psychology and Psychophysiology in the U.S.S.R.[1]

NEAL MILLER, CARL PFAFFMANN, AND HAROLD SCHLOSBERG

Neal Miller arrived first, on Friday, and was met by Professor A. R. Luria, Professor P. K. Anokhin and O. K. Tikhomirov. Tikhomirov, a candidate for the Doctor of Science degree (roughly the equivalent of an instructor or assistant professor in this country), and a protegé of Luria, was assigned as guide and interpreter. He was most helpful in carrying out the schedule of visits arranged by Professor Luria in Moscow.

Carl Pfaffmann and Harold Schlosberg arrived the following evening and were met by Miller and Tikhomirov at the airport. Inasmuch as Intourist had no record of the itinerary for the visit, Tikhomirov had considerable trouble getting Pfaffmann and Schlosberg into a hotel. (Miller was at the Hotel Ukraine.) Pfaffmann and Schlosberg finally ended up at the Metropole—an old, roomy, ornate hotel, much more conveniently located than the Ukraine. It served as our headquarters while in Moscow. On Sunday, Tikhomirov arranged a tour with a guide and car so that we could see Moscow. On Monday, we started a series of appointments that had been set up by Professor Luria. Everyone was most cordial and helpful. We were greatly impressed with the hospitality extended to us by everyone we met.

---

[1] This chapter is based on the rough notes taken by Neal Miller, Carl Pfaffmann and Harold Schlosberg during visits to various laboratories and institutes from June 6 to June 29, 1960. A single compendium of several impressions and notes was usually made each evening, often on the same day but not more than several days following each visit. Some important work is omitted or inadequately described because it did not happen to fall within the areas of our particular interests and competencies, or because other scheduled events happened to make it impossible to consolidate our notes soon enough after the visit to that particular laboratory. In no sense are these notes to be thought of as an evaluation of Soviet psychology.

Organization of Psychology and Physiology in the U.S.S.R.

We will violate chronological order by starting with the reception given for us in the Academy of Pedagogical Sciences on Tuesday, June 7. This gave us some valuable information on the background and organization of psychology and physiology in the U.S.S.R. Present were A. N. Leontiev, who is Vice-President, and A. P. Luria, who is a member of the Presidium. The Academy of Pedagogical Sciences is responsible for all the research in psychology that is carried out at its various institutes. It is also responsible for a certain amount of publishing. However, it seems to have less direct responsibility for the relatively smaller amount of research done at various universities, although many members of the Academy and of the various institutes may have appointments at universities. The Academy has a budget of fifty million rubles annually, which would be five million dollars at the tourist rate of exchange. It has about 135 full and corresponding members, largely from the Russian republic, but members of some of the other national academies are members of the Russian Academy, so that coordination is accomplished without administrative centralization.

Most research in the U.S.S.R. seems to be done at institutes. In addition to the institutes operated by the Academy of Pedagogical Sciences, others are operated by the Academy of Medical Sciences, Agricultural Sciences, and so forth. The top organization is the U.S.S.R. Academy of Sciences which also operates institutes, some of which have psychologists and physiologists.

Under the Academy of Pedagogical Sciences, there are many institutes, including the Institute of Psychology, of Defectology, of Theory of Education, of General Education, of Industrial Education, of Adult Education, and so forth.

We also learned something about the steps on the academic ladder. What we would call a graduate student works for several years in a laboratory, either of the university department or a research institute. When a thesis is completed, he attains the rank of Candidate, roughly equivalent to our Ph.D. A junior Candidate gets 1700 rubles per month whereas the senior Candidate gets 2500. The title Doctor of Science probably corresponds roughly to our associate professor, and means that the man has become an independent scientist.[2]

---

[2] One of their stock jokes is: "Why are the Candidates' theses so much better than the Doctor's ones?" "Because the Candidates' theses are written by Doctors whereas the Doctoral ones are written by Candidates."

Salaries start around 3500 rubles. The head of an institute or department may get between 4500 and 5000 rubles per month, with a possibility of dual appointments and several other privileges that were not mentioned in detail. (A new law prohibits dual salaries.)
In response to our questions, we obtained the following facts:
1. Leontiev said that the areas in need of further development in psychology were:

A. Medical Psychology.

B. Industrial Psychology. Training in industrially useful skills, similar to Human Engineering (although he didn't use the term), attempts to adjust the machine to the man. Leontiev pointed out that there was no unemployment in the U.S.S.R., and therefore no need for selection tests. Further, they do not believe in group testing. However, he did say there was great need for selection of students, which apparently is done on the basis of teachers' recommendations and oral examinations.

C. Psychopharmacology. He agreed that it was important, but there were not enough people to work on it. Some work was just getting started but he doubted that it would be pursued actively by psychologists.

When asked about expansion of training of psychologists, he said they had had too many verbal or armchair psychologists and they needed more experimental psychologists. The main problem now is improving the quality rather than the quantity.

Leontiev estimated very roughly that 100 Candidates in Psychology are turned out per year in Moscow, 100 in Leningrad and 50 outside of these two cities. Other estimates suggest a lower total number, 30 to 50 per year. For example, Smirnoff estimates that the 10 to 15 graduate students in the Institute of Psychology represent 10 to 15 per cent of all the graduate students in the Soviet Union. Since the program for the Candidate is three years, this would give a total annual output of 30 to 35. H. Pick, who was a graduate student in psychology for a year in Moscow, agrees with this lower estimate. When queried about applications of psychology, Leontiev noted that institutes are for research, but much of their work is done in hospitals and industrial situations which filters down to practical applications. Thus Luria's department does research on brain function and behavior, but all patients now in the hospital at which the institute is located were being screened by his unit, which he likened to that of Hans-Lukas Teuber. Apparently no patients are admitted to brain surgery until one of Luria's staff has given them an examination. Furthermore, the institutions in the provinces have a relatively much greater proportion of service to research functions. Students trained at the Research Institutes go out to work and make practical applications in these outlying institutions.

2. Leontiev pointed out that there are two major lines or trends in Russian psychology from an historical standpoint. Both of them stem from the physiologist, Sechenov. One line runs through Pavlov to modern physiology or physiological psychology, of which E. N. Sokolov is a representative (see below). Another line goes through Vigotsky and stresses the developmental-historical-sociological factors in behavior. There are other individual trends, such as the interest in "set" in Georgia (see below).

3. A subsequent conversation stressed the "second signal system," which Luria succinctly said was "speech." However, it is not purely motor or verbal speech, but rather the culturally derived meanings and concepts that are characteristic of human beings. Much research in psychology is devoted to this subject. However, Luria related with considerable amusement the naive idea that one could distinguish between physiology and psychology by assigning the basic Pavlovian conditioning, or first signal system, to the physiologist, leaving the second signal system for psychologists.

INSTITUTE OF PSYCHOLOGY

The whole institute has a total of about 70 professional people, 20 assistants, and about 10 to 15 graduate students, making a total of 100 plus some visiting scientists. The Director is A. A. Smirnov. About 15 per cent of the psychological graduate students in the U.S.S.R. are at the Institute.

There are two ways to become a scientist in the Soviet Union:

1. Via post-graduate training at the university.

2. By becoming a *laborantum* (which is a higher level of technician after graduation from the university.

The number of students is variable. Smirnov, in reply to a question, pointed out that clinical psychology is largely in the medical school; some of this, however, was done by Luria and A. N. Leontiev. He also pointed out that the Russian Psychological Association is primarily for research workers, not for those who apply psychology as a profession.

Laboratory of Psychophysiology

This laboratory, which is seven years old, is well equipped with devices such as electronic counters, adequate EEG and polygraph equipment, audio signal generators, adaptometers, automatic visual perception projector, and several dark rooms. In addition to the Director, B. M. Teplov, there are eight people, all of whom have desks in the same room. There are also two students working toward the

Candidate's degree. The laboratory's basic research problem is the study of individual differences in relation to Pavlov's types of nervous system. These types are based on three factors:

1. Strength of excitation and inhibition.
2. Mobility of excitation and inhibition.
3. Equilibrium of excitation and inhibition.

Most of the work has been done on the first of these factors, some on the second and very little on the third. The presentations of the research problems were all phrased in rather similar formulae. Some of the specific experiments in progress are:

Conditioning of Light Adaptation. The conditioned stimulus, a sound, is turned on for five seconds and then paired with a light for an additional ten seconds, both of them going off at the end of this period. After such training, the conditioned stimulus alone will produce an increase in the threshold to light equivalent to about twenty to forty per cent of that normally produced by the unconditional stimulus. In an individual with a "strong nervous system" the conditioned decrease in sensitivity will survive ten paired presentations under massed practice (two minute intervals). On the other hand, an individual with a "weak nervous system" shows considerable extinction under such massed practice.

Caffeine has also been used to determine the strength of the nervous system. The threshold for light or sound is not affected by caffeine in people with a strong nervous system, but there is a marked change in those with a weak nervous system.

The Orienting Reaction. This is measured in a dark room by changes which auditory stimulation produces in the EEG, GSR and breathing. The extinction (and size) of the orienting reaction probably depends on the equilibrium of E and I rather than the strength of either. Subjects with dominant E have more orienting reactions and slower extinction than do those in whom I is dominant.

A Short Method for Measuring the Relative Strength of E and I in Reaction Time. The curve which relates reaction time to stimulus strength (auditory stimulus) is relatively flat for those who are weak in E, whereas those with strong nervous systems show a steeper slope. These results were based on 20 Ss. When questioned about the probable distribution with a larger sample of subjects, the investigator thought that the distribution would be normal, rather than bimodal, i.e. "types" represent the extremes of a distribution.

Another experiment was reported at this time using forty Ss with twenty-one measures on each. A factor analysis yielded a high correlation on the first factor, "Strength of Nervous System," equivalent to somewhere between .40 and .60, but we were unable to find out exactly how this was computed. Another factor was found in these tests, with high loading on the orienting response, which was presumably "Equilibrium of E and I." (Some reports on this work were given at the 14th International Congress at Montreal.)

An Effort to Measure Mobility. Dr. B. Kh. Gurevitch exposed a series of letters in a projection tachistoscope with the instructions, "Don't respond to X after K." The negative instructions produce an inhibition which may last, in sluggish individuals, as much as ten seconds, measured by longer reaction time to letters appearing within this period. Mobile subjects may lose the inhibitory effect in one or two seconds, and may also show a reversal or induction effect. They were also studying other problems, such as the effect of positive stimuli, shorter time intervals between stimuli, and reversal of instructions after S's reaction measures had reached an asymptote.

Measurement of the Adequate Optical Chronaxie (the time required for seeing a light stimulus of twice the threshold intensity). This is believed to be a measure of mobility. Exposures were made by a pendulum, somewhat like that of the Dodge pendulum photochronograph. The chronaxie ranged between 75 and 105 milliseconds. Those values correlated .64 with critical flicker fusion. They are now running 50 subjects with 21 different measures of mobility to be factor analyzed.

Laboratory of Higher Neural Dynamics

This laboratory was founded in 1954. The Director, E. I. Boyko, was out of town at the time of our visit.

In this laboratory five people are working on complex processes, based on Pavlov's first and second signal systems. They are attempting to apply laws of animal conditioned reactions to people and to discover additional, peculiarly human laws. They have a large reaction panel and visual display panel providing stimuli and reactions of various degrees of complexity, ranging from simple reaction time to those involving thinking and problem solving.

Laboratory of Child Development

In addition to the Director, Dr. A. V. Zaporozhets, there were five Candidates (two without degrees, and three post-graduate students) in this laboratory. They described some examples of their work and findings.

When a young child is first presented with a new situation, his exploration is chaotic. After repeated presentations, each signal elicits not only its own orienting activity, but also anticipatory orientation to the next signal. They interpret this as objective evidence that the child has acquired imagery. The fact that entrance into blinds of a maze becomes progressively shorter on later trials is additional evidence for images. The main function of the orienting response is to form images. Children with strong orienting responses learn and transfer better.

As children grow up they seem to pass through three stages of learning a maze:

1. The youngest child can't benefit much by visual inspection, but has to carry out gross trial-and-error, even after he sees the maze. This seems to be due to two factors: first, the child can't learn from inspection, and secondly, he is forced by curiosity to explore the maze.

2. Somewhat older children can learn from visual inspection.

3. Finally, still older children can learn from verbal instructions.

These researchers didn't like our standard tests because different children can achieve the same result in quite different ways. Our tests, they feel, show nothing about the process of the child's problem solving, which they believe to be most important for remedial training.

Laboratory of Speech and Thinking

This laboratory, under the direction of A. N. Sokolov, is devoted to electrophysiological recording of silent speech responses. Records are made from under the tongue, and from surface electrodes on the lips, larynx and jaw. Recording was from a shielded room. Sokolov had two 4-channel EEGs with ink writers, cathode ray oscilloscopes, and magnetic tape-recorder. With auxiliary equipment, he can read both frequency and amplitude directly and can also integrate, analyze or count.

There is a marked increase in general muscular activity of the vocal apparatus at the start of inner speech. Silent reading of foreign texts shows more activity than one gets from native material, but the activity falls off again if the material is so difficult that S gives up.

In silent counting there is a reduction in activity as one repeats the easy task of counting forward, but less with repetition of the difficult task of counting backward. There seems to be a general law in mental activity—effort or activity decreases with practice. There is also more activity with high interest and effort. One gets the same type of results from recording during listening. But the discussion brought out the idea that such increases in activity were largely specific to the speech mechanism in verbal thinking; that is, there was not a general increase in the activity of the whole body unless the S was under emotional stress. Furthermore, the tongue works with the hand in writing. The same seems to be true for nonverbal perception. A book, *Psychology in the Soviet Union* (now being translated), includes a paper based on a speech by Sokolov, summarizing this work. He is beginning to apply cybernetics and communication theory to his research. In a later discussion Sokolov agreed:

1. That all inner speech need not be vocal; it may be central.
2. In reply to the question as to whether the visual image belongs under the second signal system, he said "Perhaps," but added that he was not an expert on this question. He also objects to the simple motor theory of Watson.

DIVISION OF PSYCHOLOGY AND HIGHER NERVOUS ACTIVITY,
BIOLOGICAL DEPARTMENT, MOSCOW UNIVERSITY
Laboratory of E. N. Sokolov

E. N. Sokolov is considered to be a psychologist who is also trained in neurophysiology. His general program combines physiological studies of the nervous system, using EEG and other electrophysiological measures in animals (both acute and chronic), for comparison with studies of the same phenomena in man, using vascular, motor, and EEG responses.

Researches include: (a) Sensory processes, emphasizing dynamic properties in the waking and responding organism. (b) Orienting response and conditioning.

His laboratory is very well equipped, including three 4-channel EEGs and two Grey Walter Analyzers, as well as integrators, cathode ray oscilloscopes, cameras, electric counters, Leeds and Northrup-type recording potentiometers, acoustic signal generators, and so forth. He has adequate assistance, including four technicians (two of whom have fairly good electronics training), and one man with a higher level of electronics training.

Relationship Between Orienting Reflex and Arousal. The basic situation for human subjects is a reaction time setup, in which the subject is told to press a key as soon as he hears a sound. (Incidentally, it took a little questioning to discover that this was what he meant by "conditioned reflex"; the Soviets seem to use the term conditioned reflex for any type of SR relationship, and usually make no distinction as to how it was set up.) The orienting reflex was recorded by eye movements, GSR and breathing, and the arousal response by the EEG. Correlation between physiological arousal and orienting response is high so that these are considered signs of the same response pattern. All appear in the early stages of establishing the CR, and all tend to drop out with further practice and habituation.

Parallel studies with the dog utilize recording from ear muscles for the orienting response and EEG as a measure of arousal. The electrodes for EEG were put into different parts of the dog's brain under direct visual control, by the window technique developed in the Brain Institute, which will be described later in this report. Essentially the same results were obtained from animals as from man.

After habituation to a single tone, a change of 50 cycles will evoke the orienting response. This can be used to get pitch DL in dogs. Nembutal will raise this DL to ten times its normal value.

He also found that if two tones are presented separately until habituation occurs to both of them singly, the two when presented together as a pattern will evoke the response. Similarly, if habituation occurs to a sequence of tones, and then one component is omitted, the orienting reflex will be evoked. From the response to omission of a tone, he concludes that some form of sensory integration and comparison must be involved. Thus the orienting reflex is elicited by any failure of the stimulus to comply with the animal's "expectations."

Under light anesthesia and sleep the dog will respond with the orienting response only to his name. Other louder but meaningless stimuli are not effective. In this case, cortical arousal *precedes* subcortical activity, showing that the subcortical reticular formation is not the sole mechanism for the orienting response.

They theorize that habituation is due to the build-up of inhibition which outlasts the excitatory effect of each stimulus. Sokolov suggested a relationship to the concept of reactive inhibition of Hull. In other words, each stimulus starts a self-inhibiting process by feedback which grows while the stimulus continues. Eventually this inhibitory feedback becomes conditioned to the cue being habituated. Evidence for this is the late appearance of sleep waves in the EEG to a habituated stimulus after the initial evoked response has occurred.

Photic Driving. Sokolov believes this to be primarily a nonspecific effect of the reticular formation rather than one in the specific cortical sensory system.

1. Driving is influenced by the orienting response. The subjective report is not so affected.

2. The driving response follows the level of activation or excitement.

3. The driven response is more stable subcortically than in the cortex.

4. Alpha harmonics (as seen by the Grey Walter Analyzer). When the EEG indicates that the S is aroused, one gets more high harmonics above the rate of the photic driving stimulus; when the S is drowsy,

one gets more low harmonics. This change is not associated with any change in subjective report.

Sensory Reflexes. There is a change in the electroretinogram with the orienting response. This is an effect of the unspecific system on the retina. Sokolov believes in applying the reflex concept to sensory processes, with a feedback to the receptor itself. This concept of sensory reflexes is a general principle; thus the receptor process may be conditioned (compare conditioned visual adaptation in Teplov's laboratory, above).

Sokolov described another technique, very specific pickup by concentric electrodes insulated except on the tip. The laboratories shown to us by Sokolov are very well equipped, mostly with Russian-made equipment. The experiments and data are good. Sokolov is well informed. He seems to have an excellent laboratory by any standards.

Laboratory for Phylogenetic Study of Higher Nervous Activity

This laboratory, under the direction of L. G. Voronin, has excellent equipment crowded into a number of rooms. The following experiments were discussed:

1. Specific evoked responses from reptiles up to higher animals. Here, both the form and the polarity are the same throughout.

2. The olfactory system may be activated by visual and auditory stimuli. Veronin believes that the midbrain reticular system is distinct from the olfactory arousal system. Therefore, there are two arousal systems.

3. Phylogenetic study of the reticular response and conditioning. Here, essentially the same phenomena are found from birds to the higher mammals.

INSTITUTE OF PEDIATRICS, Clinic of Child Development

This Institute, under the direction of Professor N. M. Schelovanov, is part of the Academy of Medical Sciences. It deals with both the experimental and clinical study of normal as well as abnormal children. The Institute now has 200 beds. As soon as the new wing is completed it will have 500 beds and much more laboratory space.

In addition to research on children, much work is conducted on cats and dogs in an effort to improve diagnosis and treatment. Experiments include:

1. The effect of damage during pregnancy or birth which might be produced by endocrine disorder in the mother (stress, asphyxia, birth trauma, etc.). A particularly important problem seems to be the effects of attempted and unsuccessful abortion on the embryo, typically using quinine.

2. A special interest in the neonate, for it is easy to analyze the mechanisms of the CR in the young.

3. Development of movements, emotion, speech, sleep and waking. They have a wealth of data from 40 years of research. The conditioned reflexes they study are sucking, defense (eyelid), and the orienting reflex (anticipatory movements of the eye and head). Only a few receptors will give conditioning before one month. Smell and taste work in two months. At three months, discrimination develops. For example, a DL for sound cannot be obtained before three months. By six months, the child can discriminate halftones and can do well with colors. This shows that the analytic function of the cortex is rather well developed at six months; "Therefore," they say, "education should start early!"

A typical experiment uses either light, sound, smell or taste for the conditioned stimulus. The eye-blink to the unconditioned stimulus, an airpuff, is recorded by a microphone on the nose. The response to food is recorded by a pneumatic system on a nursing bottle. Typically the conditioned stimulus lasts for three seconds and then continues paired with unconditioned stimulus for ten seconds, with a one minute intertrial interval.

Attempts at conditioning to sound have been started on the eleventh day, but the CR develops only by the fourth week. Another type of CR uses labyrinthine stimuli as CS. By the seventh day, the infant will show a conditioned feeding reaction when held in the nursing position.

At two or three months vision is dominant, so the subject is distracted by shadows. Therefore, they use a dome-shaped box that gives a uniformly illuminated visual field when they wish to study the orienting response. This is elicited by throwing a spot of light on the dome and recording either the eye or head movements. (The latter is done with an ingenious swivel support to hold the head.) Thus they can study the development of space perception which they think seems innate. At birth, coordinate eye movements occur in the dark but break up when there is a visual field. By two months, coordinated following is acquired for simple objects, but complex objects requiring convergence may take six months.

Schelovanov, who was trained at the Bechterev Institute, commented that movement CRs are easier to control than the secretory CRs. We also saw another set-up with multiple unit recorders to get movement as well as vegetative reflexes. A Chinese professor from Shanghai was studying certain effects with this equipment.

Doctor Kistiakovaia was studying the development of movement. For example, there were photographs of the hand, grasping an object, from zero to six months; in the one-month-old, the act is very slow. She "explains" left or right-handedness as a result of practice. They seem to have tried to develop left-handedness in children by favoring the left hand in early life, but found that it disappeared very early when the training was discontinued and the child met a normal right-handed environment. They see no disturbance produced by changing dominance. Emphasis here, as elsewhere in the U.S.S.R., is obviously on learning rather than heredity.

In addition to the behavorial work, they have done extensive work on the capillary system in the brain. Dr. Kosofsky is chief of the laboratory for brain development. Apparently the cerebrospinal fluid participates in the nourishment of brain cells during early development, but not later on. Incidentally, they do not believe that asphyxia is less damaging to the neonate than to the adult.

DEPARTMENT OF PSYCHOLOGY, UNIVERSITY OF MOSCOW
Laboratory of Professor Leontiev

Professor Leontiev observed that human audition is profoundly affected by social training in speech. Past studies show little correlation between pure pitch discrimination, as measured by the classical DL, and musical ability. Because of the role of timbre in speech, he studied pitch perception in tones of different timbre. For example, when the sounds "E" and "O" are sounded at the same pitch, E is judged higher by a large number of subjects, showing the importance of timbre in pitch discrimination.

Pitch and timbre tests divide people into three groups: 20 per cent show the same threshold for pitch despite variations in timbre, 50 per cent show that variations in timbre elevate the pitch threshold by a factor of two, and the remaining 30 per cent show a 20 to 30 fold increase in pitch threshold.

The ability to discriminate pitch, in the presence of variations in timbre, did correlate highly with the ability to sing a note that matched a tone, while conventional tests of pure pitch discrimination did not. Training by a passive discrimination method improved performance only for the specific timbres involved. Even after training on several timbres, there was little transfer. But it was possible to teach subjects to judge pitch and timbre independently by training them to discriminate by intonation training (a type of singing). Training on a few notes transferred to all frequencies. Comparable effects were produced when the subjects were trained to control frequency in the presence of timbre variations, by hand pressure on a key. But the pitch discrimination of such Ss could be disturbed if they were using their hand for writing during the test.

Leontiev then went on to discuss this general area still further. He pointed out that each sensory system depends on its motor effects. Thus there is no pure sensory attribute of pitch, but it is learned through the characteristics of language. If speech in a given language is tonal, then the person can make good tonal discriminations. On the other hand, a person who speaks a language which is articulatory is better at timbre discrimination. This distinction can be observed in those who learned Indo-European languages as against those who learned Chinese or Vietnamese.

B. Zeigarnick's Clinical Research Department

Dr. B. Zeigarnik, who has long been well known for her early work with Lewin, has three psychology research associates (two of whom have finished their thesis). Recently, she had a seminar of 70 clinical psychologists from all over Russia, including nearly all the psychologists who work in Russian hospitals. She herself works in clinical psychology from the standpoint of pure psychology. Her organization is a research institute and her major area is schizophrenia and hypertensive psychoses. The main researches include:

1. Therapy involving comparison of the patient before and after treatment. One of her interests concerns what happens to professional ability during mental illness. She pointed out the usefulness of her work, although she is engaged in pure science. In such evaluation she uses many tests such as the Vigotski, the Rorschach and records of speech.

In reply to our question, she suggested that therapy is mostly by drugs, but told us we should ask a psychiatrist, since psychologists do no therapy. But psychologists may use work and education as an aid to recovery, as for example, reeducation in aphasia. (She has a course in psychopathology for fourth and fifth year students, who take a practicum with her.)

2. Destruction of thinking and emotion, particularly in schizophrenia of children.

Different types of destruction of thought processes studied here included:

(a) Loss of concepts or abstraction. Classification by concrete attributes (i.e. color, not animal versus vegetable). These people don't understand proverbs. The loss of concepts is related to epilepsy and also to deep tumors. Schizophrenics show broad classification and loose association.

(b) Dynamics of the loss of conception. They seem to have no goal. This is characteristic of the arteriosclerotic person.

(c) Impairment of will. This is characteristic of frontal lobe lesion.

(d) Specific losses which are not regressions, in a Freudian sense.

SECHENOV INSTITUTE OF PHYSIOLOGY

Dr. P. K. Anokhin is Chief of this Institute, which is under the Academy of Medical Sciences. He is interested in studying integrative mechanisms, but definitely goes beyond Sherrington (see his book, *Reports on the Problem of Center and Periphery in the Physiology of Nervous Activity*, 1935, Gorki; State Publishing House, Moscow).

Return Afferentation. Anokhin's basic idea is that a functional system is a dynamic system set up for adaptive results, utilizing feedback. For example, if one picks up a pencil, the feedback from visual and tactual receptors is of extreme importance. He says that the return afferentation completes (in the sense of sanctions or closes or verifies) the act.

Problem of Systemogenesis. Work on the ontogenesis of functional systems was begun in an embryogenetic laboratory in 1935. Here, researchers are attempting to correlate the morphological with the physiological functions on amphibians, birds, mammals and man. (230 human embryos, premature babies from three to eight months after conception, have been studied.)

The grasping reflex is the earliest response they have observed, presumably because of the importance to the newborn primate of clinging to the mother. The motor nerve to the flexor develops and is myelinated first, along with the corresponding cells in the spinal cord. The development of one system ahead of others in the same neural tracts and nerves is called "hetero-chronic development."

The same thing is true for all links of the sucking reflex. The first fibers to myelinate in the facial-motor nerve (cranial #7) are those supplying the sucking muscles. The nerve, as a whole, does not develop at a given time, but only certain fibers which are part of a specific functional system. He calls this systemogenesis, as contrasted with organogenesis.

To study sucking response, a special bottle was used to present milk or one other test solution alternately by a stopcock to the nipple. The responses were recorded via a tube to a tambour. When shifting from milk to a noxious agent, the sucking stops in one-half second, even before the child has had any experience with natural sucking. However, after eight days nursing from the mother, the defense reaction, i.e. stopping nursing, takes five seconds. This is due to the fact that the infant has developed a conditioned response during nursing so that the touch of the nipple and fluid on the tongue is the conditioned stimulus for nursing. It takes some time for the bad taste to inhibit sucking. By appropriate recording the latencies of the various senses involved were tested. Touch and temperature have a relatively short latency, whereas taste has a much longer delay. Thus in normal nourishing, there is an interval between CS (touch of the tongue), and US (taste), which is an adequate temporal sequence for establishing a conditioned reflex.

Another example of systemogenesis has been found in the crow and chicken. The earliest signs of development in the spinal cord are in the cervical region for crows, but in the lumbar region for chicks, since chickens have to stand up and walk from hatching. There are some other interesting early developments in the crow, such as the early development of that portion of the organ of Corti which corresponds to the spectrogram of the mother's cry. Analysis of the early feeding reaction (for which there is early developing innervation) in the crow shows that the response of gaping is due to three factors: (1) the mother's cry, (2) the air breeze on the back of the baby's neck produced by the mother's wing, and (3) bouncing of the nest. These summate, as can be shown in experiments in which all three (artificially produced by clever gadgets) give a shorter reaction time for gaping than does any one of the three. The musculature and innervation of the mouth, neck, legs, and tail (all of which participate in this act of gaping), are parts of the same system, and mature early. (Note that this is opposed to Coghill's principle of cephalo-caudal development.)

Another exception to cephalo-caudal development is found in the guinea pig, where hopping (in which the front legs are useless) is an early reaction. In this stage, one bundle of spinal fibers is developed ahead of the others, with myelinization following in the same order.

Anastomosis of Nerves. Another research effort involved anastomosis between the vagus and the radial nerves in the dog. After recovery from the surgical procedure, when a certain area of the skin is stroked, the animal will cough· Similarly, pinching the muscles in the leg produces vomiting, a specific response. Thus there is no modification of central function when the peripheral connections are changed. Anokhin criticized Weiss for his experiments on amblystoma and his concept of resonance of the center and the periphery. We saw the dog cough when stroked, and discussed some of the details of the operation.

In another experiment, he produced an anastomosis between the phrenic and the lingual nerves. The taste buds regenerated, but he didn't test for function by electrical recording. The lingual nerve showed respiratory rhythm in tongue movements, but no salivary secretion. However, electrical stimulation of the nerve produced salivation. Therefore the *pattern* of the nerve discharge is important for synaptic transmission to the effector.

Relation of Reticular Formation to Cortex. Another area of work involves the use of micro-electrodes for investigating the reticular formation and its relations to the cortex. Anokhin believes that generalized or nonspecific ascending activation is an artifact of electrical stimulation; he believes that natural stimuli produce more specific responses.

Furthermore, if two different systems (such as feeding and defense) are both widely represented on the cortex, wide-spread desynchronization by activating either system may be obtained, although the detailed connections of each system are specific.

That something like this occurs can be shown by establishing a defense and a feeding CR in the same rabbit. Administration of electric shocks produces prolonged desynchronization and the rabbit will not eat. Injection of chlorpromazine slowly restores EEG so that desynchronization to situational stimuli is lost. Then, if food is presented, the rabbit will eat, but there is a strong desynchronization to food. Anohkin maintains that the two desynchronizations must be different because one accompanies defense which inhibits eating and the other accompanies eating.

Similarly, all narcotics block the waking center, but have different effects on other parts. of the reticular formation. For example, urethane will cause sleep but does not reduce the defense response. Conversely, chlorpromazine reduces defense and alerting, but does not induce sleep. Thus a central problem is to determine how generalized desynchronization is able to activate specific systems.

Cortical Potentials as a Function of Age. This work was conducted on a baby rabbit by a Daghestan girl named Fatima. Instead of the usual shielded room, the baby rabbit was in a small drawer in the recording table, adequately protected by foam rubber. It was a very handy arrangement.

At birth the rabbit shows only the negative component of cortical evoked potentials, produced by stimulation of the sciatic nerve. On the eleventh day, the positive component comes in. In a fifteen-day-old rabbit, urethane removes the negative wave. Explanation: the first fibers to develop are horizontal surface ones from the nonspecific system. Later, fibers develop from specific thalamic nuclei to the lower layers of the cortex and produce the surface-positive wave. Urethane "knocks out" the surface fibers, leaving only the positive wave.

Physiology of the Conditioned Response.[3] Anohkin stresses the

---

[3] See in English, P. K. Anokhin, *New Conception of the Physiological Architecture of the Conditioned Reflex.* (International Symposium on Brain Mechanisms and Behavior, Montevideo.) Edition of First Sechenov Medical Institute, Moscow, 1959.

role of sensory feedback in the conditioned response. He believes that the CS comes to evoke an afferent integration of all the stimulation which habitually follow it. If this stimulation actually occurs, the congruity serves to reinforce the whole conditioned response; if not, the interference tends to produce extinction. He has demonstrated this in an experiment in which the dog has two food dishes: CS_1 is reinforced by meat in the first food dish, and CS_2 is reinforced by bread in the second food dish. After this is thoroughly established, putting bread in the meat dish, and vice-versa, causes obvious signs of disturbance. The dog looks from one dish to the other. The actual sensory feedback is incongruent with the conditioned afferent integration.

Further evidence for the complexity of the CR is derived by having the dog stand in a device which records the weight on all four legs when he is trained to raise a single leg in a defensive CR reinforced by electric shock· The first response to the CS is a change in posture, after which the dog is able to lift his leg without being thrown off balance.

Quality of Equipment. We saw at least eight EEGs, some up to 17 channels, including both polygraph and EEG, with associated CRO. Equipment was mostly French (Alvar) and Danish. The most striking thing was a prototype (Russian made) inkwriter that responded up to 1,000 cycles. Its speed could be increased further by built-in multispeed tape storage unit, which effectively makes the limit of recording that of the grain of the tape, for the tape can be played back at slow speeds.

INSTITUTE OF NEUROSURGERY

This is a unique institution in that it has 400 beds, all devoted to brain lesions. Difficult cases from throughout the U.S.S.R. are sent here, and from seven to ten operations on the brain are performed per day. The major research with which the Laboratory (under the direction of Professor Luria) is concerned is localization of function in the cortex by strictly psychological methods. In the Neuropsychological Laboratory, one goal is pure science, the other is to improve diagnosis.

Functional Qualitative Analysis of Deficits. When there is a local lesion, all functions suffer, but they suffer differentially. Furthermore, performance on a given task may be impaired by two lesions, but the same end result may have been produced by different deficits, which require different types of remedial, compensatory training. For example, in writing, the following things happen (depending on the location of the lesion):

1. Temporal lobe damage makes it impossible for people to differentiate phonemes; there is very poor acoustical analysis.

2. If the lesion is a bit further forward in the lower somatosensory motor area, patients don't articulate well. This is a motor deficit, but it interferes with the perception of speech.

3. Lesions in the occipital-parietal region disturb spatial relationships, yielding reversals and transpositions, as well as trouble with all sorts of relationships.

4. Lesion to the premotor area produces perseverative errors.

5. Lesions in the frontal area produce perseverative deficits in visual tasks, which are only quasivisual. For example, when given a sequence x, x, x, o to copy, he will copy it x, x, x, x.

Luria makes similar analyses of reading, thinking, and perception. He holds that:

1. Goldstein's alleged primary law of abstraction in cortical damage is actually secondary, resulting from specific losses in primary functions.

2. Hemispheric dominance is relative, which may result in partial loss of specific functions when one region on a given side is damaged.

Thus a detailed analysis of the specific defects of a patient is essential before his reeducation is started, so that other functions can be substituted for damaged ones. For example, a patient with specific acoustical defects is taught with the aid of diagrams (and in front of a mirror) to substitute visual cues. First, the patient might be said to have substituted lip reading for hearing. Later, the process becomes short circuited so that he can write from dictation with his eyes closed.

Frontal Lesions Affect Relationships Between First and Second Signal Systems. Contrary to his original expectation, Luria [4] found that Pavlov's theory of types did not prove useful in differential diagnosis of functional losses from localized brain damage. More fruitful was a study conducted by O. K. Tikhomirov (who was our guide). Since speech is so important, he studied the relation of the second to the first signal system. In a two-year-old child, speech will initiate behavior, but may not stop it. For example, if a child is given verbal instructions to press a reaction key to a red light, but not to a green one, he will tend to press both. At three years he will make the discrimination verbally (by saying "press" or "don't press" appropri-

---

[4] A. R. Luria, *Rehabilitation of Brain Function after War Trauma*, Pergamon, London.

A. R. Luria, *Higher Cortical Function in Man*, Grove Press, N. Y.

A. R. Luria, *Regulatory Role of Speech in Development and Pathology*, Pergamon Press, London. See also Macy Foundation Conf., 1960.

ately), but when instructed to combine verbal with manual responses he will continue pressing both the red and green lights. At a somewhat later age, speech really does begin to control behavior, so the child will not press when he says "don't press."

Dr. E. D. Khomskaia is applying this technique to find out which lesions disturb the relationship between the first and second signal systems. She performs three different sorts of tests:

1. Manual discrimination reaction time to two lights presented in rapid succession.
2. Verbal reactions to the same series of lights.
3. Combination of manual and verbal reactions.

In this experiment some verbal control is maintained by all except frontal lobe cases in which the verbal control is almost gone, that is, words and actions seem independent. He may say "yes" or "no," as is proper for the stimulus, but react by pressing the key every trial.

Parietal cases may make errors in responding directly to the lights, but verbal responses will markedly decrease the errors. Professor Luria's theory of frontal lobe function is that it has to do with preliminary integration of stimuli, feedback, and integration and control, particularly of restraint of behavior by one's own speech.

Another related line of research is the study of the orienting reflex measured by EEG, GSR, or plethysmograph to repeated stimuli, such as two tones of different pitch presented in random sequence. Responses thereto normally adapt. But when it has reached an asymptote, showing complete adaptation, the task is changed so that subject is to respond by discriminating the stimuli, calling each stimulus either "high" or "low." The orienting reflex immediately returns and persists until the subject is allowed to drop the discrimination task, whereupon it adapts to its old level. As a control, the S can be asked to delay his report but the reflex will appear immediately to the tones, indicating that it is elicited by the task of discriminating rather than by the vocal response.

Frontal lobe cases, doing this task, will show habituation in spite of the request for a discriminative response. A cerebellar tumor may give intracranial pressure and other symptoms of a frontal lobe tumor, but the subject will not habituate while discriminating. The frontal lobe case, on the other hand, doesn't even show a GSR to an error, either in the above test, or in counting. From this comes the idea that the frontal lobe is a preliminary organizer of behavior.

Luria believes that, as a basic principle, the correction of behavior by speech is the first step in control of voluntary behavior.

PHYSIOLOGICAL LABORATORY OF THE U.S.S.R. ACADEMY OF SCIENCES

In addition to some work on the CR, which we will discuss later,

207

there is a great deal of work on the general neurophysiology of the recovery of function after damage, especially to the CNS, which has been in progress for 25 years. For example, much work has been done on semi-section of the cord and the medulla at various levels. The semi-section may be done in any plane. The same animal may also have partial denervation or removal of the legs. Lesions are also produced in the brain stem. Then the recovery is followed. One important question is the role of the cortex in recovery of function. This is studied phylogenetically from frog to dog.

After recovery, they may remove one hemisphere of the cortex and find that recovery is lost. The animal recovers again, by way of the other hemisphere, but when the second hemisphere is removed, there is no recovery over a period of five years. In one-sided operations, the side of the lesion matters only with regard to asymmetrical functions, as of an arm or leg. After decortication, reflex activity is possible, but there is no voluntary activity.

Using electrodes (including micro-electrodes), activity in damaged areas during recovery is studied. The effects of decortication in six-month-old puppies are milder than in adults, and there is better recovery. The same differences are found in phylogeny; the lower the animal the less are the effects and the more rapid the recovery. Such animal experiments have relevance for brain surgery in man, particularly in relation to the vital centers of the medulla.

The Director of the Laboratory, Dr. E. A. Asratian, citing the work of Windle, stated that another group in his laboratory is studying different ways of stimulating central nervous system regeneration.

Dr. Asratian has a book of lectures to the British Royal Academy, for which Dr. Corson in the United States is trying to obtain funds to translate. (Dr. Corson is also trying to obtain funds to translate one of Anokhin's books.)

Role of Cortex in UR. This is a study of the neural and humoral control of salivary, gastric and tendon reflexes. One cortex is extirpated and the results in symmetrical organs are compared—one side is a normal "control," and the other side is the "experimental" side. With unpaired organs, it is necessary to remove both hemispheres and to use another dog as a control. In general the reflexes remain, but are weaker. Bilateral removal has a similar effect with common or bilateral responses and it also eliminates differential responses of digestive secretion to sham feeding of bread versus meat versus milk.

The cortex also controls the adjustment to mild blood loss—thus the decorticated dog dies more easily as the result of injury. In addition to weakening responses, decortication also increases fatigue and disturbs the adjustment of reflexes. On the other hand, actions initiated by humoral agents are potentiated by cortical removal, just as they are with denervation. That is, after the operation, a small amount of adrenalin raises the blood pressure much more than before. His scheme of the organization of the nervous system is essentially the loop system, in which successively higher centers control the lower ones. Thus the cortex is part of the unconditioned reflex pathway as well as of the CR pathway.

Switching. Much work has been done on setting up two different CRs and analyzing the factors which support them. For example, a dog may be taught to respond to a bell followed two or three seconds later by food in one room, but in a different room he may be forced to make a delay of one minute. This is said to indicate two types of response: a tonic one with the phasic one superimposed. The room determines the tonic response, and the CS signal seems to release the phasic response, depending on what tonic response is being maintained at the time.

It is possible to set up a flexion CR in different legs in separate rooms, that is in one room the right leg may be flexed, and in the other room, the left leg. When in a given room, there is a tonic discharge in the motor area of the ipsilateral leg; that is, the one that is not to be shocked. They didn't fully understand this. (Harold Schlosberg suggested that the unshocked leg was being braced to support the weight in preparation for lifting the shocked leg.)

In another type of switching CR, light is CS for food and bell is CS for flexion from shock in one room, and vice versa in another room (M. Strutchkov, experimenter). B. Pakovich, in trying to set up a simultaneous CR, found that a CS-US interval of 100 milliseconds was not good, whereas 500 milliseconds is very satisfactory. If a forward CR was established and then gradually shifted to a simultaneous one, the CR was weakened. This principle can be used in balancing reflexes.

Dual CRs. M. Ye. Varga worked on an interesting problem. Both food and shock conditioning were used in a sequence so that food was followed by shock to the foreleg. Thus food was the unconditioned stimulus for salivation, and a conditional stimulus for leg withdrawal. It is equally possible to set up the reverse situation by giving shock before the food, in which case a shock will produce both flexion and salivation. In a sense, two conditioned reflexes were formed, a strong one for the sequence in normal order, and a weak one for the stimulus sequence in backward order. By varying the time interval between the two stimuli (or the proportion of the time that one comes first), one might balance the strength of the reflexes at any desired ratio, thereby producing various proportions of the two responses.

Comments. This was an active, well-equipped laboratory with interesting ideas. In addition to the director, there seems to be one doctor of science, four working toward that degree, twenty-one degree candidates, and thirty technicians. We have the names of M. Ye. Varga, Ya. M. Pressman, Simonoff, and Sakhniulina.

THE INSTITUTE OF DEFECTOLOGY

This institute is under the Academy of Pedagogical Sciences. A. R. Luria is the head of the Scientific Council, which is composed of leading staff members. There seem to be 60 members of the scientific staff (including 40 teachers and 10 physicians) plus 20 technicians including the electronics engineers. We spent some time discussing the method of handling a blind-deaf-dumb individual. Education required 15 years for the course, which starts with modeling in clay, to teach the nature of the world by touch and kinesthesis. The technique is extremely interesting.

There are many departments or functions:

1. Blind and partially sighted. One part of this department, under Professor I. A. Sokolyanski, deals with special devices (of which Luria mentioned two). One of them is a reading machine that transforms print into tactual pressure, produced by a Braille contactor (see page 211). Another is a photosensitive element, a sort of radar which gives distance by pitch and is said to be very useful. This section directs a system of schools for the blind and partially sighted.

2. Another department is doing work on rehabilitation of the deaf, dumb and blind. (One researcher, O. I. Skorokhodova, is a fifty-year-old woman who graduated from the school and is now a scientific worker at the Institute. We saw her and heard her talk Russian to a translator, and think she is superior to Helen Keller. She has written several books about her experience.)

3. A third department deals with the deaf. It is under Dr. Rau, who pointed out that in England and elsewhere many deaf children are in homes for the feebleminded. Dr. Rau has a technique to separate the hard of hearing or deaf from the true cases of feeblemindedness, resulting in a decrease of about 30 per cent in those diagnosed and treated as feebleminded.

4. Speech disorders, aphasia, etc.

5. Phonetics and acoustics.

6. The Department of Education of the Feebleminded (organic damage constitutes the only type of feeblemindedness recognized in the U.S.S.R.).

7. The psychology of feebleminded children.

8. The Department of Clinical and Physiological Study of Feebleminded Children.

9. Electrophysiology.

The EEG is used for diagnosis to separate the feebleminded from the deaf. The normal child can have his alpha wave driven at 10 to 20 cycles, but the feebleminded only goes up to 5 to 10 cycles. When higher driving frequencies are used, feebleminded children show slow waves.

Another research area is the distinction between specific and unspecific factors in the cortex. If an animal, for example, is blinded and isolated for a year or so, the electrical activity of the cortex is slowed and weakened after some time, but the reticular formation may become more active. Depression of cortex is measured by the frequency of the background activity, driving to flicker, and excitability of the motor cortex to direct stimulation. After several months of deprivation the threshold increases to two or three times the normal value. It is assumed that this basic change is directly cortical, not reticular. The blind show a lowered cortical tone (as measured by alpha rhythm) which is not found in the deaf and dumb.

The device for reading text material had been sent off to another city and was not available for inspection. Essentially, it scans a line of text and converts the dark part of the letters into tactual pressures by way of a small transducer with six points, arranged like those on a six spot die. The pick-up device can be arranged to cover the height of the line by an appropriate adjustment, as monitored by the activity of all six transducing points. Sound has been used as a transducer, for use with the blind, but it was more difficult than the Braille pattern transducer, described above, since most blind people were familiar with the latter.

We discussed the training of the blind-deaf-mute at length. At first, the child is described as not really a human being, but rather like a scared animal. His interest is maintained by rewarding him with things that satisfy his hunger and thirst. The first thing is to teach the child about the world of things. They maintain that verbal learning is useless until he has discovered the world. Thus thinking can occur without the second signal system, which is added much later. The researcher described very clearly the progression from individual gestures to common gestures to words to letters. They object strongly to what they call "word fetishism," which holds throughout the world. Introducing words before the child knows the world of things is useless. (They referred to the importance of the pioneering work of Dr. Howe in the United States.)

211

Institute of the Brain of the Academy of Medical Sciences

The Director, C. A. Sarkisov, was out of town, but we were received by L. G. Trofimov. The Institute has approximately 60 professional people, plus five or six administrators, a total of about 120 persons counting technicians. Those present were: V. N. Zworikin, M. Y. Rabinovich, O. S. Adrianov, and Scribicki. The Institute studies different parts of the brain by morphological, histological, biochemical, physiological and clinical methods. There are six laboratories, devoted to Cytology, Anatomy (with an interesting museum), Pathology, Clinical, Conditioned Responses (Adrianov headed this) and Electrophysiology (under Trofimov). We visited the anatomy museum, conditioned responses and electrophysiological sections.

The comparative method, exemplified particularly in the museum which was set up by Dr. M. Ye. Vareshov, showed brain sections covering both macro- and micro-structure from invertebrates to man. Outstanding in this museum was a series prepared largely by Dr. I. N. Filimonov, which showed cytoarchitectonics reconstruction of brain areas for a large number of human brains. This demonstrated clearly that there is considerable difference from person to person. (This work has been published by C. A. Sarkisov and I. H. Filimonov, et. al. in an *Atlas of Cytoarchitectonics of the Cortex of the Forebrain of Man*, Medical Publishing House, Moscow, 1955.)

Much of the work of the conditioned response laboratory was devoted to localization of function. They are studying vision, audition, and motor function extensively in several different breeds of dogs. O. S. Adrianov and T. A. Mering have published an *Atlas of Dog's CNS and Brain*, Medical Publishing House, Moscow, 1959. This consists of three sections: (a) microscopic structure from spinal cord through the thalamus; (b) the cytoarchitectonics of the cortex; and (c) a stereotaxic atlas for different sized dogs.

In one series of experiments they extirpated the temporal cortex and found that auditory conditioned responses persisted. After a large part of the geniculate body was destroyed the CR still remained. But by including the brachium of the inferior colliculus, the conditioned response was destroyed. This showed that the auditory cortex is not essential for auditory CRs. The temporal cortex seemed necessary only for fine auditory discrimination.

Another series of experiments involved the interrelation between two different regions of the cortex in conditioning. A visual and tactual stimulus was a positive CS, whereas either alone was inhibitory. The response was based on food reinforcement in some cases, shock to the foreleg in others. After the CR had been established, the white matter between the visual and tactual areas was cut down to the ventrical—but the patterned conditioned response (i.e. that to both stimuli together) persisted. They compared this with Lashley's work in a similar vein.

When fibers from the thalamus to the somesthetic areas are cut no defense motor conditioned response remains, but the respiratory CR is undisturbed. A previous worker at the laboratory, Nekhludova, a woman, is planning to repeat some of these experiments on monkeys, at Sukhumi.

Another experiment involved the cortical localization of the food center. It seems to be in the insula and surrounding anterior composite gyrus, for if these are removed, the salivary conditioned and unconditioned responses are diminished.

They had a clever combination of the traditional Pavlov's stand and a free situation. The dog stands on a starting platform until a signal is given and then runs to the food magazine on a platform, eats and then returns to the stand for the next signal. It is possible to record the movement from the first platform to the food magazine, as well as salivation during the run, or to substitute a traditional Pavlov's stand, plus a clever device which records leg lifting by using an easily-moving potentiometer as a transducer.

Researchers here have developed a special method for implanting sub-cortical electrodes in dogs, using visual control. They open up a large bone flap (4 x 5 centimeters), reflect the dura and push the median sinus to one side. Then the two hemispheres are separated down to the corpus callosum, taking care to coagulate the blood vessels. The occipital lobe is then separated and electrodes placed in the thalamus, midbrain and reticular formation by forceps (judging the locus by visible landmarks). The electrodes are made of 20 micron insulated wires, bipolar, with tips one millimeter apart. The twisted, insulated leads pass through a limiting bead, which determines the depth to which they are permitted to penetrate the brain.

It is also possible to place electrodes in the medulla by trephining the hole in the supracondile surface. Through the hole, one can see the VIIth, VIIIth and IXth nerves and can insert the electrodes in appropriate relationships to these landmarks.

As many as 25 electrodes (chronically implanted by this method) can be used to study defense and feeding conditioned reflexes. The evoked potentials to the conditioned stimulus (a series of clicks) become larger as the CR develops. They also studied CRs in different layers of the cortex· They used defense CR to auditory stimulation. At first the response shows up in all layers of the cortex. When the CR is established, the response is strongest in the fifth layer. With experimental neurosis there are great slow waves in the second layer of the auditory cortex.

Conditioned inhibition seems to show a decrease in the motor cortex layer 5 and the auditory cortex layer 2. (Published results include those by M. Y. Rabinovich, "Electrical activity of different cortical layers of motor and acoustic analyzer when elaborating defensive CR," *Journal Higher Nervous Activity,* VIII, (1958), 546-559.)

JOINT TALK TO SOVIET PSYCHOLOGICAL ASSOCIATION

Our last evening in Moscow, June 17, was spent talking before a meeting of the Soviet Psychological Association. Harold Schlosberg presented a short paper on the dimensional analysis of facial expression, prepared for presentation at the International Congress of Psychology at Bonn.

Carl Pfaffmann reported on his research on the gustatory sensory system, and its relationship to motivation. Neal Miller summarized many of his experiments on motivation, including the work with self-stimulation. The program took about two hours, and seems to have been favorably received. There were somewhere between 50 and 100 psychologists present. The meeting was held at the building of the Academy of Pedagogical Sciences, and we joined some of the officers of the Association at supper, served in one of the offices after the meeting. It was a very pleasant affair with every evidence of good international friendship.

LENINGRAD
INSTITUTE OF PHYSIOLOGY OF THE ACADEMY OF SCIENCES, U.S.S.R.

Studies conducted here, in the Acoustical Laboratory of Professor G. V. Gershuni, included work on hysterical deafness and electrophysiological studies of auditory systems.

Hysterical Deafness. This was studied by conditioned reflex method, using either GSR or vascular changes. (The research was apparently done by Avakian.) Although it is possible to get a threshold or audiogram this way other reactions are needed for a difference threshold, since vascular responses don't discriminate. The eyelid CR gives both the RL and the DL, for both pitch and loudness. To record the eyelid reflex a photocell and lightweight diaphragm attached to the lid is used. The lid movement closes the diaphragm, and the response of the photocell is fed through the normal EEG amplifier for recording purposes. Normally the tone lasts for one second, and the unconditioned stimulus, or puff, lasts for about one-tenth of a second at the end of the tone. Apparently anticipatory responses appear in the lid after seven to ten reinforcements. The audiograms obtained this way are essentially the same as those obtained by verbal report.

However, the vegetative response (GSR or the alpha wave) is more sentitive than the verbal response, i.e. in responding to subthreshold stimulation. In hysterical deafness, the eyelid response indicates a rise in lower threshold, but the GSR shows a normal level. In deliberate malingering, thresholds by both responses are normal, but in real deafness both are greatly raised. Some experiments were also carried out on hypnosis.

Electrophysiological Studies of Auditory Systems. These involved the general problem of the deterioration of frequency discrimination in man, due to inattention and similar factors. In other words, how does the nervous system lose discriminating capacity? In animal experiments, electrodes were implanted (using penicillin rather than aseptic technique) in the cochlea through the bulla, as well as in the geniculate body and cortex. The electrodes are insulated constantine wire.

Dr. V. A. Kozhevnikov, collaborating on this project, developed electronic methods of analyzing low magnitude responses against backgrounds of neural "noise." His analyzer consisted of a series of band pass filters in conjunction with a four-to-eight-channel EEG. These filters feeding the recorders gave ink tracings of each frequency band, along with an integrated record below each band, in the form of tallies or blips. The tallies could also actuate counters. The frequency distributions with no stimuli then could be compared statistically with those occurring with weak stimuli. (This work is mentioned in an American edition of Sechenov's journal.)

Similar analysis can be performed on EEG records on human beings so that alpha block, conditioned to sound with light as the unconditioned stimulus, can be used to obtain a threshold function for hearing. This yields a steeper function than does verbal report; that is, the cutoff is more rectangular. A computer operating during the experiment shows (a) when enough readings have been obtained to give a reliable threshold, or (b) when more trials are needed, or (c) that the variability is too great to ever yield a reliable threshold. This procedure is based on a cross-correlation method for detecting weak signals against "noise" (fairly standard radar procedure). The equipment is now made in Moscow and has also been licensed for production in Hungary. Another ingenious device provided a two dimensional visual display of potential changes converted to spot intensity modulation, and coupled with a "Raster" sweep. The resulting photographic plates can be read by a photoelectric densitometer.

In waking animals, with implanted electrodes, there is clear evidence of depression of the first VIIIth nerve response during prolonged stimulation with clicks. But this suppression does not depend on the reticular formation, because activation of the reticular formation doesn't suppress the first response. Removal of the auditory cortex eliminates this inhibition. Thus there must be a specific inhibiting mechanism within the specific sensory system. Such effects are thought to be related to changes in sensitivity and selectivity, observed in attention and inattention.

The nature of the true speech element is being investigated by Dr. L. A. Chistovich. Her original interest seems to stem from the hope of developing a machine which would typewrite spoken speech. This forced her to attempt to identify the true psychological units of speech on the assumption that the conventional phenomes were not adequate. Her basic technique was to take the reaction time or time delay for repetition of a sound imbedded in a series, as in repeating dictation. It was assumed that this time delay would be at least as long as the psychological unit. She found that in continuous dictation, the listener can repeat the dictated material with a time lag of about 150 milliseconds, which is about the duration of a vowel. This raised the question of whether or not S was merely repeating the sounds or was responding to them as speech elements. So she set up two lists of vowels, presumably on tape, so that one list was made up of normal, clearly-spoken vowels, and the other list was made up of sounds that resembled vowels. An observer listened to the tape and repeated it to a second observer. By comparing the responses of the second observer with those of the original tape it was clear that the false vowel sounds had been corrected by the speaker so that they were much more like the conventional vowels. That is, the observers were not simply repeating sounds, but were classifying them as vowels.

Another way of getting at the unit of speech was to plot speech sounds in terms of so-called visual speech, which is a vertical spectogram of the sound. It was possible, using this method, to break up a sequence into several specific phases, each phase maintaining a relatively constant sound. The reaction time is short enough so that the response to the first segment may appear before the second or third segment is presented, showing that the reaction is made to the segment.

How does S ordinarily store up past segments; is each stored as a sound or true segment, or as a decision? To answer these questions, Chistovich tested to see whether there would be a difference between sequences of three pure tones, or one syllable consisting of three separate sounds. The subject had to identify each sequence, as "high, medium high, low." It was found that the response to syllables was much faster; i.e. the information was absorbed more rapidly. Then she tried tones that resembled speech sounds, and these were reported as speech sounds; they were reported almost as rapidly as were syllables.

Her conclusions: (1) there are segment decisions; (2) there are phoneme decisions; and (3) there are larger units which must be studied later.

Earlier, she had studied the minimum interval between two clicks to be reported separately. The interval must be about 150 milliseconds, for 75 per cent correct report, when the difference between the intensity of the two clicks is 35 decibels.

PAVLOV INSTITUTE OF EXPERIMENTAL MEDICINE IN LENINGRAD
(Pavlov's "Towers of Silence" Are Located Here.)

Investigations of this Institute (under the direction of P. S. Kupalov) included work in experimental epilepsy; experimental neuroses with free movement in room; and independent ipsilateral CRs by externalizing the mucous membrane.

Experimental Epilepsy. A dog trained to stand in a Pavlov frame was used in these studies. A weak light is flashed six times per second in one eye and five times or less per second in the other eye, for twenty minutes a day. In two weeks the legs start to tremble, the tremors appearing first in the forelimbs, but bearing no relation to stimulus frequency. Then the tremor settles in the side that gets the higher rate and increases through myoclonia to a tonic reaction like the Babinski reflex in form. Next the tremor leaves the forelimbs and appears in the hindlimbs. Eventually the dog trembles on each return to the room, before the light has been turned on. Although there is the typical spike and slow-wave EEG pattern, like that in epilepsy, there is no loss of consciousness. The same effect can be produced with sound, using an interrupted tone. This state can definitely be conditioned to a stimulus, but is usually conditioned to the whole environment. (See the report in the *Journal of Higher Nervous Activity*, "Changes in Behavior of the Dog by Intermittent Photic Stimulation," Volume 8, 1958, by J. W. Danilov.)

Experimental Neurosis with Free Movement in a Room. This employed what would be called "shaping and chaining" of behavior, using a large room marked off in squares like a checkerboard. For example, a dog is first trained to get food when a new dish is rotated into place. Then he is trained to go to a specific spot when a light is on to operate the food device. Then he is trained to lick the light stand to turn it on, return to correct spot, orient to direction from which a metronome will sound, and then run to the food delivery magazine. This behavior seems to be established very much as one would shape behavior in a Skinner box. Normally, there are ten trials (all rewarded) per session and the animal is trained for one month. At the end of this time, if one item, e.g. the locus of the light, is moved, the dog is very apt to develop an experimental neurosis. He howls, won't eat the food, and tries to escape from the room if the door is open. Thus a neurosis can be obtained *without restraint*. The neurosis may disappear of its own accord, if the original conditions are replaced after a rest, but it may be necessary to start training fresh. (We were told to write Professor Kupalov, who was away at the time of our visit, for reprints; this was characteristic of the Russian laboratories, where there is often a high regard for proper channels.)

Independent Ipsilateral CRs. These were obtained by K. S. Abuladze, who externalized both sides of the mucous membrane from the back of the tongue, including the taste buds. By this operation, the taste surface on the two sides of the tongue were accessible outside the mouth. He was able to set up two different conditioned reflexes, each dependent on stimulation of a different side. Thus defense secretion on one side might be stimulated by acid, and alimentary salivation on the other side by food. The possibility of setting up two independent salivary CRs, each based on a different unconditioned stimulus, offers interesting possibilities. (K. S. Abuladze has written a book describing these experiments.)

BEKHTEREV INSTITUTE OF NEUROLOGY AND PSYCHOLOGY

We saw Dr. V. N. Miasischev, the Director, and talked with two neurologists and three psychologists. Unfortunately, through a slip-up in arrangements, we allowed far too little time for this visit.

Problems of neurophysiology in animals and man are studied here in the tradition initiated by Pavlov and Wedenski. In psychology, they are interested in the experimental diagnosis of speech disorders, movement and reaction, and particularly in interpersonal relations, because the latter, especially, are disrupted in neuroses and psychoses. Personality is a complex of social relations, as Marx pointed out, rather than the product of instincts and drives. The group here tries to synthesize neurophysiological and sociological factors in understanding people.

Dr. Tonkonogy talked about aphasia, apraxia, and agnosia. They study speech and thinking, using electrophysiological techniques. One approach is by means of non-verbal problems in different forms of aphasia, especially amnesic. (They referred to the work of Goldstein.) The relationship between kinetic speech activity and various aphasias is also studied. They are interested in lesions in the supplementary motor areas (as described by Penfield) and in special speech disorders from lesions in the thalamus and the brain stem. (Some of this material has been published in the U.S. in 1959 and in the Congress of the Neurological Association.)

Another research effort is concerned with the EEG in aphasic patients. Electrodes are placed on various areas of the skull, and potentials recorded while S is solving verbal problems. Muscle potentials from lips, heart rate and GSR are also recorded. Analysis is difficult however and more work is needed.

Finally, we discussed therapy. The methods used are the conventional European ones, except that they emphasize observation of syndromes and symptoms rather than inferences about psychodynamics, in an effort to see how these are shaped by treatment. Some drugs are used. A given drug may have a different effect on the same symptom depending on the syndrome of which each symptom is a part. Thus chlorpromazine reduces defensive CRs but not positive ones. It does not relieve hallucination in paranoia because the patient is satisfied with his ideas, but it does reduce hallucinations in schizophrenia, because they involve fear and aggression. The assumption of the differential effect of chlorpromazine was verified on animals and man by conditioning techniques, in which the galvanic skin reaction, salivary secretion, and so on, were recorded. Food reflexes were not affected by chlorpromazine, but defense CRs were. For human conditioning they used a neat Krasnagorsky salivation device about the size of a dime. The rim provides suction holding the device to the cheek, the center section collects saliva, and the back has holes for squirting USs such as lemon juice into the mouth. They recorded with an excellent polygraph system; the laboratories are well equipped.

INSTITUTE OF EVOLUTIONARY PHYSIOLOGY

Professor B. B. Kasatkin, the Director, was away but we were received by Dr. A. I. Karamyan. He pointed out that the ideas of evolutionary physiology derive from Darwin, who gave the general scheme of evolution. This was followed in 1903 by Pavlov's report on the higher nervous processes and in 1909 Lucas emphasized the importance of evolution for physiology. Hughlings Jackson and a number of others have brought out the same point. The idea of this institute came from Orbeli about 30 years ago. There are three lines of research: (1) comparative physiology; (2) ontogenetic physiology; and (3) experimental and clinical pathology in human and animal subjects, to trace the disintegration of complex functions.

In addition, they utilize bio-chemistry, neurophysiology and morphology. There is a special laboratory for pathology of higher nervous processes and another one for pathology of children. The laboratory studies only vertebrates, using the methods of CR, extirpation, EEG and histology to study the highest nervous activities. Professor N. N. Traugott is particularly interested in studying both the highest and lowest functions in neurotics. He studies the CR and the UCR in acutely developing depressions, as affected by various pathological agents, drugs and electroconvulsions. He also studies (1) the order of depression of various functions. (For instance, under what conditions do primitive reactions appear?); (2) the interaction of lower functions, i.e. the reticular formation and the cortex, and how such interrelations are affected by chlorpromazine and barbiturates; (3) cardiac disturbance in neurosis; and (4) aphasia.

The interaction between the reticular formation and the cortex has been studied with many drugs. Chlorpromazine does not disturb old conditioned reflexes, even when the patient is almost at the sleeping level (by "old conditioned reflex" he referred to a voluntary response to a stimulus which had been practiced repeatedly, as in reaction time). Chlorpromazine strengthens an inhibitory conditioned reflex but doesn't raise the threshold of stimulation. However, defensive reflexes cannot be formed under this drug. In fact, already-formed flexion CRs to electric shock disappear. If one attempts to set up a conditioned flexion reflex while under the influence of this drug, there will be amnesia for the event and no traces of the voluntary CR set up by instruction. There will be traces in the depression of the Alpha rhythm, however, for both voluntary and CR flexion. The effector side is depressed, vegetative reaction is partially depressed and generalization is narrower. Chlorpromazine depresses the tonus of the cortex. (Adrenalin has roughly the opposite effect: defense reflexes improve; generalization is wider and amplitude is greater.)

Chlorpromazine also depresses the reticular formation in both the brain stem and the thalamus and it intensifies the inhibiting influence of the cortex on the reticular formation, but not on specific pathways. It also depresses the secretion of hormones of the hypophysis.

Barbiturates depress the reticular formation in the brain stem, but not of the thalamus. Generalization of the conditioned reflex is broadened by barbiturates, but narrowed by chlorpromazine. Of course, deep narcosis by either of these drugs will knock out most everything.

Three separate functions must be distinguished: (1) non-defense movements; (2) defense movements; and (3) Pavlovian inhibition.

Karamyan studied birds, rabbits and cats. In the cat the cortical alpha rhythm was abolished, but could be restored by adrenalin when the sympathetic system was knocked out by crushing the stellate ganglion and the cervical ganglion. Chlorpromazine acts in much the same way as does sympathectomy. The recruiting reaction of the suprasylvian gyrus of the cortex, reflecting stimulation of nonspecific nuclei of the thalamus, is abolished by chlorpromazine but reappears as the drug wears off. In the pigeon, destruction in the hypothalamus depresses alpha rhythm, but there is recovery in 45 days.

The localization of evoked potentials in the fish, frog, rabbit and bird were studied in relation to the principle of encephalization. In the cat, destroying the paleocerebellum augments, while damage of the neocerebellum diminishes the conditioned reflexes, (the latter connected with the cortex through the thalamus, whereas the former goes via the reticular formation). There was also some study of DC stimulation of the cerebellum, which inhibits monosynaptic reflexes from the sciatic nerve to the ventral root of the spinal cord, but after habituation the same stimulation restores it.

Researchers here have an apparatus for producing vestibular stimulation in various animals, using it as a conditioned stimulus for salivation, defense reactions, etc. The pathways involved in vestibular stimulation are being studied by extirpation techniques.

In general, they had excellent equipment, including 12-channel EEGs, 'scopes, cameras, several conditioning chambers, etc.

Masking of Weak Tones by Louder Ones. The masking tone was found to be effective (by Samoilova) even when it *followed* the masked tone by as much as 100 or more milliseconds. Indeed, the curves of forward and backward masking are fairly symmetrical. The results suggest the importance of central rather than peripheral factors in a relatively simple perception.

She is now starting work in a similar fashion on the auditory perception of words.

Histological Study of the Olfactory System. V. G. Vimikov gave us a book summarizing his work (using histo-chemical methods, tissue culture and embryology) on the history of the olfactory organ entitled, *Studies in Histology of Olfaction*, 1957, Leningrad.

He is presently interested in the cochlea, studied by his special method for removing it *in vivo*. The isolated organ can then be stimulated by any frequency, intensity and duration for a prolonged period. Such stimulation depletes acetylcholine, the remainder of which can be visually assayed by staining techniques. There is evidence of localized loss, depending on frequency. He has sent descriptions of his method to Davis and Bekesy. It was demonstrated in considerable detail at the 1959 Soviet Exposition in New York City.

PAVLOV INSTITUTE OF PHYSIOLOGY (AT KOLTUSHI)

This is a branch of the same Institute (the Academy of Sciences) which we visited in Leningrad, when we saw Gershuni. It was begun in 1932, when Pavlov was ill and came to the country for a rest. At first, he had a simple wooden structure with two scientists and a few dogs. But others followed him from the home Institute and the Koltushi laboratory was gradually built up to good size.

General problems here are more biological (those in the city are more medical). Researches here include:

1. Influence of environment on properties of the nervous system.
2. Heredity of properties of the nervous system.

Laboratory of V. K. Krasussky

Experimental work here deals with:

1. Types of the nervous system and methods to measure higher nervous activity.
2. How properties of the higher nervous system are formed under the environment and how they are transmitted by heredity. *Thus far, they have no proof of inheritance of acquired characteristics.*

In one experiment various breeds and types of dogs were studied. Half of the puppies (18) were isolated from the environment, and the other half (19) had close contact with the environment. The isolated dogs spent 40 days locked in single chambers with no access to other animals and with no view of the caretaker except for 15 minutes daily for cage cleaning. However, they could hear barking and other sounds very clearly; lighting was normal but they could not see the other dogs because of a solid wall between cubicles. After a year and a half, the two groups behaved quite differently, but special tests showed no difference in basic types of neural organization. All isolated dogs showed some sign of passive defensive reaction. The dog is frightened, cautious. But in spite of these differences, when given special tests the dogs showed evidence of what was presumably their original strong or weak types of nervous system. It was concluded that the type is congenital, i.e. the type was largely that of the dog's parents.

Weak dogs never lost the passive defensive response after the period of isolation, whereas strong dogs showed some recovery. In reply to Miller's question about use of correlation, it appeared that the type is determined in a clinical, or general descriptive fashion. One way to determine types is to determine the amount of nitrogen in the saliva. This is produced with food as US, but not with acid. The test is to

222

give acid repeatedly, and then substitute bread. The strong type shows rapid change of saliva; in the weak type it takes more than an hour to shift over to the appropriate type of saliva. (In reply to a question by Schlosberg, researchers here said they had not yet studied the second generation.)

At present they are working on breeds that vary in mobility of nervous system. They plan to study behavior types and mobility in hybrids and continue more work on determination of types. It now takes from one to one and one-half years to determine the type, so a faster method is needed. (They hope to get this through unconditioned responses.) The general viewpoint is that any function of the organism, if there is a method to investigate it, reflects the type of nervous system. They also study general activity, biochemical changes, heart, circulation, metabolism and the course of inflammatory reactions, all of which reflect types of the nervous system. They study 40 dogs per year and find 25 per cent strong, 25 per cent weak, and 50 per cent intermediate.

Most of their publications appear in the *Journal of Higher Nervous Activity*, Moscow Academy of Sciences. It often has a summary in English and it is now being translated by U.S.P.H.S.

The laboratory has 16 experimental chambers; 20 in the whole of Koltushi. They are completing a new building, which will have eight more chambers.

The Department of Experimental Genetics
of the Higher Nervous System

This department (directed by Dr. V. Federov) uses pure breeds of rats in searching for inherited characteristics on a number of generations. Thus far they have had no positive results.

Another approach is to study irradiation effects on parents and offspring, using cobalt 60 of rather weak strength. They found no effect on the first filial generation, but did find some on the second and third, with continuous irradiation of the parents of each successive generation before breeding, but not during actual breeding. There was a high percentage of neurotics and of excitable animals in irradiated compared with control groups. In general, experimentals were more sensitive to stimulation and more prone to convulsions. The third generation showed lack of adequate growth.

Biochemical studies were in progress. They were starting to repeat the work of Krech and Rosenzweig on acetylcholine and behavior.

We saw a clever set of automated training boxes for rats and mice. An avoidance-training apparatus (Figure 1) consisted of a small, rotating circular starting cage bisected by a partition. At the begin-

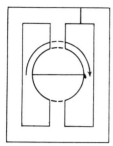

Figure 1

ning of a trial the animal was on the near side of the partition. At the conditioned stimulus of a bell, plus the opening of a door, the animal ran straight forward to a choice point. The right side of a runway which formed a square was blocked and the left hand side allowed him to run around and back down a central alley to the half of the rotating cage opposite to the one from which he started. The floor of the apparatus consisted of a grid; the rats ran to avoid (or, if they were slow, to escape) electric shock. At about the time for the next trial, the center turntable rotated, changing the animal from the safe goal position to the dangerous starting one.

In another similarly automated apparatus, the animal ran from a start when a light began to flash, to a goal box to secure food, and then ran by another path back again to the start to avoid electric shock when a bell started to ring. In both pieces of apparatus, programming was controlled by tape and time and errors were recorded automatically. (These methods were published in 1954 in the *Journal of Higher Nervous Activity*.)

Laboratory for Psychopharmacology

In this laboratory (under the direction of G. I. Tsobcallo) conditioning in rabbits was studied in a device similar to a Skinner box. The response is pulling a ring with the teeth, which moves a small food pan into place. The rabbit is shaped to this behavior by smearing the ring with carrot juice. The positive CS (S_D in Skinnerian terms) is a light bulb, and the negative one (S_{Delta}) is a lantern (but sounds are sometimes used). The latency between the onset of the light and the pull is usually about two to four seconds. Two minutes elapse between trials and one and one-half hours constitute a maximum session. A ratio of four positive stimuli to one negative stimulus is usually employed. During the session, drugs may be injected. (See Malinowski, 1952, Russian *Journal of Physiology*. Tsobcallo's modification of the device appeared in the *Journal of Higher Nervous Activity*, 1956.)

In another experiment dogs were used to study the effects of a morphine-like analgesic. Experimental and control days were alternated. (The depressing effect of the drug is minimal on "strong" dogs, larger on those with a "weak nervous system.") The method is a typical conditioning one, with four minutes between trials and four or five positive stimuli and one negative in a 20 minute session.

Another drug, Jen Shen (Chinese), acts as a stimulant, increasing the amount of conditioned salivation. Moderate doses of procaine were a stimulant, strong ones a depressant. Morphine eliminated the CR but as its effects wore off the first responses to appear were those to the negative cue. Individual differences in rabbits were studied, as well as classical pharmacological effects in acute experiments.

Interoceptive Conditioning. Kosoff reported on the work of E. S. Airapet'iants,[5] who was ill with phlebitis. The research was concerned with the cortical localization of the visceral interoceptive analyzer in dogs using the conditional reflex technique. The CRs are elaborated by excitation of different parts of the stomach, intestines, bladder, uterus and kidneys as CS. Interoceptive stimulation is obtained by introducing balloons, which can be filled with air for pressure, or liquid for temperature stimulation. In general, the unconditioned stimulus is avoidable shock; unavoidable shock was found to be less satisfactory. After the CR is established, a lesion is made in the motor or premotor cortex, which leads to a temporary loss, or disturbance, of the CR. Control lesions in the occipital lobe have no effect. Hence one pathway is by way of the frontal cortex. No CR, either intero- or exteroceptive, can be set up after complete removal of the cortex.

Another long series of experiments has involved the effects of removal of the spatial receptors—visual, auditory, smell, vestibular— on behavior of animals. The general results:

1. Simultaneous removal of receptors in the adult produces a very lethargic dog.

2. Multi-stage removal in the adult yields an active dog.

3. Simultaneous removal in the puppy yields an active dog.

Monkeys seem somewhat more resistant to these effects. In one experiment a baboon was conditioned to sit on a shelf against an air nozzle. An air puff, which serves as tactual stimulus, is the CS to go to another area in the chamber to pull a lever, which produces food The animal then returns to his original sitting position for the next trial. Animals without eye, ear, nose or vestibular organs don't lose the habit, if they have been pretrained before the sensory loss.

We saw one dog, now two-and one-half-years-old, that had been completely decorticated as a puppy. She has had two litters of normal puppies, but didn't eat the placenta—she had no maternal behavior. No conditioning is possible. She is quiet and does *not* show sham rage. Rage seems to be found *only when thalamic damage occurs.*

In the discussion, we asked for an explication of the differences

---

[5] See E. S. Airapet'iants, Die hohere Nerventatigkeit und die Rezeptoren der Inneren Organe. *Veb. Verlag Volk und Gesundheit.* Berlin, 1956.

between intero- and exteroceptive conditioning. In general, it seems that interoceptive CRs are more slowly established and extinguished, and more variable, but the similarities between the two types are more striking than are the differences. (Much of their earlier work is available in English in *The Cerebral Cortex and the Internal Organs, by* Konstantin M. Bykov, M.D., translated and edited by W. Horsley Gantt, M.D., Chemical Publishing Co., Inc., 212 Fifth Avenue, New York, N.Y., 1957.) Apparently they are not doing any extensive work here or elsewhere using any visceral responses other than salivation. Kosoff studies vestibular CRs and UCRs using rotation as a stimulus and chiefly records nystagmus by eye potential technique, using chronic electrodes placed under the skin around the orbit of the eye.

In a letter, Pick, an American student at Moscow State University, reports the following work from Airapet'iants' laboratory: "The method of study with dogs involves using saliva flow as an unconditioned indicator of a taste stimulus. Problems include threshold determination before and after ablation of part of tongue or part of brain. In addition, Zubkova has conditioned discrimination to taste stimuli in dogs, but finds this very difficult to establish and has done little with it. In her experiments, the under part of the jaw is operated upon, exposing the bottom of the tongue. The stimulus is applied here so that there is no entry of the stimulus into the digestive tract —it flows away. The work with humans also involves the use of saliva flow as an unconditioned response. A rather neat vacuum device draws the saliva off. A stimulator enables separate sides of the tongue to be stimulated independently. Apparently saliva flow is somewhat specific to the side of the tongue being stimulated, i.e. different rates of saliva flow can be evoked simultaneously by different magnitudes of stimulation. Bacusseb has also obtained verbal reports from subjects when the two sides of the tongue are being stimulated simultaneously by different substances. He reports some masking effects. He also has made other physiological measurements under conditions of taste stimulation, e.g. EEG. In this respect he didn't find the dissynchronization effects associated with auditory and verbal stimulation. However, he hadn't finished working on this yet. His next problem will be a study of the effects of temperature on saliva flow and presumably verbal reports of taste."

SUKHUMI

INSTITUTE OF EXPERIMENTAL PATHOLOGY AND THERAPY OF THE U.S.S.R., ACADEMY OF MEDICAL SCIENCES MONKEY COLONY SUKHUMI
  We were shown around by Ye. M. Cherkovich, an able woman. The Institute (under the direction of B. A. Lapin) was founded in

1927, and has several sections: cancer, general biology, physiology, isotopes, microbial infectious disease, pathology, radiobiology, cytology, biochemistry. On an area of 71.8 acres they have about 1400 monkeys, worked on by 60 scientists who are assisted by 340 assistants, caretakers, etc. Most of the monkeys are macaques and baboons, raised at the Colony, and some of them are in the fifth generation of captivity. There were at least two large open areas where groups of females were segregated with one male, for breeding purposes. We entered the baboon compound, and found them extremely tame, begging for candy.

There is no work presently being conducted in this Institute that they called psychology. However, there is some research on the effect of experimental neuroses on hypertension and on other circulatory disorders. It is difficult to set up an experimental neurosis in a monkey by the classical Pavlovian methods of discrimination, but they employ two techniques:

1. In the male, if he is housed with several females for a period, and then the females are moved to a nearby cage with another male, the isolated male develops a neurosis, either an aggressive one or an inverted one, (he withdraws, circles, and shows it in his learned behavior). He may also show tics or hallucinations in which he acts as if he were trying to catch a nonexistent fly. He will lose weight, and may lose his hair, develop hypertension, cardiac symptoms, and insomnia. (A physiologist, D. I. Miminoshvoli, who died recently, developed this method.) Sometimes males living alone may develop cardiac symptoms without the formal jealousy treatment.

2. With both sexes and infants, a neurosis can be produced by changing the light-dark cycle to six hours light and six hours dark, repeated indefinitely. This sequence is reversed every four days, and a neurosis may result in a month.

One of the tests for experimental neurosis is a lever-pressing situation. (They have been using lever-pressing as long as they can remember and believe that Pavlov originated it in his work with monkeys.) We saw several animals put through this. There is a simple lever in a large cage. The animal can obtain food if he presses this lever, but only after a signal has come on. There is also a negative signal. Thus if a bell rings, the monkey is supposed to press the lever, and the experimenter gives him some food, either meat or fruit. However, if a buzzer sounds, he will not be rewarded for pressing the lever. The same animal also learns to respond to white and red lights as positive and negative stimuli, respectively. There is a two to three minute intertrial interval, and the stimulus is on for ten seconds.

Animals are tested one day a week in order to monitor the development of the neurosis. The behavioral signs of neurosis are increased restlessness and emotionalism in the experimental situation, failure to respond to the positive stimulus, sometimes responses to the negative stimulus or extra responses between trials. Errors are made first to the lights, then to the sounds. With restoration of a normal light-dark cycle, responses to the bell may appear in ten days and to the lights in two months.

The basic interest in this Institute is in the circulatory disturbances which develop during the neurosis in healthy young monkeys without arteriosclerosis. These monkeys show an abnormal EKG, with the T-wave indicating cardiac insufficiency. They also show brachycardia—slowing of the heart rate from a normal 160-200 per minute to as low as 75. These symptoms slowly return to normal after the monkeys have been returned to normal conditions. Monkeys may also show hypertension, fibrosis or necrosis in the heart muscle, and they have two cases of cardiac infarct. We saw slides of some of the cardiac damage and records of the EKG, as well as records of the disturbance in the day-night cycle of activity. The mixed up day-night cycle also produces a loss of appetite and weight.

Another setup consisted of a chamber with a narrow end, which was gridded. The animal had to cross a charged grid to get to either food, or to see a toy which was displayed in a window (orienting reflex). The whole box was soundproof. The animal could turn off the charge on the grid by pressing a lever, thus giving him free access to a second lever which produced the food. The equipment was intended to study the relationship between food, orientation and avoidance reflexes. A hungry monkey will refuse food to look at a toy. The appearance of a toy follows a signal (note: he cannot handle the toy, only see it). The experiment has been conducted for about two years, but we didn't learn of the results because it was not the experiment of the person who showed it to us.

We also saw a Pavlov stand for monkeys. It used a sling to keep the monkey in a dog-like position, with his head and sometimes his shoulders through a stock. The macaque will tolerate this but not the baboon. It was used for animals with implanted electrodes because it was thought to be a more natural position than the sitting one used at N.I.M.H. They are also studying cortical and sub-cortical structure as related to the circulatory system, i.e. what part of the cortex is disturbed by neurosis so that it produces coronary insufficiency and so forth. They use the EEG and chronic implants, but since they are just starting, no results have yet been obtained.

In addition, there were some other complicated experiments which required the animal to push a lever up or down in response to different stimuli. This task will sometimes produce a neurosis in monkeys, because it is very difficult; but usually it is difficult to set up neuroses in the laboratory, except by the techniques mentioned above. A monkey has considerable ability in dealing with stimulus sequences, in which the animal can respond with ease to chains from three to five stimuli as a pattern to be discriminated from the same stimuli in a different sequence. Furthermore, it is easy to set up four food stimuli and four inhibitory stimuli and then to reverse the behavior by training.

In spite of the free-ranging condition of the breeding colonies, there apparently has been no study of social reactions. Most of the recent work has been medical, not psychological.

TBILISI

INSTITUTE OF PSYCHOLOGY OF THE GEORGIAN ACADEMY OF SCIENCES

The Institute was founded in 1941 as part of the University. When the Georgian Academy of Sciences was founded in 1945 it became the first Institute of the Academy. The Director is Professor A. Prangishvili; his interest seems to be in general psychology. A. Bochoroshvili is interested in history of psychology, and I. T. Bzhalava in clinical and pathological psychology. There are also groups interested in genetic and pedagogical psychology. The basic emphasis in all divisions is on the psychology of personality. The key approach is the study of "set," as developed by Usnadze.

They began their exposition with a demonstration of the Fechner illusion, in which several pairs of figures are exposed, in a tachistoscope, with an interval of several seconds between each pair. The Subject is asked to judge on which side the larger one is located and to say it aloud promptly. After a half dozen or so pairs are exposed, with the larger one on the right, there appears an equal pair. However, the Subject immediately reports "left" larger. This illusion is said to be due to the disequilibrium between the set and the environment. We have a set for inequality, so this set makes equal objects seem not equal. Similar illusions can be shown with balls held in the hand. These illusions furnish a way to study set. (They gave us a book entitled, *Experimental Investigations of the Psychology of Set,* written in Georgian.)

This is the basic fact. What are the principals?

1. One can transfer set from tactual to visual modality; as from held balls to seen figures. Hence set is not in a single modality, but involves a "wholeness," for they regard it from a "holistic" approach. For instance, Usnadze established a set for inequality under hypnosis

229

and it showed up in post-hypnotic states. One can also establish such a set by saying, "Imagine a heavy ball in the right hand, lighter in the left." Repeat this 15 times and then test by giving the subject equal weights. It will work, for the subject will judge the left one as heavier. Actors seem to show this illusion unusually well.

2. Unity of directionality. Set can be established with each pair of figures different—squares, triangles, circles, etc., and a test such as a diamond. In an experiment by Pogalla, the Subject was asked to read aloud lists of German words, but there was a familiar Russian word in the middle of the list. The Russian word was invariably pronounced like a German word, despite the fact that it was printed in Russian letters. Set is relational and directional.

Set is the "mode of being, the essence of personality, at every given moment. The essence of personality is its various sets." How can one describe and measure set?

1. *Instigation* is a function of the number of presentations used to establish set.

2. *Durability* can be determined by the time between the establishment of the set and its testing—that is, memory.

3. *Stability* is shown by the length of time it takes to extinguish a set. There may also be an overshoot into a reverse set. Some personality types, such as epileptics, have difficulty getting over the illusion —it may appear for a week or month after the original exposure.

Professor Navakitze investigated individual differences in children. Professor Bochoroshvili studied variations in set, and Bzhalava studied its pathology.

There has been some controversy with Piaget, who studied the Usnadze effect as a function of age. Piaget thinks it develops late but the Georgian researchers think it is present very early—the phenomenon appears wherever one gets discrimination. Piaget limits the phenomenon to the sensory-motor sphere, but the Georgian group considers it quite general.

In another test for set the infant is fed from bottles of different sizes. The child prefers the larger bottle and after several trials with the large bottle to the left, chooses the right when presented with equal bottles. This was done on pre-school children under five months.

Finally the phenomena of set are to be viewed in terms of demands of the organism in a situation. Set emerges as a new entity, as an interaction phenomenon between the Subject and the environment. Therefore, set is not merely subjective. Hence all laboratory research here revolves around this problem.

Urie Bronfenbrenner [6] asked them who, in America, had formulations like theirs. They replied that perhaps a dozen people in general psychology, and a few more in social psychology, had similar views, but nobody else does research on it. They mentioned both Allports, as examples, but they thought Lewin and his "vectors" left no personality core.

Set is a new relational entity which emerges from interaction of the organism in the environment. It is unlike Marbe's *Einstellung,* which is subjective. The essence of set is a combination of the subjective (phenomenal) and objective containing a tendency to action. They hold that disposition toward action is imminent in set—in contrast to the old view that action *follows* perception.

Bronfenbrenner asked what research they were doing in personality, and they replied that they were just starting and there were too many problems for too few hands. In differential psychology the relation between set and character has been worked on, but we never got to this in detail.

Set and Temperament. They employ the four-way typology of Hippocrates. In one study they divided people into four classes on the basis of clinical interview, observation, biographical data, and so forth. Then they took 50 to 60 "pure types" out of about 200 people originally studied. These pure types were tested from a standpoint of set; that is, for speed of establishment and recovery and so on. The distribution of these people and types is given in the book. There were 20 sanguine, 15 choleric, and so on. The sanguine people reached the asymptote of set in about 15 trials. They seemed to have dynamic sets, that is, after the first reversal, they went through a series of others, like a pendulum returning to equilibrium. But the over-all recovery is relatively quick.

In the melancholic, the effect appeared very quickly, reaching an optimal value after two trials. While 90 per cent of the sanguine reached the optimum at 15 trials, 100 per cent of the melancholics had it at two trials. The melancholics might retain the illusion for one hundred trials, and it often lasted for a month without further practice, but the illusion was getting weaker.

In the phlegmatic, optimum is high, occurring after about 25 trials. Set gives a strong illusion very slow to extinguish.

In the choleric, arousal is easy, after about two trials. The extinction, when it occurs, is a sudden, an all-to-none return to normality,

---

[6] This was one of the times when we crossed paths with Dr. Urie Bronfenbrenner (see Chapter III). His excellent knowledge of Russian was especially helpful in the Georgian Academy.

rather than the progressive return characteristic of the other types.

Extinction is explained by the existence of two factors: (1) the higher corrective process, and (2) the lower one producing the set.

Consider the immediate impulsive set "I am thirsty." The higher conscious level says, "The bottle is dirty," or "I won't drink." Set is the impulsive level and the recovery (or extinction) represents a conflict between it and consciousness, i.e. the objective situation. Temperament is at the impulsive level so it can be studied by set. (Incidentally, set is more resistant to extinction under alcohol.)

When asked if their typology was the same as Teplov's, they replied that his was neurological, following Pavlov's, but their own is psychological. However, both take four types as "given."

The mentally ill are not disturbed in a limited function—hence the disorder must be studied by a holistic approach. Until recently, psychology has made little purely psychological contribution in this area—it has acted as a handmaiden to psychiatry, using and developing psychiatric tests. The experiments of the Gestalt psychologists were too segmental to be of much use. However, set is global and generally psychological, not psychiatric, so it offers a new and promising approach. They have studied hysteria, epilepsy and schizophrenia.

In hysteria, sets are variable. Sets may even fail to develop. The differences are intra-individual so that the individual is essentially unpredictable. There is also marked lability, that is, long-time change in these cases.

Parenthetically they pointed out that Luria has found brain-injured individuals don't show the set effects on imagined weights consistently. They also pointed out that set phenomena appear in chimpanzees when trained with two plates containing unequal amounts of food and tested with equal plates.

Epileptics are very stable and slow to extinguish. Even when told that the stimuli are equal, they don't believe it. Touch is especially effective. Set is not transferred across modalities or from hand to hand. Epileptics don't even transfer set from right eye to the left eye. Hence set is localized in epileptics. Incidentally, all of these statements apply to 75 per cent of the epileptics, which are those of unknown origin—or "essential epilepsy." The other 25 per cent are organic and they don't fit the general picture. The group has worked for ten years and studied 350 epileptics.

In schizophrenia, there is an excessive spread or generalization across modalities. Set will easily carry over from two held balls to two visual lines. They are surprisingly stable in that they will see a difference for 75 trials after *two* establishing trials. There is no reversal of phases. They are weak in the effects of imagination, however. Subtypes among schoziphrenics can be distinguished.

They think the phenomena of set becomes a useful technique for diagnosis. (See a book *Neuropsychiatry of War,* published in Moscow.) A gentleman who wasn't present, Chartishvili, published a monograph on motivation of voluntary behavior, a copy of which was given to Urie Bronfenbrenner.

They have three trained workers in the library who have the responsibility of calling the Staff's attention to developments abroad related to their interest.

Professor Bochoroshvili is interested in the history and philosophy of psychology. They consider it a core problem and asked us how much we did in America in this area. We made a long defense of our relative lack of interest in history of psychology and philosophy, especially the Mind and Body problem, but we don't think they were convinced.

In response to a question on Social Psychology, they replied that problems of Social Psychology are central to the whole Marxist-Leninist approach. Psychology formerly was involved in this a little and then was out. Now psychologists are being called upon for some work of this kind in Pedagogical Institutes, as a result of the recent change in the educational law combining practical work with academic education. It is too early to have definite results yet, but one can anticipate that there will be increasing use of psychologists, not only with respect to cognitive, but also with respect to social-psychological problems. Social Psychology is presently in the Academy of Philosophy, especially in the sub-section on History and Dialectical Materialism. The approach is largely deductive.

In response to a question as to whether they ever made special studies, for example, of a new collective farm or factory where things were going especially well, compared with one where things were not going as well, the reply was they "study such things all of the time in every farm and factory." There are inspectors coming from outside, whose duty it is to look into such things. Keeping track of how things are going is the duty of the Party members. Furthermore, everyone participates in sessions of self-criticism. Extensive reports from these sources are continually going to the section on History and Dialectical Materialism. Typically, long before any trouble develops, they know that it is likely to come and why. "Our whole system is geared to evaluate the results of such social experiments."

BERITASHVILI INSTITUTE OF PHYSIOLOGY,
GEORGIAN ACADEMY OF SCIENCES, GEORGIA

This lab is under the direction of I. S. Beritashvili. (He was known

233

as Beritov in Moscow, but on his return to Georgia he again took the original spelling of his name.) He is a dapper and energetic man of perhaps 75 years, and was a very cordial host. (Georgia is famous for longevity and hospitality!) A younger colleague, T. Ioseliani, acted as our guide and interpreter. There is also an administrative director, S. P. Narikashvili. In addition to his Institute position, Beritashvili (who studied under Wedenski and Magnus) is Chairman of the Department of Physiology at the local University. The Institute has been operating for 25 years. There are 35 scientific workers, and 20 to 35 technicians.

When we arrived at the laboratory Beritashvili outlined the general program of the laboratory. Some of the major problems included:

1. Influence of cortex on interaction of subcortical structures. Last year they studied evoked potentials in the subcortex after cortical stimulation. This year they expect to study the effect of cortical stimulation on the subcortical interaction between the specific and nonspecific pathways. They will also study the effect of drugs on this interaction.

2. Regeneration of the cortical tissue, which may occur in young animals.

3. The orientation reflex.

4. Influence of cerebellum on paleocortex.

5. Afferent connections of caudate nucleus.

6. Effect of bilateral removal of caudate nucleus.

7. The role of the orbital cortex in emotional reactions.

8. Effect of subcortical stimulation on conditional reflexes.

9. Histological study of cortico-reticular connections.

10. Cortical circulation.

11. Source of ammonia during neural activity.

The last three of these problems are morphological. Study of structure is important but very complicated, and needs much cooperation. (The next triennial symposium of physiologists in Georgia will be devoted to this problem.)

Beritashvili commented on the stellate (or star) neurones in the cortex; many seem to have no long connections, but feed back into themselves. Do they have something to do with consciousness or with images? Their potentials differ from those of the pyramidal cells. Cortical layers III and IV have a very great number of these cells. It is also true that there is an increasingly large number of star cells as we go up the animal scale to the apes and man (cf. Jasper and Li.). Beritashvili thinks that most memories are localized in the sensory area. (See his paper in *Comptes Rendus (Doklady) de L'Academie des Sciences de L'Urss,* "Studies on Central Nervous Activity," Moscow, 1939, 23, No. 1, pp. 30-76.)

The stellate cells are assumed to be activated by sensory input, but also can be reactivated by feedback from other cortical areas. Beritashvili's theory of the stellate cells as the basis of the image, in some ways resembles Hebb's theory of cell assemblies.

Beritashvili pointed out that he did most of his present research on the role of images in behavior at the University. He agrees with Pavlov that UCR and CR explain behavior, but he thinks this applies only to automatic behavior. Such automatic acts may not even involve vision. For example, a typical CR such as a dog responding to a stimulus by lever-pressing for food, actually involves a chain of CRs. But there are still higher types of behavior. A delayed reaction with a one-day delay, for example, is not a CR. The same is true of detour situations. This behavior is controlled by images. The same thing may be seen in dogs, chickens and rabbits, and was demonstrated in a movie. Thus if a dog sees food behind a barrier, the next time he goes to the room he goes directly to the barrier. In non-automatized behavior the animal has an image of food location; if the location is changed the animal searches for it. The image, once it arises, lasts a long time. The delay may be as long as a week. (cf. reprint in English.)

Behavior is a more inclusive term than "conditioning" and is roughly comparable to *adaptation to the environment. Reflex* is a simple response to stimulus. Thus after pinching a leg there is a *flexion reflex,* followed by the *behavior* of escaping. Such behavior is made up of S-R connections, but it has a goal. To study this behavior we need other methods (particularly allowing free motion). There is often one-trial learning. This he calls "individual behavior." Behavior is directed by psycho-neural processes produced by the environment.

Images based on a complex of processes in the "star" or stellate neurones with short axons, in layers III and IV of the cortex, are projected into the environment by vision and labyrinthine perception; that is, there is spatial organization. Stimulation of any one part of this complex revives the whole image (i.e. as in the old concept of redintegration, the smell or taste will evoke the whole,the perception of an orange). Beritashvili emphasized the importance of the labyrinth for spatial perceptions; it seems more important than vision. Muscle receptors are not important except in automatized behavior.

Schlosberg asked if Soviet psychologists objected to the use of the word "images." Beritashvili said, "Only the Pavlovian psychologists and physiologists." Then Beritashvili himself objected to Köhler's concept of "insight."

We then saw a movie on delayed reaction, made in 1938. Dogs, rabbits, and hens were shown a goal object in one part of a room, and then moved to a standard starting stand. They were able to return to the goal object as soon as they were released by a stimulus or by opening the door. In one particularly interesting series of experiments, the animal was shown one food, removed to the stand, and then shown a second food in a different place as much as three minutes later. After return to the starting stand and release after a delay, the hen and the rabbit invariably went to the second food, even though the first one was normally preferred. However, the dogs go to the preferred food, even if that was the first one shown.

A second movie showed the extreme importance of the labyrinth in orientation. If the labyrinth is destroyed in animals, there is complete disorientation. Special experiments eliminated the role of olfaction and vision. The labyrinth is equally important in both active and passive movement; i.e. it doesn't matter whether the animal is pulled across the floor, walks, or is carried in a box. The movie also demonstrated the role of certain cortical areas in orientation, especially those related to the labyrinth. The cerebellum is very important as a transforming mechanism. If the vestibular area of the cortex is destroyed, the cerebellum isn't enough to permit orientation. However, if the cerebellum is damaged, but the cortex is intact, orientation is disturbed.

Most of these generalizations were based on dogs, using passive movement in a carrier, often under a blind-folded condition. The basic technique was to carry the dog in a box to a certain place in the room, let him see food, and then to carry him back to a different starting place. The intact animal, even when blindfolded, will leave the box when the starting door is opened and go to approximately the location of the food. However, in certain cases, when the box was placed a considerable distance from the food after some movement, the dog would not leave the box until the door had been closed and the box moved nearer the food. When the labyrinth was removed, often by cauterizing, the dogs performed very poorly in the tests.

Similarly, deaf children can orient as well as do normal children, if the labyrinth is normal, but they are disoriented in blindfold tests if the labyrinth is damaged. One experiment in the movie showed a blindfolded child being carried around in a semi-circle and then released. The child can either backtrack to the starting position on a semi-circle, or he can return to the starting position by the shortest route, direct from the place where he is put on the floor. Children with normal hearing, but blindfolded, could hear the experimenter walk from their side to follow a large Z painted on the floor (each path measured about 8 feet long). The children could then follow this path surprisingly well, showing that they had localized movements of the experimenter quite accurately in space by auditory cues.

There were some experiments on obstacle avoidance by the blind, roughly similar to those of Dallenbach, but more extensive. Among other things, it was shown that if the sense of hearing is disturbed by earphones, the ability to avoid obstacles disappears.

We had a discussion of the possible effect of previous experience on the dogs and other animals in the movies. Beritashvili pointed out that each specific experiment shown represented the first time the animal had tried it. However, there had been a good bit of previous experimentation of the same general sort, and we were reminded of Harlow's "learning to learn." There was also the question as to whether or not the previous life experience of the animal would be important. (It might be interesting to try some of his spatial orientation studies in cage-reared animals.) The experiments in the movies prove their point, irrespective of the role of experience in acquiring the ability to respond in this way; the role of experience would be an additional problem.

Complete Regeneration of the Cerebral Cortex. According to a report by N. Dzidzishvili, complete regeneration of the cerebral cortex seems to be possible, in puppies and kittens, if the operation is performed early enough. The electrical activity in the regenerated cortex appears normal. He removed one hemisphere at a half- or one-month of age (two months is too late for good or complete regeneration). The operation was done carefully using either a spoon or suction to remove the tissue, but some portions of the cortex remained, presumably fragments. If the basic structures below the cortex are untouched, these isolated bits of cortex grow or regenerate, so that after one month, you can't tell the normal from the regenerated cortex.

He plans to study the relation between the regenerated cortex and the reticular formation, using both electrophysiological and histological techniques. From present evidence, they know that there is rapid proliferation of cells in the first few days. But they do not know how the gyri, connections, etc. develop. He pointed out that Kogan, at Rostov, has studied the same thing in the visual cortex. (Pfaffmann reports that Bob Benjamin, at Wisconsin, a former student of his, has tried this type experiment, and has had no evidence of regeneration.)

A. Roitbak reported on evoked potential studies of conditioning. He has found that the evoked potential produced by a stimulus changes when this stimulus becomes CS and back again when the CR is extinguished. (He has a paper about to appear in the *Canadian EEG Journal.*) Now Roitbak is studying the orientation reflex (most authors consider it mainly reticular in origin). He has found that electrical stimulation of the auditory cortex produces the orienting reflex and that it will adapt out. Also, the medial geniculate body shows the same phenomenon. The medial geniculate body produces both electrical and behavioral arousal. He thinks arousal and orientation are related; the typical sequence is sleep, followed by arousal, followed by orientation. Stimulation of the geniculate body, he believes, affects the auditory cortex, which stimulates the reticular formation, which in turn arouses the whole cortex.

Experiment on Reaction Time. Reaction time varies from time to time. The cause of this variation has been unknown, but Roitbak thinks he has found one cause. Reaction time is associated with phases of breathing. During the inspiration phase, reaction time is shortened by as much as 100 milliseconds (visual or auditory RT), using a key pressure as a response. There seems to be no relation between RT and EEG.

In an attempt to check on some of the physiological factors involved, he used animals, with electrodes on the auditory area. A click, set at threshold level, does not produce a primary response in the auditory cortex except on the inspiratory phase of breathing. The animals were either under light anesthesia, with special electrodes on a thin portion of the skull, or implanted electrodes in a chronic experiment. Schlosberg pointed out that there might be some relation between these experiments and the old belief that the optimal fore-period was about two seconds, which would just about give a person time to take a breath and brace himself for the response.

M. A. Nutsubidse reported on studies of faradic stimulation of the orbital cortex, which produces signs of anxiety in cats. Combining stimulation of the orbital cortex with a new stimulus produces conditioned anxiety. For example, it was possible to cause a hungry cat to avoid food. If the neocortex is removed, a fear CR can still be set up, but it is forgotten after about a week; normal animals retain this much longer. Removal of the neocortex increases rage and pleasure (purring) but decreases fear. Later, she seems to have said that complete removal knocks out all pleasure responses. She has never been able to condition rage, but has conditioned fear.

Ablation of the orbital cortex produces sensory-motor feeding difficulties, presumably fundamentally motor. However, removal of the uncus, without damage to the orbital cortex, gives aversion to eating and drinking, with no motor deficiency.

Beritashvili believes that the hypothalamus cannot form temporary connections, i.e. mediate conditioning, but it can be involved with higher areas, where such connections can be formed (the discussion mentioned Masserman, and Neal Miller's work). That is, the hypothalamus has no separate role in conditioning.

Beritashvili then asked us what we thought of Penfield's concept of the centrencephalic system, namely, that diencephalic centers are the seat of consciousness. He quoted as negative evidence the case of a microcephalic girl who behaved as unconscious, but histological examination (post mortem) showed the diencephalon to be normal. (He mentioned a book of his in press, translated by Liberson, *Neural Mechanisms of Behavior*, to be published soon by Little, Brown.) He then asked another question, "Can any cortical stimulus serve as CS?" Schlosberg said that he doubted that one of the frontal lobe could, and Beritashvili agreed, but Miller disagreed. Roitbak promised to put a student on the problem.

Miller then asked Roitbak how his theory explained the fact that extinction is speeded up when reinforcement is omitted. Roitbak said he believed reinforcement excites the lower section of the reticular formation, which he thinks is antagonistic to the thalamic nuclei of the reticular formation which are responsible for inhibition. Narikashvili doesn't agree. Beritashvili thinks that in a free-movement situation, there is an image of absence of food, which causes S to avoid the place of non-reward. This would account for one-trial extinction. Pavlov found one-trial extinction in a dog which had undergone many reversals of conditioning and extinction. It is especially apt to happen when the dog isn't hungry.

We must comment on the extremely hospitable way in which we were entertained, in keeping with a long-established Georgian custom.

GENERAL IMPRESSIONS OF THE SOVIET SCIENTIFIC SCENE

1. We were greatly impressed with the large number of Research Institutes, in which the personnel are free to devote their whole time to pure-science research. Some of the Institutes were at Universities; a considerable number of them were separately located. Some of the members of these Institutes also have teaching appointments and some students are working for advanced degrees at these Institutes; but the new plan of combining practical work with study may send other students to work at these Institutes as technicians. However, the primary mission of these Institutes is research.

2. We were also impressed with the level of technical assistance given to psychologists and physiologists, especially at the Research Institutes. Apparently, it is possible to give not only the leading creative scientists, but also their collaborators and technicians at all professional levels a secure career in such Institutes. Many women are working in the laboratories. We were impressed by the number of our Soviet colleagues who have special secretaries, who are graduates of the Language Institute, to assist them in keeping up with English, German or other Western literature.

3. Although some of the equipment is ingeniously homemade or only fairly adequate, a great deal of the equipment is absolutely top-notch. The physiological laboratories seemed to have a somewhat higher priority than the psychological ones on equipment, but both are usually well equipped.

4. We were impressed with the high prestige given to scientists and, generally, to intellectual and artistic activities, as well as with the amount of reading engaged in by the general public.

5. Apparently, everybody uses *conditioning* as synonymous with *learning* at all levels of complication. Thus conditioning may refer to a classical conditioned response, to a natural learned response (such as a rabbit eating a carrot thrust at him), to an instrumental response (such as pushing a lever for food), or to pressing a key to a signal after having been verbally instructed to do so. Rather than responding freely, however, the subject almost always is required to respond to a special signal, and often to differentiate a positive from a negative stimulus.

6. There is widespread interest in the reticular formation and the arousal response. There is considerable interest in searching for submechanisms involved in more specific types of arousal and in differentiating among the various nuclei of the reticular formation. There also is interest in looking for structures, other than the reticular formation, which participate in arousal.

7. There is a good deal of interest in what Pavlov called "the orienting reflex," and considerable tendency to equate it with arousal via the reticular formation. Other groups seem to be using the orienting reflex as a basis for studying phenomena which we might describe as "curiosity."

8. There is frequent use of the EEG simultaneously with the conditioning technique and/or verbal reports. Many studies involve recording from electrodes chronically implanted in animals.

9. Often both salivary and motor responses are recorded simultaneously.

10. There is considerable interest in the modification of sensory

thresholds or afferent mechanisms by CNS influences. There is considerable interest in afferent integration, feedback and imagery.

11. Sensory activity is regarded as a sensory-motor reflex.

12. The term "motivation" is rarely used. This concept is referred to as "idealistic" and "of Freudian origin."

13. There is a widespread interest in individual differences, usually based on Pavlov's typology, which goes back to the choleric, phlegmatic, melancholic and sanguine temperaments of Hippocrates, but has been given a physiological slant.

14. Much work that might be done in psychological laboratories in this country, is done in physiological laboratories in the U.S.S.R.

15. We were struck with the extent to which our first-hand observations contrasted with our preconceived notions of the U.S.S.R., and believe that many of our Russian colleagues would experience similar surprises on visiting the U.S.A.

16. In many respects the people in the U.S.S.R. are especially similar to Americans; in fact, they seemed to us like a group of happy extroverted Texans, proud of their State and its accomplishments.

APPENDIX

Visit to Warsaw

Department of Neurophysiology of the Nencki Institute of Experimental Biology

In general, the people at the Institute publish in English. Complete reports are published in an Annual, *Acta Biologicae Experimentalis,* Polish Academy of Sciences, Nencki Institute of Experimental Biology, 3 Pasteura Street, Warsaw. Current volume is XIX, 1959. Short papers and preliminary reports are published in *Bull. L'academie Polonaise des Science. Serie des Sciences Biologicques* now in Volume 8, No. 2, Warsaw, 1960. Sometimes longer reports are published (primarily in Polish, but sometimes in English) in *Acta Physiologica Polonica.* All of these Journals are available on request.

In addition to ablation and brain stimulation, there are a great many behavorial experiments on both instrumental and classical CR conducted here. The Director, J. Konorski, thinks ablation techniques are crude, but necessary at times. But if conditioned reflex tests can be used for analysis of the effects of the operation, some progress may be made. He thinks tests such as the maze and some of Harlow's experiments are too complicated to be related to physiological processes. He prefers tests where physiological principles are clearly understood. (By physiological, he means concepts such as "inhibition," as used by neurophysiologists like Eccles, but not as used by Pavlov, whose neurophysiology he described as an imaginary one.)

Techniques of Instrumental and Salivary Conditioning. The instrumental response for food which is used in this laboratory consists of a pressure, usually with the right forefoot, on a panel measuring approximately 6 by 6 inches, mounted in a horizontal position slightly above the floor of a platform. The platform contains a disc that rotates to expose one food cup at a time under a hole. The dog is trained to make the paw movement to the CS. Initially, on certain trials his leg is moved passively to the CS, but passive movement is omitted on other trials, with no food unless the dog makes the movement himself. This is reported to be an economical method of training.

Salivary secretion is obtained from the externalized orifice of the salivary gland. Instead of transplanting the mucous membrane, only the duct is externalized. A blunt wire is thrust into the duct to keep it open during the operation and subsequently is withdrawn. The end of the duct is slit so that it can be sewed down on the adjoining skin, which has been gently scraped to expose raw flesh to which the duct will grow. Careful postoperative care is required to avoid blocking of the duct until it has healed thoroughly. It is especially important to remove all caked saliva.

The connection with the exteriorized salivary duct is made *via* a disc attached with the traditional (but not altogether satisfactory) hot cement. Saliva is siphoned through a tube to a reservoir (which prevents it from gumming up the recording apparatus). As the saliva is sucked into the reservoir, water flows down a tube to actuate the plunger of a small insulin hypodermic syringe mounted vertically at a lower level. The plunger is very free moving; a little rubber cup attached to the top of the syringe and filled with water serves a dual function of lubrication and sealing. A light pulley arrangement, mounted on the plunger, doubles the excursion of the recording pen writing on a smoked drum. They take care to see that no air is trapped in the system since this would produce a lag in recording.

Soltysik and Zbrozyna have improved this technique still further by externalizing the salivary duct close to where it leaves the gland and by extirpating certain small associated glands which secrete mucus. This eliminates muscle artifacts (as in chewing, and so forth). As a result, Soltysik can observe latencies of one second, whereas the old Pavlov technique, with its inertia and included air, usually had a lag of ten seconds. This is extremely important, for it determines the minimum CS-US interval in conditioning, and the lag of Pavlov's equipment may have accounted for the typical experiment in which the so-called simultaneous CR has an CS-US interval of ten to twenty seconds—an interval still typically maintained in the Russian experiments.

Defensive instrumental CRs are established to acid in the mouth or a puff of air or a shock to the ear. They deliberately chose a noxious stimulus which does not intrinsically elicit the avoidance movement (paw lifting) as a UR. But when this movement (passive or accidental) follows the CS, no noxious stimulus is delivered. Otherwise, it is delivered.

Once a good defense CR has been established in which the CS is terminated by the CR, a normal dog needs no further reinforcement. Furthermore, the noxious stimulus doesn't have to be strong.

In addition to the leg movement, breathing and heart rate are often recorded. We saw Soltysik record the latter by a tiny microphone on the carotid artery which had been externalized in a protective sleeve of skin to form a "carotid cuff."

Removal of Cortical Taste Area for UR. Santibanez, a visiting

Professor of Physiology from the University of Chile, used dogs whose unilateral taste area had been removed. Each dog had an instrumental CR to get food (panel press), plus a salivary CR. The CS-US interval was ten seconds plus five seconds overlap, with a two minute intertrial interval. The typical results show that experimenting can be started six days after the operation, and that both sides are depressed for as long as ten days. The CR and UCR of the homolateral side continue to be depressed, but the contralateral side shows increased activity. This holds for both food and acid, for conditioned and unconditioned reflexes. If the cortical area in the other hemisphere is then removed, there is again a general depression, but eventually facilitation (which they had not expected) on both sides. This is interpreted as some kind of release phenomenon. After operation, the variability is also markedly increased as measured by the "sigma" of the distribution of scores.

Lesions of Premotor Cortex. In an experiment by Stepien, using instrumental CR for food, the premotor cortex (corresponding roughly to area 6) had been removed, producing a CR analog of apraxia. When we saw it, the dog acted essentially normal (the lesion may have been too small, so that recovery had occurred). A more typical dog shows deterioration for a few days after the operation, often making intertrial responses. Then there is recovery, but with some intertrial movements, and more or less chaotic behavior.

We also saw an instrumental CR of the defense type, in the same dog, but in a different room. He made frequent and fairly regular intertrial responses of either leg. (Left leg flexion, in one room, avoided shock to ear. In another room, right leg lifting produced food.)

With the next dog, ten weeks had elapsed since the operation, but he worked somewhat better. (After operation, steady retraining is essential, one session per day, shifting between alimentary and defense CRs.) This dog made no intertrial movements, but seemed to have trouble "making up his mind to lift the leg." There is, typically, some gradual recovery from a disturbance like this, although it is variable from dog to dog, and may last over a year of training.

The preceding operation, especially if the entire sensorimotor cortex is removed, gives disreflexia. The animal is variable for both positive and negative stimuli, for both defense and alimentary motor responses with many intertrial responses.

Recent Memory. The experiment of Chorazyna is concerned with the physiology of recent memory; the ordinary CR deals with stable long-term memory. Konorski's laboratory has a strong interest in immediate memory. A good test of it was carried out by Mrs.

245

Karolja, who presented two tones as the CS. The first tone came on for three seconds, then there was a pause of up to five seconds, and then the second tone came on for three seconds. If both tones are the same pitch, the animal is reinforced after the second tone, and eventually this becomes the positive CS. If they are different, however, the animal is not reinforced, and the combination is negative. This means that the animal must remember the first tone until the second tone comes, so they may be compared. Extending the interval between tones to seven seconds is likely to produce a neurosis. Incidentally, Konorski pointed out that they are not interested in studying experimental neuroses, so they make every effort to avoid this complication. After such training, they remove the anterior and posterior sylvian gyri (the fourth acoustic area). In this case, the animals react positively to both stimuli, regardless of whether they are the same or different.

If the difference between the two stimuli is one of pitch, there is very little recovery after six months of continued training. However, if the difference is one of loudness, there is some recovery, but not to the level of perfection. (The dog we saw had been trained for three months on a four-second delay.)

Other comparable experiments show visual loss when the temporal-occipital association is removed, and some areas more lateral and ventral. Both visual and auditory systems show loss on this task when the hippocampus is removed.

As indicated previously, other variations on this test for recent memory were tried. One method used a given tone for a given day as the positive CS and one higher as the negative CS. This is very difficult for the dog, who seems to have absolute, rather than relative, pitch. Chorazyna now uses three negative to one positive stimulus, which avoids the effect of food on the negative stimulus. The method is an improvement.

An Analysis of Delayed Reaction. This experiment, conducted by Lawicka, was conducted in a fairly large room (approximately 25 ft. square), converted into a rough oval with the aid of screens. The starting platform was located near one wall, with food delivery devices in the center of each of the remaining three walls. E stood at the starting platform, which also had a chain to hold the dog's collar. The experimenter leashed the dog at the start and then sounded a buzzer, for example, at food station No. 2. The dog was restrained for one minute; when released, he went directly to station No. 2 where food was then delivered, ate, and returned to the start. (The delay can be longer if necessary.) The dog does not always stay pointing, but may move around in various positions. Nevertheless, he went

246

consistently to the proper food platform when he was released. We saw several dogs perform in this fashion.

If the prefrontal cortical areas are removed, the dog loses the ability for correct delayed response without maintained orientation. However, he can still respond correctly if allowed to remain pointing. They are now investigating the effects of removing portions of the prefrontal area.

Hunger Elicited by Electrical Stimulation of Goat's Brain. We visited a research laboratory of two women, W. Wyrwicka and C. Dobrzecka, for the study of behavior in goats. Dr. Wyrwicka, one of Konorski's former students, now also heads the laboratory at Lodz, which Konorski left some time ago.

The goat has several advantages as an experimental animal. One is that permanent electrode attachments can be firmly attached to the horns for supports; another is that they will stand quietly so that electrodes can be implanted with only local anesthesia. They can be tested immediately, or the electrodes changed at any time without further anesthesia (i.e. raised or lowered). The electrodes are adjustable Hess-type, with three parallel units which can be moved to the correct depth during the experiment. For eating, the electrodes are placed in the plane of the bregma (about 3mm. laterally).

In the experiment we viewed, the goat received bread from a plate if he pressed with his left foot, but did not get fed if he pressed with his right foot. He worked very regularly.

The purpose of this research is to understand the role of the hypothalamus. One goat, who had an alimentary CR to the general experimental situation, had been trained daily for a month or more with every response reinforced. Then electrodes are inserted into the hypothalamus and stimulated by a train of square waves, 50 per second, with 1 millisecond duration. (This was the only pulse duration produced by the only stimulator available, although 5 milliseconds would have been better.)

Electrical stimulation in a certain area of the hypothalamus produces very good eating and lever pressing by satiated goats. The usual latency for this response is ten seconds, with a variation between five and twenty. The latency tends to be longer at the beginning of the experiment, and to decrease after a few trials.

If a discrimination is established with normal hunger, there will be disinhibition, indicated by responses to the negative stimulus, when the hunger is greatly increased. Similarly, during a period of continuous moderate electrical stimulation, the animal will respond only to the positive stimulus, but if the current is turned up, he will also make some responses to the negative stimulus. After ordinary experimental extinction, goats show similar disinhibition if the period of food deprivation is lengthened, or the current is strengthened.

In another experiment, the researchers stimulated two centers, one in the lateral, and the other in the medial hypothalamus. The medial center stops the hungry goat from eating—it spits out food, but it does not leave the food tray. Hence, the central stimulation doesn't seem to elicit a defense response. With strong stimulation in the medial area, postinhibitory rebound will show up—the moderately hungry animal presses and eats more rapidly than before for a period after the stimulation is turned off.

It is possible to balance E against I points in the hypothalamus, giving simple algebraic summation, with some rebound when the I is turned off.

A panel-pressing CR to electrical stimulation will continue for a long time if the food is given, even though the stimulus (which keeps the animal from eating the food) is turned off before the animal eats. But, if the food is omitted, prompt extinction occurs.

In one experiment, the animal received food by pressing the left foreleg in the front of the cage, and water by lifting the right hindleg in the back of the cage. Stimulation of the alimentary point, which is related to hunger, produced left foreleg flexion in front of the cage, and never the hindleg flexion in the back of the cage. This shows that the hypothalamic point is specific for hunger.

Aggression sometimes accompanies eating at some electrode locations. For example, the goat when stimulated may attack a dog and then appear to be surprised.

They are now working on defense escape reaction to stimulation of certain points in the hypothalamus. Will the goat respond to turn off electrical stimulation of the brain?

The Laboratory of Physiology at Lodz [7]

Mrs. Wyrwicka is Director of this Laboratory. In it they are experimenting on rabbits with lesions in the region of the ventromedial nucleus of the hypothalamus. They use lever pressing to the general situation. Mrs. H. Balinska reported that such lesions increase the rabbit's preference for grains. This was interpreted as an increase in preference for protein. A. Ortowski used a metronome as an inhibitory stimulus and reported that the operation did not produce appreciable disinhibition even though it increased the food intake by 400 per cent. But an increase in hunger to 48 hours did not apparently produce much disinhibition either, nor did metrazol or strychnine convulsions. Pre-

---

[7] These researchers came to Warsaw to visit us.

liminary results suggest that chlorpromazine does not produce disinhibition.

Mrs. K. Lewinska has studied the amount of food consumed as a function of the duration of food deprivation. She finds that before the operation, the maximum occurs at approximately 24 hours, but afterward it occurs at approximately 66 hours.

J. Wojtczak studied the defense reflex as influenced by medial hypothalamic lesion in both dogs and rabbits. If the rabbit has an alimentary and a defense reflex (such as jumping onto a safety island to avoid shock) both are disturbed by the operation, but the alimentary is most disturbed. In hyperphagic rabbits, there is eosinophilia (a stress effect). Before the operation, ACTH drops the eosinophil count in the blood by 50 per cent, but after the operation ACTH gives a 100 per cent decrease (i.e. to zero).

Experiments of Soltysik in Konorski's Laboratory. We have already referred to Solytsik's improvement in recording the salivary response by placing the fistula much nearer the gland to avoid muscle artifacts, and by means of a completely air-free system to insure quick response.

Previous experimenters had found that, if they first trained an instrumental response to one stimulus and then trained a classical response to a second stimulus, the instrumental response automatically tranferred to the second stimulus. Since his improved method records salivation with a shorter latency, he was able to use a shorter CS-US interval. This shorter interval did not produce such transfer.

Earlier work of Soltysik showed that instrumental CRs are very dependent on the degree of hunger. Now he is studying the effects of satiation on the strength of both the classical and the instrumental CRs for food, described above. We saw him producing satiation by double sized reinforcements, giving about one per minute.

He finds that the unconditioned response shows little satiation effect, measured either by salivation or by pulse rate. The conditioned response shows satiation as measured by both of these effects, but the instrumental response is usually the most subject to satiation. However, with certain stimuli (which he calls "very motogenic" ones), or with more training trials, or shorter delay of reward, the instrumental response may be persistent. He believes that stimuli on the leg and the flank are more motogenic than auditory stimuli, and hence are more resistant to both satiation and experimental extinction.

Experiments in which he varied the size of the portion show that the UCR varies with the amount consumed, rather than with the number of trials, but the trials with either one-fourth or twice the normal size of portion, apparently produce faster satiation of the CR. Discussion by Konorski of Experiments on De-afferentation. The chief statement in Miller and Konorski's original theory might be phrased as follows: "The animal performs the movements when feedback from movement is a signal for food. He stops the movement if movement is not reinforced." At that time Konorski thought (as do the vast majority of psychologists and physiologists today) that the chief difference between autonomic and voluntary responses was the presence of feedback in the latter rather than the former. This seemed so obvious that when some of his students proposed an experiment to test it, he told us that he did not feel it was a good investment of time, but refrained from discouraging them too much in deference to freedom of scientific investigation. E. Jankowska and T. Garska established a scratch reflex in cats, as an instrumental CR to get food. They de-afferented the leg, but the conditioned reflex persisted.

Konorski asked them to try the experiment by setting up the CR after the operation. The CR could be learned after de-afferentation. Thinking that cats, perhaps, might be special, he had the researchers try it on dogs and found that even extensive de-afferentation doesn't interfere with instrumental conditioning. They concluded that proprioception isn't needed for voluntary movement, it only makes the movement more precise.

One of the more recent experiments by R. Tarnecki was to de-afferent the leg in a cat before training. Then the response to be conditioned was elicited by stimulation of the motor cortex and used as an instrumental response for food. Such conditioning occurred when reward was given but not if reward was omitted.

Soltysik on Conditioned Fear. One of the main parts of the second afternoon session was a presentation on conditioned fear, by Soltysik. In the dog, foreleg lifting would turn off or prevent shock to the ear. Soltysik recorded the heart rate classical CR by aid of a carotid sleeve, as well as the leg movement. His results:

1. Lesions involving the caudate nucleus, internal capsule and some of the anterior thalamic nuclei abolished both the instrumental avoidance CR and the heart rate acceleration. These could not be retrained, although both unconditioned responses were intact. These animals seem disoriented.

2. In a normal dog with a weak instrumental avoidance CR, the occurrence of the motor response could be predicted from the degree of heart rate acceleration to CS. There seemed to be a definite threshold effect, below which the motor response did not occur. Soltysik then established a discrimination and found that when the

heart rate acceleration to S — had extinguished below the level that ordinarily predicted the instrumental response, the instrumental response to S — dropped out. Hence, he concluded it was fear, not a defense response, which was extinguished on S —.

Soltysik's Explanation of Resistance to Extinction. Soltysik observed, in well-trained animals, that there was a correlation between the occurrence of defense response and beginning of cardiac deceleration back toward normal after the initial acceleration to the CS. Thus the stimuli produced by the defense response acted as an inhibitor for fear. Can activation of an inhibitory center help to preserve activity of the fear center?

In order to test this theory, he trained a food response recording leg, heart rate, saliva and breathing. Then he set up a conditioned inhibition, and presented a positive stimulus, followed in three seconds by the negative stimulus for 100 trials, with no simple positive trials at all. Early cardiac acceleration (coming before the negative stimulus) showed no sign of extinction. When the negative stimulus was omitted on the following test trials, all parts of the conditioned response had the original strength. He concluded that this proved his case. (There were some people, however, both in the laboratory and among us three, who were not completely convinced.)

GENERAL DISCUSSION

On a second afternoon, all of the staff, the scientists from Lodz, and the few local psychologists met for another discussion. Konorski began by saying that motivation as a concept was not needed for classical CR, and went on to show that he thought the concept was not needed for an instrumental conditioning either. In place of motivation, Konorski uses terms like "states of excitation of feeding centers," etc. Schlosberg commented that he agreed completely with Konorski, except that he thought motivation was a convenient loose term or chapter heading for drive-incentive relationships. Konorski agreed.

Somewhere in the discussion the fact came out that when hemidicortication knocks out contralateral responses, a naturally learned response immediately transfers spontaneously to the other side, whereas laboratory CRs do not. Possibly this is because the natural CR may involve alternate use of either side, whereas the laboratory CR is limited to one side.

There followed a long discussion on this and other related topics, in which everyone seemed quite free to express agreement or disagreement with anyone else. There was no need for a translator, for essentially everyone in the laboratory appeared able to understand English.

Konorski's laboratory shows what can be done with brains, originality and enthusiasm, despite shortage of funds. We don't think we saw a decent EEG apparatus while we were there, although one of his students, who is going to study for a year with Don Lindsley, has been told that the Academy will give him $5,000 for such equipment when he returns. 90 per cent of the recording is done with old wide-drum kymographs, although there are a few home-made inkwriting kymographs. There is almost no electronic equipment, and Konorski laughingly remarked that "nothing electrical works in Poland, except electric lights, and they are a bit better than candles." There seems to be plenty of room, including adequate quarters for over 100 dogs. But, in spite of simple equipment, they do excellent work.

CHAPTER VIII

Soviet Life and Soviet Psychology
GARDNER MURPHY AND LOIS MURPHY

After short visits to Japan and India, we took an Aeroflot jet plane on Saturday, August 27, 1960, across the vast stretch of the Himalayas. In late morning we landed in Tashkent in Uzbekistan—a glowing tropical sun-and-desert country, which through the extensive use of four large rivers has been irrigated and transformed into a very rich agricultural area. We were put up at a good Intourist hotel and supplied with an excellent interpreter and guide.

The visit, even in 48 hours, gave us a tremendous sense of the rapidity and depth of institutional changes. We were taken on Saturday afternoon to an interesting historical museum, where we were given an intelligent and intelligible account of the life of the region from prehistoric to contemporary times. In the fine arts museum we were confronted by the great modern paintings of Benkov and his students. He had gone to Uzbekistan to share his perceptions and his skills with a people who had no representative arts before.

YOUNG PIONEER PALACE

Sunday, the 28th, was a memorable day. We visited the Young Pioneer Palace, the only example of the extracurricular activities for children we had an opportunity to see in the U.S.S.R. We heard children enthusiastically recite slogans for the new group life, as they do when they greet their teachers at school (schools were not in session until September 1). We were graciously led by the arm by mid-adolescent girls to the room in which band practice was going on (anybody with a musical skill can play, so that there were eleven accordions in a group of forty pieces, but they played with spirit and vigor and reasonable competence) on into a very charming show of five-year-olds learning the first ballet steps—Russian children mixed with Uzbek children, that is, white with brown—and that great grace which one thinks of in terms of Russian dancing.

Then on into the children's parks. We saw everywhere health and agricultural slogans and posters, a statue of Lenin and a quotation to the effect that the strength of government is based on the people's understanding: "a government is strong only insofar as the people are free to know everything about everything."

In one area there was a place for quiet play at large tables, with games and toys from a "lending library" of toys, operated as we would operate a lending library. That is, a child signs out a doll or toy which he ordinarily could not afford and plays with it for a period and then turns it back for some other child to use. Elsewhere in the playground we saw children playing group games and we joined in one of the simple dances. We also watched a delightful blind-man's-buff game in which a tiger boy and a bear boy (with appropriate masks) chase a girl who has castanets, which she must keep sounding to help them chase; of course, they stumble and bump into one another many times before they succeed in touching her.

In another part of the playground we saw children between the years of five and mid-adolescence playing chess, including a young Korean, apparently not more than five or six years of age (reputed to be quite a master for his age level), playing a Russian child. A few hundred yards away we saw another open space in which peace exhibits, flags of many nations and pictures of white doves were prominently displayed. The whole feeling was one of pride, confidence, sense of social participation; much planning for the children, and joyful response of the children to it.

We enjoyed these busy, skillful, happy children in the Pioneer Palace and the children's parks of Tashkent.

The attitude of Tashkent was like one we can remember from childhood: let us do our very best to show the visitors what a nice school we have, combined with the feeling of warmth and pleasure in being visited. Photographs were permitted indoors and out-of-doors in every part of these parks.

Here, and in Moscow and Leningrad, we got the strong impression that education is not just a matter of schools. The beautiful posters dealt with ways of building good health, varieties of vocational choices, and the importance of peace. The emphasis is on bringing up children to develop health, and skill in one's work. The U.S.S.R. wants more and better workers; and to become a good worker, one who does his task well, is a basic expression of patriotism, or devotion to the Soviet state.

On Monday morning we left by jet for Moscow, where Intourist placed us in the Leningradski Hotel, a large, rather comfortable, traditional "continental European" hotel, with slow, but fairly adequate meal service (aside from fruits and vegetables). At the end of August and early September we shared the traditional problem (both in the hotel and outside) of coping with the cold and damp. We had a splendid guide (again a young woman) who very conscientiously and competently helped us plan all that we did. She was even more eager to convince us that the Soviet way of life was the best in history. Finding that neither Professor A. R. Luria nor Professor A. A. Smirnov was available at the time, we used the first afternoon to see the Pushkin Museum of Fine Arts, magnificent with its Italian Renaissance and Dutch masters, including some Rembrandts.

ACADEMY OF PEDAGOGICAL SCIENCES

On Tuesday we saw Professor A. N. Leontiev, Director of the Institute of Psychology, Academy of Pedagogical Sciences, who had sent us a cordial letter and a copy of his book, *The Problems of Mental Development* (now scheduled for translation into English). We had a free-ranging conversation on psychology, in French. In describing, briefly, the Academy of Pedagogical Sciences, Leontiev said that it has a broad view, integrates experimental studies and theoretical development of concepts, establishes principles which are suitable for adaptation and application to local conditions in the separate republics. The Academy provides professional training, a program of research on working youth, including not only their working skill, but also their esthetic and personal development.

There were, according to Leontiev, 50 to 60 schools for "verifying principles of learning and education developed in the Institute," but these were not strictly experimental. They are directed by the Minister of Education, but the Ministers in different republics have the opportunity of applying the principles arrived at in the central institute, in different ways suited to the needs of their different republics. The autonomous representatives of the separate republics determine the details of application for their own areas.

Leontiev further stated that physical education and artistic education were available for everyone and that sports are encouraged as a way of fostering national esprit. Physical education is under the Ministry of Health. (We saw groups of high school children doing setting-up exercises, track, etc., on the streets, after school started in Leningrad. Emphasis on physical education is implemented in many different ways, both by the resources in the parks, school sports activities, posters of physical development and sports, etc.)

Leontiev's own work in the Institute of Psychology also includes preparation of teachers for guidance work, and industrial studies which involve training men to grasp general work principles. Take, for example, the use of tools to cut metal. It would be absurd to teach extensor movements, flexor movements, separate types of eye-hand coordination, etc., when the fundamental problems of cutting metal remain at a higher level of synthesis and must be so understood. They transcend specific manual operations. Working skills must be taught at a high level. He emphasized the need for systematic experimental work and made what we regarded as an excellent statement about psychology as a systematic experimental science. Cooperation, he said, was possible within the experimental field between workers in different countries, but cooperation between experimentalists' work and people occupied with work at a "verbal level" was much more difficult. Dominance here will remain with experimental approaches, but clinical, social, etc., are still needed. Interdisciplinary cooperation is very important, but there are many complexities. First, it is necessary to have a common problem and terrain.

Cognitive and motor functions had been systematically studied in psychology, he said, but not the feelings. When we asked why one must exclude Freud with reference to feelings, he said that undoubtedly there was a "great deal there to be learned," but also that it was impossible to sift out what was true and useful. As to learning theory, he accepted our view that some learning occurs without reinforcement, and that some is instrumental conditioning of the perceptual act or the act of attending; he agreed cordially to all of these propositions. He gave us several volumes from the work of the Academy.

On Tuesday, the 30th, we talked with Professor A. A. Smirnov through our guide-interpreter. He described his own experiments on memory, which emphasize different kinds of balance between first and second signal systems in normal and oligophrenic children.

Memory, he said, is best not for things easy-to-learn but for things that occasion difficulty or frustration; the second signal type of memory is largely verbal rather than imaginal. There is a great increase of ability to learn and remember as a consequence of training to grasp broad principles.

Wednesday was largely spent in a visit to the Tretiakov Museum, with its historical sequence of pre-revolutionary, revolutionary and post-revolutionary painting and sculpture. We also visited a department store, the Children's World, spoken of with much pride in Moscow, and the Folk Art Exhibit. The great variety of wood, ceramic, woven and embroidered products in the latter met a consistently high standard of artistic and technical excellence.

TRUE AND PSEUDO OLIGOPHRENIA

Professor Alexander Luria, having come back to Moscow late Wednesday, spent some time with us on Thursday.[1] We talked about

---
[1] Notes on this meeting were taken rapidly and probably are not very accurate.

his summer, during which he had been finishing a book on development. He said that his own research interests were now largely in neurophysiology.

There are no real mental defectives, he stated, except those with a physiological defect. As we understood him, there are a few *true* and many *pseudo* oligophrenics arising from social-emotional factors. True cases of oligophrenia showed distinctive EEG in response to photic driving. When asked, "What conditions produce emotionally disturbed children?" he responded, "Every kind of emotional conflict." Differential diagnosis by electroencephalogram and photic driving—differing responses to high and low frequencies—differentiate oligophrenic from normal. EEG's are obtained on normal children from ages eight to twelve. Abnormal EEG of frontal lobes appears in 10 per cent of the youngest children, but in 50 per cent at the age of 13 among mental defectives; alpha rhythm and slow waves, especially, show abnormalities. "Rhythmic activities of the cortex (especially under photic driving) can be used as diagnostic signs because the cortex of the feebleminded is in an inhibited state." Spontaneous rhythms can be used in diagnosis of high and low imbeciles.

When asked if "pseudo oligophrenia" can be helped most in the first five years, he said, "Yes, much work is being done with them now." Soviet results are said to be similar to ours. (Data will soon appear in English from Pergamon Press, in London.)

We then went with Professor Luria to the Institute of Defectology, where we met Drs. Zh. Shif and G. N. Soloviev and exchanged ideas with them regarding emotional conflict and the simpler types of therapy which are suitable. Doctor Shif was particularly interested in Western research. She emphasized work with "pseudo oligophrenics" who often have some partial defect in hearing or sight, or have speech difficulties, and so forth, which leads to retardation.

Dr. Shif also said there were more schools for the hard-of-hearing and for the retarded than there were for the blind. We saw briefly a young man who was interested in work with a Braille reading machine, which converts auditory into tactual equivalents of printed Russian characters, and also, if desired, visual into tactual, so that the blind, or severely handicapped with respect to vision, can "read" through touch without requiring a separate Braille book in every instance. He also showed us objects made in the process of tactile education of blind children who are helped to "see" with their fingers.

THE ORIENTING REFLEX

On Friday, we saw E. N. Sokolov[2] at the University. He took us about his laboratories, explaining what he was doing, listening carefully to our questions, and showed an interest in building bridges between physiological and psychological disciplines.

He began by describing the "orienting reflex" and its relation to "arousal." There is new work in collaboration with Vinogradova on oligophrenic cases, utilizing the alpha rhythm, the galvanic skin response (GSR), the electromyogram (EMG), and eye movements.

"Any *change* in the stimulus situation may produce orienting responses." There is high biological priority: the first thing the organism must do is to "know" whether the environment is changing or not. Ultimately, Sokolov hopes to get this at the level of the *individual neuron*. He describes all of his work so far recounted as the "objective study of sensory integration." It will be noted, however, that the term *integration* does not necessarily always mean an intercellular event.

In further discussion of the orienting reflex he describes the use of the plethysmograph, with vasodilation in the forehead and vasoconstriction in the finger. Asked if the just-noticeable differences for the orienting response are stable for the individual, he replied that the verbally-reported *JND* is similar to the threshold for the orienting response, but not absolutely identical; both of them, as we understood him, reflect a struggle between the defense reaction and an inhibition of the orienting reflex. With auditory stimulation autonomic indicators occur before the motor.

We emphasized that we were particularly interested in all the different kinds of studies of orientation, since our behavior records in the Coping Study at The Menninger Foundation had contained a good deal of material on the orientation processes as seen at a behavior level. Sokolov replied that the experimental procedures in the U.S.S.R. are focused on the degree of excitation, and the degree of newness, difficulty, etc., related to excitation; the habituation and drop in the level of excitation with habituation to a specific process. "Thus after twenty to thirty stimulations of the retina with a new stimulus, all components of the orienting response which occurred initially disappear. This refers to the various physiological measures used as indicators of the orienting response." His interpretation is

---

[2] This is the man whose name is more carefully transliterated by Razran as Ye. N. Sokolov, author of *Perception and the Conditioned Reflex*, Moscow, Moscow University, 1958, a book referred to by Razran as "probably the most significant Soviet contribution to psychology . . . of the present decade by a single author." It is now being translated into English.

that the orienting responses occur when there is a lack of coincidence between the brain models and the pattern of the stimuli, and the orienting responses disappear when the new model is elaborated in the brain.

With the infant and young child there is at first a small and then a big GSR response. After habituation this drops out. They also recognize individual differences due to the level of excitation in different children. They have used both the EEG and GSR in studying the orienting response, forehead vasodilation and vasoconstriction. If a stimulus is too strong, a defensive response amounting to vasoconstriction can be seen in the form of a drop of the plethysmographic record. "Sub-threshold responses can be studied by vasomotor measures also."

A reference was made to Bronstein in Leningrad, who has found that if a baby is stimulated with sound, sucking stops; that is, the orienting response inhibits sucking, and also the conditioned response and defense responses. Through these methods the capacity for spatial localization of sound can be studied in newborn babies as young as two hours.

"If the orienting response is strong, it can support motor reactions, but if it is too strong it inhibits the motor response. The orienting response reflects directly the level of excitation."

We asked further about these orientation responses at two or three hours of age. Sokolov replied that the child's orientation response to auditory stimulation proves the presence of hearing, even when audiometric determinations cannot be conducted. The orienting response can dominate even a very intense stimulus in the CR setup. He is studying the number of times the stimulus needs to be presented to give habituation. "The orienting response reflects directly the inhibitory relation; it can indicate the real presence of inhibition."

Before we left he introduced us to a young woman who is helping him in EEG work, and showed his equipment, some of which is French, some Russian.

Friday, we went to the office of Professor A. A. Smirnov, as planned, and found that he had arranged to have us meet a number of his associates. Dr. Jacobson showed us an article on his work with moral judgments, comparing nine to eleven, twelve to fourteen, and fifteen-to seventeen-year-old children by a method involving verbal expression of moral judgments, somewhat like that of Piaget (though he felt that Piaget's studies dealt mainly with moral feelings rather than judgments). Ingenious use was made of motion pictures to catch the facial expression of the child without the child's knowing it. At this point, Dr. D. B. Elkonin came in and we had a few moments of talk with him about his interest in helping the child to understand ("the more conscious the response, the better") and trying some meaningful arrangements of language work (breaking Russian words into components and doing this three years earlier than it had been done heretofore). Dr. Elkonin said that the time required for mastering reading and writing was reduced to 50 per cent by emphasis on increasing the awareness of the child, first at a practical level and then intellectually. As part of this, they are helping children to understand how words are built, doing this in the second grade, where formerly this was held over until the fifth grade. With this foundation of understanding how words are built with prefixes and so forth, syntax and grammar are given in the fifth grade now. Formerly they studied rules of arithmetic in the fifth grade, now they experiment with giving rules in the second grade. (In all this discussion of grades it should be remembered that in the second grade the children are eight-to nine-years-old. Children do not start formal schooling until seven or eight. Up to the age of seven, activities are mostly play and games.)

PROCESSES WHICH CAN ASSIST MEMORY AND LEARNING IN CHILDREN

According to Smirnov, there is considerable study of memory and the processes which can assist memory and learning in children. One technique involves giving two phrases, sometimes correct, sometimes incorrect. The task was to think about whether or not the phrase was correct. This process of thinking about the correctness of the phrase produced better memory than control techniques which included (1) being asked to remember, (2) being asked merely to correct the spelling rather than the idea. If the sense of the statement is evaluated by the child, memory is better. Also, when the task is more difficult, memory is better.

In studies of spontaneous memory, one method used was to ask the person what he was thinking about on the way to school or to work. Professors who acted as subjects were not able to remember what they thought about although they could remember actions and obstacles they overcame.

Investigations are also being made of the balance of memory of images over words, images being regarded as belonging to the first signal system, and words belonging to the second signal system.

It is easier for nine-year-olds to remember complex pictures than it is for adults. Adults remember abstract words better than complex pictures. Children in art schools remember complex pictures better than other children. The balance between the first and second signal system is different for them. He referred to Pavlov's statement that artists have developed the first signal system more than have other people.

They have also studied the role of speech-movements in memory. The lighter the task, the less the inner speech and the less excitation. Methods of memory are compared both in children and adults, and, according to Smirnov, adults tend to divide tasks into different parts according to their sense. The child tends to "take it as a whole." The adult helps his memory by giving names to the subdivided groups, which the child can't do. He can't label the groups, but every sentence is important. This is true up through the third grade, after which they do develop the ability to divide material into groups in order to help themselves remember it. If the teacher teaches the children to divide up material, the sequences of stages move faster.

Similarly, children and adults differ in their tendency to go back over material and reread it. The adult sorts out the harder parts and focuses on these parts in successive reading, whereas children ordinarily do not. He gave an example of one bright boy who, however, did go through successive stages which he described with an analogy of the different stages of washing.

Smirnov said that not all children are born the same, but the most important differences are due to the way they are handled. However, musical gifts are more a matter of inheritance than, for instance, talent in physics. Achievement in physics is more a matter of environmental influence.

At the Institute of Defectology, in working with blind or blind-and-deaf children, one technique is the use of modelizing, using clay to make models of tactually-experienced objects. The models shown in a little exhibit case were quite precise in their balance and realism, unlike the objects which Victor Lowenfeld in this country illustrated as produced by the blind. His illustrations were of objects produced spontaneously, where we assume the results of this modelizing reflect the effects of special training.

Later we talked to Dr. L. I. Bozhovich and her assistant and learned a little about character assessments based on life history material and clinical material. [3]

---

[3] We spent a long time trying to make contact, because what we had been told that this division was concerned with, namely "upbringing," did not fully correspond with our expectations. What they were trying to do, they said, was to study fundamental character, trying to develop methods of appraisal (i.e. clinical and life history methods, not involving psychological tests). They are especially concerned with methods of developing reliability and efficiency; one of these, for use with preschool children, offered a series of pictures of daily "tasks" which could be covered as each task was completed. They asked eagerly about American work on the measurement of character.

We then went downstairs to see another Dr. Sokolov—Dr. A. N. Sokolov—who is working on the EMG with techniques very reminiscent of those of Edmund Jacobson and L. W. Max on relations of speech and inner speech to muscle tensions and to symbolic thinking.

Sokolov regards his work as new and original with respect to three points: (1) noting the fact (not in line with Edmund Jacobson) that some records show no EMG, although there is inner speech; (2) the EMG is most active when there is *effort;* and (3) the EMG disappears as the flow of activity results in less and less tension.

Muscle tensions appear at the moment of difficulty and are reduced at other times. Sokolov showed examples of myograms representing tension curves. Tension increases with new tasks and is reduced as the child is habituated to the task. The highest tension appeared in writing efforts.

Dr. Sokolov continued: "The tension curves are also studied in listening situations. There is evidence of impulses aroused by questions, and by demands for memory. The most active responses appear when the child cannot remember. Muscle tensions disappear when the test is simple. At the moment of choice the tension goes up." In studying writing, he finds that children must pronounce while they are writing. This helps them to remember the written word. In working with aphasics, pronunciation of the word aloud helps to restore the speech.

"Tension is the physiological component of speech which connects visual, auditory and other components. Muscle tension appears in different parts of the speech apparatus at the same time."

A REPRESENTATIVE EXPERIMENTAL SCHOOL

On Saturday we were able to see a representative "experimental school," one of many scattered throughout the city (serving local children, not children specially selected). At the experimental school we were told that there are about 35 children in each class in the first four grades, and the classes get smaller as the children get older. In the eighth to eleventh grades there are about 25 children in each class. Children may leave school after the seventh grade if their parents wish.

Formerly, schooling was based on a ten-year program, but since 1957, as we understand it, it has been based on an eleven-year program in preparation for university training and for entry into the special institutes such as Pedagogical Institute, Institute for Foreign Languages, etc., as well as for mechanical schools. The children study according to a program of regular liberal arts education four days a week and spend two days working in laboratories and technical schools. Some children work in factories or industrial installations in the ninth, tenth, and eleventh grades.

From what we heard and saw here, and from other communications, we acquired the following impressions: In all schools today there is some "polytechnical education" from the first to the eighth grade. In the first grade activities, handling paper, plasticene and cloth provide a foundation and from the fifth to the seventh grades the children work with wood and metal. The girls learn homemaking, learn how to sew dresses, and so on. The children make things which they can take home, useful things, and are allowed to choose what they wish to make.

In the eighth grade they study and work with machines, learning the parts and learning how to operate the machines. In this grade they prepare for working in the mechanical shops of plants or mills. On Fridays and Saturdays they have two hours of theory on the job, with four hours of physical work in the factory or mill. The factory and mill supervisors also teach in the eighth grade at the school. The mechanical shop in the school is considered part of the plant or mill, and what the children make is part of the output.

Polytechnical education now includes electrotechnical education. (Interest in this has increased very much.) The main idea of the school is to connect real life and study. Children at the school do real laboratory work for the plant. They work with great interest when doing real things and when making things for themselves.

Their vocational choice is their own. The children may choose a profession to concentrate on at the age of fifteen or sixteen; they work at this until they graduate at eighteen. They then may change their choices and go to a different institute afterward.

When we asked regarding the range of abilities of the children at the higher levels in school, and how many of them went on for advanced education, the principal said that out of 22 pupils who graduated from the eleventh grade in this school, 16 entered higher educational institutes after passing examinations. Two children who took the examinations and failed went to work at the plants where they had been working during their high school training. More than 50 per cent of them get advanced technical and professional training. Some children from the seventh grade do not go on to the last four grades, but go to a vocational school. This is generally decided by parents.

In this experimental school there was an impressive library of 28,000 books. There were several large shops with machines for turning screws and other metal work, and also machines for woodwork. Physics and chemistry laboratories were as good as any school laboratories we are acquainted with. There was a microscope for every child in a large class. There was also a natural history laboratory with a wide range of specimens, and a large birdhouse about 6' x 6' x 8', containing live birds, both imported and native; some are birds the children bring in.

We visited classes in biology and chemistry where seasoned, and rather directive, teachers were lecturing. The children sat at broad double desks, two children at a desk. As we visited the rooms, they seemed friendly and often looked up and smiled, although their attention was primarily focused on the teacher who was giving a didactic lecture. Discipline and morale seemed high. Between class periods, however, the young males "horsed around" as they do in some other parts of the world.

There is a parents' committee to observe and help children who have difficulties. If the child is not able to complete work satisfactorily, he is given an opportunity to make it up during the summer, and if he does not succeed in making it up satisfactorily, he has to repeat the grade.

In the summer there are assignments or "tasks." The children are expected to make collections which will be used for study the next fall. Individual teachers are free to set their own goals for their own groups of children, and the principal of the individual school also has considerable freedom, within the directives provided by the Academy.

We also visited the kindergarten in a Moscow housing development. We found a little two-story house with space for a three-year-old, a four-year-old, and a five-year-old group with 25 children in each group. Outdoors there were sheltered structures which made it possible for the children to be outdoors in the drizzly weather. One sheltered area had benches and a large space where the children could gather around and listen to a story or play circle games. There was also a large sandbox. There was almost no climbing apparatus or the type of jungle gym, slides, swings apparatus of the kind we saw in Hawaii, Japan and some schools in India and, for that matter, in children's parks in Tashkent. But they are aware of the lack and hope to extend their facilities. The children's daily schedule called for taking a walk. Twenty or twenty-five children can be taken for a walk by one teacher by the device of having them hold onto a rope or rings attached to a rope.

CONTRAST BETWEEN OLDER GENERATION AND CHILDREN

While faces of Soviet old people often seem resigned, tired and sad, generally the children seemed lively, friendly, confident and full of vitality. It looked as if the extent to which children were being handled in group care, under warm and understanding direction, with satisfying, challenging activities and plenty of fun, permitted them to grow up without being shadowed by the sufferings and losses of the older generation. At this point we are, of course, speculating, but in contrast with our research group here, where the effect on children of emotional disturbances of parents is so profound, one wonders whether the extensive group care doesn't provide an important buffer or protection for the child in a culture and at a period when the older generation has been taxed by terrors of war, siege, famine, change and loss. We certainly didn't see much evidence that children were growing up in a militaristic world, in a world where they were being poisoned against enemies, where they were being taught to hate, or where they learned to fear.

On the contrary, the children are being given the best. By and large their clothes seem nicer than those of grownups. The children, at least those that one sees on the streets, are healthy and vigorous. They are loved, are given many opportunities, and are in turn growing up to love their country, to be proud of it, to try to help to make it still better. One sees very little evidence of foundations for rebelliousness in the groups of youngsters we saw—whether we talk about children playing in the sandpiles, children in the kindergarten of the housing development, the children at the experimental school, or at the Young Pioneer Palace and the children's parks.

Other recent observers have commented on the foundations for deep emotional identification with the way of life of the U.S.S.R. which are laid from the beginning. The Russians are "very good to children"; the people one sees in charge of groups at children's parks, Young Pioneer Palaces, kindergarten groups moving through the street, etc., typically have a warm attitude. "Being good to children" is their phrase. When I asked in Leningrad how they chose the staff for the children's hospital, the answer was simply, "When we need new people, we try them out and if they are good to children, we keep them." It is assumed that being good to children is good for the children.

THE BEKHTEREV SCIENTIFIC INSTITUTE

On Monday, September 5, we flew on to Leningrad, assisted by the letters and phone calls of Professor Luria, who had in advance telephoned Professor V. Miasishchev, of the Bekhterev Scientific Institute. He also made contact for us with Dr. Traugott, in whose department of psychiatry Dr. Kaidonova is working. These two contacts we used to generate many other contacts in the five-day Leningrad period.

Wednesday morning, September 7, we went to the Bekhterev Scientific Institute to see the Director, Dr. V. Miasishchev; his assistant, Dr. Lebedev; his chief psychologist, Dr. Tonkonogy, and several others. We compared notes with them for some two hours as to the diagnosis and treatment of disturbed, epileptic, brain-injured and oligophrenic children, getting a great deal of vigorous participation, especially from the head of the children's department, Dr. Abramovich.

Dr. Miasishchev is especially interested in research on personality and neurosis. He and some of his staff were interested in projective tests which they said they used as association tests. But he asked us to send them reports of the use of the Children's Apperception Test. They use the GSR with word associations and study reactions to suggestions with the GSR. Their idea of longitudinal research from birth to the present is the detailed study of life history through interview with the parents.

We visited the Bekhterev Institute again on Friday morning and were shown the Bekhterev historical museum, with the many documents and evidences of Bekhterev's extraordinarily versatile career. We also saw Dr. G. B. Abramovich's wing for epileptic and brain-injured children.

Here we were told that there are four mental hospitals and clinics in Leningrad. The Institute supervises work in outlying districts, in dispensaries for out-patients. This includes diagnostic work and therapy. The Bekhterev Institute itself has a clinical section, an experimental section, and a section for children. The experimental and research section includes laboratories for neurological research and the psychiatric clinical section includes occupational therapy, which is emphasized very strongly. Play is not regarded as therapeutic.

The set-up for experimental work includes a morphological laboratory, patho-histological laboratory, EEG laboratory, and a laboratory for study of pathology or higher nervous activity. It also includes pharmacology and a laboratory for animal study. Biochemical and serological studies deal with metabolic problems, the role of vitamins, hormones, and so forth.

Children's Section of the Institute

At the children's section of the Bekhterev Institute, most of the child in-patients are from seven to fifteen years of age. Parents do not generally bring for consultation children much under the age of seven. In the U.S.S.R. they consider autism to be rather frequent, but it is not regarded as a kind of schizophrenia. There are several kinds of autism, among which autism in children with some organic defect is particularly outstanding.

They have 55 in-patients, including epileptics (handled chiefly with medication), post-encephalitics, children who have suffered traumas, and oligophrenic children. Neurotic children may have very severe anxiety and be extremely disturbed, to a degree comparable to that of psychotic children.

The group agreed that work with parents is very important. They said there was no need to have social workers because they have plenty of doctors who are able to do both the work with the parents and with the children. Each doctor has eight to ten patients, makes clinical studies, and works with the parents.

Diagnostic work on the children is based chiefly on extensive laboratory studies. Sometimes all the doctors concerned with the child will discuss all the data together; sometimes the data are sent, as requested, to one specialist. "The EEG specialists are also good psychiatrists and good neurologists, so group discussion is not so much needed." It is often not easy to separate the work of the laboratory, as such, and the clinical diagnosis.

In research they are particularly interested in problems of etiology and patho-genesis of schizophrenia, epilepsy, neuroses, and "vascular diseases of the brain."

Their emphasis on organicity is a natural outcome of the many kinds of damage to the organism which have occurred as a result of war, disease, starvation, and deprivation. If there is a long period in the society without war, without famines, without severe epidemics, it is quite possible that the proportion of difficulties due to organic pathology as compared with intrapsychic conflicts may shift, and they will be forced to pay attention to new syndromes and to study them in new ways.

The technical finesse and the originality and productivity of their application of the conditioned reflex here and elsewhere in conjunction with GSR, etc., is very high. We saw no evidence of the likelihood of early abatement of preoccupation with problems which could be illuminated by these methods, except for the amount of similarity of work in different places. As they receive diminishing returns from the problems and methods they are using now, we would expect that people of the technical caliber and originality which we saw would move into new areas.

In the Institute laboratory we learned of the use of EEG, EMG, etc., in differential diagnosis. A psychologist, still working primarily on the neurological side, is beginning to use TAT and seems interested in finding out about Western clinical psychology.

There is also the human side. Dr. Abramovich, the warm and cordial director of the children's hospital, said, "We emphasize work and love more than play. Being able to do something *constructive* helps the child."

Treatment of Handicapped Children

Wednesday, after lunch, we met Dr. Kaidonova, who took us to meet her chief, Dr. Traugott, and we all went together to Dr. Traugott's office, where we discussed the use of drugs and other biochemical and neurological techniques to be used with handicapped children of one sort or another. Only slight attention seemed to be given to psychogenic factors, and the types of psychotherapy utilized appeared to be very limited. The approach seemed to be almost exclusively a medical concern with children with neurological difficulties.

Dr. Kaidonova commented that the hard-of-hearing children can differentiate clearly what they *do* hear. Conditioned reflexes can be obtained on sounds above the threshold, and the same is true for children with visual difficulties. It is only the organ of hearing which is disturbed.

Children with sensory aphasia, however, show disturbances in conditioned reflexes. Both simple and compound reflexes may be disturbed. Children with simple disturbances of conditioned reflexes appear deaf, but are not. Parents may say they do not know whether the child hears. Sometimes he seems to hear, sometimes he does not. The child understands some phrases, even when they are not pronounced loudly. The reality is that we are here dealing with disturbance in the higher centers, cortical or sub-cortical parts of the acoustical analyzers.

Children are examined both in the school for the deaf and the school for the hard-of-hearing, in order to differentiate these groups. The diagnosis is difficult when the orienting reflex is disturbed in the child.

The prognosis depends on various matters. In the development of hearing, this state may disappear. The children are not given earphones, but are given practice in listening to varied kinds of stimuli. Further evidence of a learning factor is the fact that if the hard-of-hearing are sent to a school for the deaf, they lose their hearing. Brain function is important for perception, because perception is a thing that must be developed. It is not enough for the peripheral organ to be normal.

Children who show hearing only by reactions to sounds which cause pain could be helped to understand speech by training in differentiating sounds.

Training Through Passive Differentiation

Dr. Kaidonova has been interested in training through passive differentiation, plus conditioning of movements, for example, to get food. Perception must be *active* to be effective. When Dr. Kaidonova was asked whether children might sometimes be afraid to differentiate, and how could they be helped to overcome this, she replied that the task can be made more simple, and the child can be rewarded with sweets.

In the adult the orienting reflex is not inhibited, the reaction to simple sounds is normal; the initial development is all right until damage occurs from an illness, tumor or other cause.

Dr. Kaidonova works with children with suspected disturbances of central origin. They speak but cannot understand. If the child is backward in other respects, or emotionally disturbed, that is something different. When it was suggested that there could be secondary emotional disturbances in reaction to the difficulties the child experienced, she did not agree.

Children who can understand but cannot speak, who have motor aphasias, are more apt to be emotionally disturbed and excitable. Studies are being made of disturbances of the conditioning of motor reflexes and analyzing of kinesthetic stimuli. Some children can differentiate visual and auditory stimuli but not proprioceptive stimuli. There is a disturbance of the motor kinesthetic analyzer. There are many children with sensory difficulties like this since the war (due to illnesses, starvation, brain damage).

We asked about consequences of the siege of Leningrad. They said that all the starved children had speech disturbances, or lost their speech. When conditions were restored, speech generally returned. Speech suffered first. The activity declined, but the *structure* of speech actually did not suffer, and the effects were not permanent.

In children with motor aphasia, the structure of speech suffers. Grammar is not developed. They acquire words, but cannot use them. Those with motor disturbances cannot repeat in the correct order.

There is a difference between retardation of speech and the loss or destruction of speech by long illness, weakness, and so forth. The retarded child has normal conditioned reflexes, but his intentional cooperation is poor. The child with speech difficulties rooted in motor disturbances uses gestures and facial expressions, but does not say anything. When the child has been deprived of communication, there is no such difficulty in grammar, vocabulary, repeating speech sounds, and so forth.

Friday evening we met with about a dozen psychologists, led by

Dr. A. Yarmolenko (who acted as our interpreter), at the Leningrad University. We were asked about the organization of psychology in United States' universities, clinics, etc. E. S. Kuzmin, working in experimental social psychology, wanted to know what experimental work existed in that field.

Dr. Yarmolenko is interested in the study of personality in terms of the evolution of drives and tendencies. Needs are studied as driving forces in learning. The foci of interest are on different forms of school discipline on the one hand, and causes of disabilities in different disciplines. They are experimenting with the development of different abilities. They have a special school and kindergarten for research.

They are interested also in the physiological traits which underlie disabilities; for instance, in mathematics, poor visual memory for mathematical symbols is important. In the ability for mathematics, space perception is also important. Images in space, space memory, space imagination, and relationships between space and time are all of interest here.

Subjects are tested for their ability or disability in geometry, the ability to form general notions as well as clear, concrete notions, by the time of the seventh grade. Psychologists are also investigating the development of general notions in language.

Dr. Yarmolenko and others are also interested in studies in tactile perception in relation to industrial work. In industrial psychology they are interested in sociometry as a method of studying interrelations in the human group. They try to apply it critically. When Moreno visited, they were very much interested in the presentation of his work in sociometry. There was reference also to socialist competition: competition between groups.

In the evening, Gardner Murphy lectured on the topic which Miasishchev and he had agreed upon, namely, "Some Samples of American Experimental Psychology." Beginning with a tribute to the great contributions of Pavlov and Bekhterev, he sampled American work in perception, learning, cognitive style, personality, and social psychology.[4] With Dr. Lebedev's help, he had written a few sen-

---

[4] After the introduction, Gardner Murphy said: "Thank you. I regret that I cannot speak your language, but want to try just two sentences in Russian: The scientific methods discovered here are known all over the world. When I was working on my *Historical Introduction to Modern Psychology,* I emphasized the contributions of the great Pavlov and the great Bekhterev. I never guessed then that I should have an opportunity to visit their beautiful city."

He then followed the outline given below and read aloud the fragment in

tences in Russian to introduce his remarks. The audience was enormously enthusiastic and generous, both in connection with the opening in Russian and at the end of the lecture. A number of questions were asked eagerly at the close of the lecture. The general atmosphere was decidedly warm and friendly.

VIEWS OF SOVIET PSYCHOLOGISTS

Now to turn more closely to the thinking of Soviet psychologists. Beginning with Professor Leontiev, whose broad gauge and generous view of world psychology showed no signs of strain at all, one notes nevertheless that his current book has vast underpinning in terms of Marx and Engels, dialectical materialism, the Lenin philosophical contributions, and, of course, Pavlov and the Pavlovian school. Leontiev thinks in these terms, just as we in the West would think in terms of James, Dewey, Wertheimer and Freud. We have, however, no over-arching or dominating figure in American psychology comparable to Pavlov, and integration of our various leaders involves a good deal more equalitarianism or even anarchy in the selection and utilization of ideological components for whatever system we personally set up. Soviet psychology is more tightly structured than American psychology. As regards the emotional pressures on the individual, it is likely that these, insomuch as they involve the need to maintain

---

quotation marks at the foot. The outline:
1. Significance of Pavlov and Bekhterev for the American psychologist.
2. Desire of the American Psychological Association' for closer contact; our world tour and our recent experiences here.
3. Some strengths and weaknesses of American psychology; our conversation with Professor Leontiev regarding integration of *experimental* method with *observational* method, as in the work of L. B. Murphy.
4. Some samples of recent experimental work:
   A. Physiological psychology: N. Miller.
   B. Perception: H. A. Witkin ("field dependence").
   C. Motor learning: B. F. Skinner ("instrumental conditioning").
   D. Perceptual-cognitive learning: C. M. Solley, J. F. Santos.
   E. "Scanning": J. F. Santos (Note similarity to the ideas of K. M. Bykov).
   F. "Cognitive style": G. S. Klein, R. Gardner.
   G. Drives (Motives): H. F. Harlow (curiosity and love).
   H. Social psychology: M. Sherif and C. Sherif; E. E. Bovard.
   I. Man and environment: D. O. Hebb.
5. Some opportunities for Soviet-American cooperation in investigating man's place in space and his relation to cosmic evolution.
End: "Although there is an important place for competition in science, I earnestly hope that in the investigation of man's place in the great world of space, all nations may work in brotherhood. I hope the problem of man's place in cosmic evolution may be studied with the *united* energies of all mankind."

oneself within the Soviet economic and political system, are little greater than would be the case with reference to an American psychologist trying to get himself established. But we are not sure that this is more than a quantitative difference, and we are not at all certain that this is a very big difference. Pressure on Americans to see things in terms of the middle-class and mid-twentieth century ideas of what science is, what human nature is, the various odds and ends of nineteenth and twentieth century mechanism and the need for quantification, blended in a curious way with humanitarian and egalitarian ideas, does not amount to a tight system, but it nevertheless can have a very considerable structure-giving effect upon the mind of the psychologist. There is a great deal to be said about ways in which American psychologists are constrained, as are French, British, German or Italian psychologists, for example, by their intellectual heritage and present social situation, but this task is too big and vague to be tackled. Our net impression at this date is that Soviet science in general, and Soviet psychology in particular, are *somewhat* more constrained than is the Western counterpart, but *not very much* so.

We should like to quote in this connection an interesting sentence from a Soviet scientist whom we greatly respected. He had noted that in some of our discussions there was no mention of Freud. To this we replied that in discussing the process of learning there was already too much to cover, but some experiments on learning from a psychoanalytic viewpoint were being carried out. We were immediately asked about integrating Freudian and Pavlovian ideas. We said that many of us were attempting this. He said, "For you, this is possible; for us, it is difficult, very difficult." As American psychologists, we believe that, just because our fellow psychologists in the Soviet Union cannot always make certain necessary integrations, it is all the more important for us to maintain some kind of intellectual poise and freedom in which these specific integrations can at least be tried out.

In the meantime, we think that our visit did result in some honest interchange of opinion on matters relating to the learning process, both from the experimental and from the clinical point of view.

They did not ask us much about our own research, but they did ask us a good deal about the literature dealing both with experimental and clinical approaches to the learning process, and in many cases they wrote down what we said. We are, moreover, sending them some books and periodical literature along these lines. Those who work within the frame of reference of the Pavlov approach in the experimental field will make use of some things. Those who use the

Pavlovian material on the learning process in infancy or early child-hood, or the elementary or high school age, will likewise use what they find convenient, clear and directly applicable to their needs. They may decide that our ideas are appropriate only to our own society, and not to theirs, or they may decide that our approach is all too complicated or farfetched, or they may decide that ideas from the West cannot really be fitted into the Pavlovian system.

SPECIFIC CONTRIBUTIONS BY SOVIET PSYCHOLOGY

Now as to the specific contributions by Soviet psychology. It has been the universal testimony of those psychologists with whom we have talked and those whose work dealing with the Soviet Union we have read, that the U.S.S.R. is far more advanced in physiological psychology than in clinical, social and personality psychology. Their work on learning, particularly the second signal system, rooted in work done long ago by Vygotsky, Luria and others, is solid and im-portant. Their attempt to view cognitive processes, especially thought processes, in terms of the Pavlov concepts, is interesting and decidedly worth while.

We did not feel that their approach to disturbed children was broad or sound, except with respect to circumscribed topics, like the use of EEG and EMG, and diagnosis of brain-damaged and epileptic children, the use of drugs combined with EEG in testing out certain concepts about neural integration, etc., and notably the work of E. N. Sokolov, as noted above. We do not believe that emotionally disturbed children get a very thorough study or a very adequate type of help, except when mothering and supportive techniques are what is mainly needed. We did not, however, have the opportunity to observe these types of work for ourselves; and we remain cautious. The all-or-none types of thinking in which a child is regarded as *either* an organic case *or* a case with social etiology, and in which an enormous amount of skill goes into differential diagnosis, we heard about everywhere. We suspect that in individual conversation certain children are helped, and that in group work even more is done. But we must leave this matter with our impressions, trusting that others had a chance to see at firsthand what is being done along the lines of diagnostic and therapeutic method characteristic of modern clini-cal psychology. The fact that they are excited about the organic approaches and want to talk about them is, in itself, very eloquent. The fact that there are practically no pictures, dolls, playthings, to be seen in certain rooms we visited, where disturbed children are supposed to be under care, or other equipment natural to a child's world (by contrast with the excellent world for children in Tashkent),

273

is likewise the kind of thing which is sure to make a deep effect upon us. The fact that we did not anywhere see defective (mongoloid, microcephalic, etc.) and other types of "organic" children in the streets or in the railroad stations or in huge throngs probably means early and efficient institutionalization. Nor did we see many blind, deaf, amputee or other crippled or disabled persons. All the more reason to hope that some American psychologists had an extensive opportunity to see these handicapped groups receiving help.

We asked one psychiatrist about the effects of the one-room apartment home, saying that with us, where children sleep with parents, their fantasies about the parents' intimacies can become quite exaggerated and troublesome. He said, "It's the same with us," and later added that the crowding of family life also heightened the children's sensitivity to disagreements between the parents, especially in regard to the bringing up of the children.

But at the same time, we wonder whether the very lack of privacy does not exert an influence toward more family unity as a group. The parents have less opportunity to make an extended love affair out of their marriage. Other pressures are pushing in the same direction—devotion is directed to the state, to production, to making the U.S.S.R., Moscow, etc., the best in the world.

In an expanding society with the urgent needs in every field, women are needed as workers. A high percentage of medical and other professional people are women, as in India.

Women don't have to stay home and take care of the young unless they have several children and want to. They can be quite secure in giving the children to group care under the guidance of warm, motherly women who do like children. Since so many occupations are open to women, they do not have to work with children as our teachers often do—teaching by default of other opportunities.

At the Bekhterev Institute they asked for reports of our work, asked whether they could have records of the diagnostic process in individual cases, records of therapy sessions, and, in general, were most eager to get acquainted with what is going on in the United States.

On such a short trip, when one sees thousands of faces or people of all ages, with opportunities to talk with only a few dozen at best, and those from very selected groups, our evidence is of a special kind —the evidence of our muscles, of the antennae that we carry around with us which catch the feeling of atmospheres, of the implications of postures, of facial expressions, of tones of voice with which we are surrounded. In these terms one feels the busyness, the work orientation, the striding ahead, of the people in the U.S.S.R. "What we really want most is to get on with our work, to get to the point where we can make better housing and have better clothes."

What sort of world do the children grow up in? Not billboards screaming the dubious advantages of one car, cold cream or canned soup over others, but posters extolling the glories of the U.S.S.R., illustrating possible vocations, educating for health and for peace, physical vigor. Portraits of Lenin, like Washington and Lincoln in schools in our day; not dirty, littered streets—none of the three Russian cities was a fraction as dirty as many of our large cities; not a rushing world—meals are leisurely; not an individual or a home-centered world but a group-centered world, oriented toward the development of the whole.

Our dominant impression is that Russian children are growing up to be good members of the Soviet Union; to cherish its goals, and identify with its belief in its potential supremacy. Supremacy and achievement is the aim. They are growing up to want us to recognize theirs as the best way of life.

Our brief and fragmentary impressions, even when directed to answering such questions as the scope and achievements of psychology within the Soviet Union, could not have competed in importance with the information already available through many sources, notably the accounts of Russian psychology appearing recently in American psychological journals by G. H. S. Razran, and Ivan D. London; the piece by Alexander Mintz in the *Annual Review of Psychology,* 1958; the lists of areas of activities available in the *International Directory of Psychologists.* It must be remembered that much which we call psychology in America is assigned in the U.S.S.R. to the general domain of the physiological sciences and that, although psychology has its affiliations there, as here, with education on the one hand, and with physiology on the other hand, it is not a fully autonomous science anywhere.[5] But in the U.S.S.R. most basic psychological work, including the many studies of the learning process, are carried on within special scientific institutes intimately related to physiology or medicine. Pavlovian studies have enormous prestige everywhere, as already noted. They comprise, not only the conditioned reflex studies, but also studies of the orienting reflex. They heavily emphasize both the first signal system and the second signal system. All this,

---

[5] Mintz comments: Pavlovian concepts of analysis and synthesis are much more directly relevant to educational research than is conditioning. Salivary conditioning was characterized by Pavlov as a technique for the study of brain physiology. Pavlovian physiology emphasized the role of induction relationships between different brain mechanisms, and the formation of stereotypes.

of course, is embodied in studies continuously published by the hundreds. These are the areas which receive the maximal emphasis in Soviet behavior research. What appears to be refinements of conditioning procedures and the application of these procedures to learning situations generally, such as those which occur in schools and in industrial establishments, surely make up a large proportion of the published material. We believe that we in America can learn much from these studies of the learning process.

NAME INDEX

SUBJECT INDEX